high function ing

Overcome Your Hidden Depression
and Reclaim Your Joy

Judith Joseph, MD, MBA

Foreword by Mel Robbins

LITTLE, BROWN SPARK
New York   Boston   London

Little, Brown Spark
Hachette Book Group
1290 Avenue of the Americas, New York, NY 10104
littlebrownspark.com

First Edition: April 2025

Little, Brown Spark is an imprint of Little, Brown and Company, a division of Hachette Book Group, Inc. The Little, Brown Spark name and logo are trademarks of Hachette Book Group, Inc.

The publisher is not responsible for websites (or their content) that are not owned by the publisher.

The Hachette Speakers Bureau provides a wide range of authors for speaking events. To find out more, go to hachettespeakersbureau.com or email hachettespeakers@hbgusa.com.

Little, Brown and Company books may be purchased in bulk for business, educational, or promotional use. For information, please contact your local bookseller or the Hachette Book Group Special Markets Department at special.markets@hbgusa.com.

Book interior design by Marie Mundaca

ISBN 9780316577298
A Library of Congress Control Number is available for this title.

Printing 1, 2025

LSC-C

Printed in the United States of America

For Zara, my only child and the reason that I want to make the world a better place

Contents

CONTENTS

Foreword

by Mel Robbins

I'm so proud of you for picking up this book. In it, you'll learn about groundbreaking research into one of the biggest things that busy, successful, high-functioning people like you struggle with.

If you've ever found yourself feeling "off" without being able to put your finger on why, or if you're constantly busy but don't find yourself fulfilled, you're in the right place. This book is the ultimate guide to creating more joy, fulfillment, purpose, and happiness.

Dr. Judith Joseph knows exactly what you're going through, because she's lived it. She's also spent years studying it. Her pioneering research into high-functioning depression, conducted in her Manhattan Behavioral Medicine research lab in New York City, finally gives a name to the exhaustion, numbness, and restlessness you feel when you keep it all together for everyone else while your own joy slowly fades away.

Dr. Judith's insights have changed my life, and I know they will change yours too. As the host of the wildly successful *Mel Robbins Podcast*, I have the honor of connecting with listeners in 194 countries, so I know how common it is to feel like you're not reaching your potential and to want more in life. I want that for you too. I also have the unique experience of meeting experts at the top of their fields and learning from them every single week. Dr. Judith Joseph is so good that I have invited her back on the show not just twice but three times, because her incredible research-backed insights and tools truly change lives.

What I love most about Dr. Judith isn't her expertise or her groundbreaking research. It's her ability to make you feel seen and understood. In one of her appearances on *The Mel Robbins Podcast,* she explained that happiness isn't a grand destination; it's a series of small moments—"points of joy," as she calls them. It's the text you send to a friend when you're feeling lonely, the rest you give yourself when you're tired, the connection you seek when you need to feel supported.

This simple yet profound concept struck me, and I hope it will make you pause too. How often do you rush past those small points of joy because you're so busy jumping right into the next thing? And how often do you ignore what you're really feeling because you think you don't have time to feel it? For a long time, I was addicted to busyness, until I truly faced the impact that constant motion had on my life—and Dr. Judith was a core part of my journey of change.

If any of this resonates with you, you're about to feel something extraordinary as you read this book: relief. Relief in understanding why you've been feeling the way you do and relief in knowing you're not alone. Most important, you're about to learn that no matter how far away joy feels right now, it's not gone. It's waiting for you.

This isn't just a book. It's a road map back to yourself. I can't wait for you to read it and experience all of Dr. Judith's research, insights, and tools.

high
function
ing

Introduction

"Judith? Is everything all right?" my associate asked nervously. She had knocked on the door to my office and popped her head in to check on me. Her eyes were squinting at me above her N 95 mask. She was looking at me in that way—you know, where you can tell the person is concerned about you. Her instincts were right. She should've been worried about me. I was worried about me, too. But I nodded confidently to her that I was fine. That wasn't true.

It was April 2020 in New York City, and these were the dark days at the beginning of the pandemic. Days when you could walk through Times Square—one of the most bustling intersections on the planet—on your way to work and see only two or three other people. When storefronts on the world-famous Fifth Avenue were about to start boarding up their windows because owners feared them being smashed by protesters. It seems like a movie now. Except it was real, we all lived it, and, by the way, we're still coping with the trauma from it.

Even though we were all in survival mode, I have to admit that many things in my work life were going extremely well. Mine was the only doctor's office in my building that hadn't been shut down due to the pandemic because my lab was working on important studies that the FDA wanted to move forward with. My media career had taken off because everyone wanted to talk about emotional well-being during the pandemic; I was at the point of turning down appearances. I had more patients than ever before because the country was in the midst of a mental health crisis and healthcare professionals needed all hands on deck. Not to mention I had just been invited to be one of five people joining an elite group of women in medicine at Columbia University.

But with all of those accomplishments came a tidal wave of overwhelm. There was a day-in, day-out pressure that came with work. There was a perpetual responsibility to show up for everyone in my life. If you're reading this book, I know you can relate. Just like me, you're likely the person in your family or circle whom everyone looks to as the strong one — even if you're pouring out energy from a nearly empty cup.

Back then, I never got to just be Judith. At any given moment in time, I was a boss whose employees were counting on her for a steady paycheck to survive this economic crisis. I was Dr. Joseph, with clinical trial participants who were terrified of this new disease and patients who needed help with new coping mechanisms. I was a mom and wife whose family was falling apart under enormous pressure. Every day I had to push through the stress, and I worried that boss/researcher/doctor/wife/mother Judith was failing them all. Sound familiar?

That April, my associate and I were scheduled to give a joint Zoom presentation — from separate offices, of course — to two hundred healthcare practitioners and their families at a major healthcare system. The night before, I was working on my PowerPoint for the presentation, called "Coping with the New Norm." With the clock ticking closer to 8 p.m., my stomach starting to rumble, and my eyes getting heavy, I recognized the irony. I was highly aware that coping was something I was barely doing. In fact, while I was organizing my slides, I pulled my hands away from my keyboard, looked away from the screen, and said aloud to myself in an empty office: "I think I'm depressed."

I'm a psychiatrist and even I was caught off guard by the self-diagnosis. The next day wasn't any better. If you didn't know me, you would have assumed everything was fine during my part of the Zoom presentation. You wouldn't have noticed the flutter in my voice or my hurried breathing while talking about emotional trauma. You wouldn't have caught how my eyes darted around my office in an effort to hold back the tears that were welling. I was supposed to be focused on healing the people on the call, but I realized that I needed healing myself.

Most of the faces on my Zoom screen belonged to overwhelmed healthcare workers, many of whom were scribbling notes or dropping fears into the chat ("The other nurse on my shift has been drinking a lot after work" or "My co-worker is constantly breaking down in tears"). But one of my associates left her computer and came over to my office to check on me while I was off camera. She could see that I was teetering on the edge of my emotions and about to topple over. That's when she asked, "Is everything all right?"

Until that presentation, I hadn't realized that I was depressed, because I didn't check all the boxes for depression. I could still get out of bed in the morning. I wasn't bursting into tears on the subway (and even if you do, New Yorkers will politely ignore you). I still organized my daughter's birthday parties and brought in bagels for morning meetings at work. And, remember, I was not only showing up for work, I was killing it at work. But I felt an inner restlessness. A need to stay busy. I was sure that if I slowed down something bad would happen. I couldn't quite put my finger on what this feeling was. Unlike most people with depression, I was functioning. More than that: I was high-functioning! What the heck was going on?

STARTING TO UNMASK HIGH-FUNCTIONING DEPRESSION

After that moment in April 2020, I went on a search to understand what was happening to me, and it led me straight to High-Functioning Depression (HFD). I didn't find what I was looking for in scientific journals because medical literature is usually miles behind what people in the world are actually experiencing. You don't see High-Functioning Depression in the *Diagnostic and Statistical Manual of Mental Disorders, 5th Edition* (*DSM-5*), the most recent edition of the book that psychiatrists live by for diagnosing conditions. HFD isn't officially recognized and there hasn't been a definition for it...until now.

I kept reading experts saying that High-Functioning Depression isn't real. They're wrong. In fact, it's one of those conditions that get missed by most doctors because, I believe, many of them have had or currently live with High-Functioning Depression themselves. Think about it: medicine is a profession where you're conditioned to work long hours, put others first, ignore your own needs, and delay happiness, all the way from high school through medical school and residency. (See all seasons of *ER*, *Grey's Anatomy*, and *Chicago Med*.)

Those experts pointed to the fact that there was no research on High-Functioning Depression and it didn't exist in the *DSM*. But we all knew that burnout was a real thing long before it was classified as a condition by the World Health Organization in 2008.[1] Does that mean no one had it before 2008? We all acknowledge that imposter syndrome exists even though it's not in the *DSM*. Does that mean we should wait until it gets classified to help people overcome the constant inability to believe their success is deserved or a reflection of their skills? These conditions, just like High-Functioning Depression, were showing up in people when they came to therapy sessions. In short, I knew High-Functioning Depression was real because patient after patient I saw was experiencing it.

Though the term "High-Functioning Depression" first started turning up on the Internet in the early 2000s, it didn't really enter the public consciousness worldwide until 2016. Websites incorrectly labeled it as persistent depressive disorder (or dysthymia), but it's not the same, because both of those conditions require a significant loss of functioning.[2] HFD is present in people who are very successful, manage to run a household, and keep up appearances instead of being overcome with sadness throughout the day. In fact, the term resonated with people who didn't identify with feeling depressed at all.

What they did identify with was feeling guilty, because despite the fact that they were producing a lot at work—even if it meant taking calls in the bathroom or falling asleep with their laptop in bed—they never felt like it was enough and they never enjoyed the results. They identified with always making sure to take care of their loved ones and friends but never taking care of themselves. They identified with being tired all the time but unable to sleep because of all their anxious energy. They identified with feeling incapable of spending their spare time relaxing or engaging in fun; instead, that time was spent cleaning the house, or planning the family vacation single-handedly—in part so they could make sure the hotel Wi-Fi reached the pool area and there was a business center somewhere in the building. And they identified with never sitting still, because if they did, they'd realize that they were feeling empty and that the things they used to enjoy didn't give them pleasure anymore.

High-Functioning Depression might be a new concept, but it's as real as any ailment listed in the *DSM-5*. That's why millions of people—just like me—have been walking around with it, undetected.

The more I read and the closer I looked at the patients under my care, I could see that High-Functioning Depression was everywhere. But people couldn't go to their doctor and ask for a diagnosis or a prescription for antidepressants for it. If they did, the doctor would run through a quick screening tool for depression that looks for lack of functioning and acute distress. They'd ask, "Is living this way impacting your life? Are you showing up for work? Are you able to take care of your family? Well, then, what's the problem?"

There was a problem, though.

High-Functioning Depression didn't just come with the danger of sliding into low-functioning depression and bringing our lives to a full stop. It also kept us living life with our eyes closed. Most people with High-Functioning Depression don't realize that they have it. They're not fully aware that the joy has been removed from their life. And even if they do realize something is off, like I did while working on that PowerPoint, they don't know how to get back on track.

This book sounds the alarm that the millions of us suffering from High-Functioning Depression are all forgetting something absolutely essential: how to enjoy life. We are walking around on autopilot without wondering where our path is taking us. We are all in danger of waking up one day burdened by an existential crisis, trying to figure out, "What did I do all of this for? Whom and what was I sacrificing for?" We are at risk of opening our eyes, perhaps a little too late, and realizing that we built the wrong lives and allowed ourselves to be used by everyone we encountered, and now it might be too late to reclaim some pleasure in life for ourselves.

There is also the possibility that we'll collapse under the weight of all the pressure we have been putting on ourselves. Take, for example, journalist Cheslie Kryst.[3] By the age of thirty, Cheslie had no shortage of career accomplishments. The Emmy-nominated television correspondent wasn't just stunning enough to win the Miss USA pageant in 2019; she was also brainy enough to earn an MBA and a law degree, and respected enough to interview Oprah. But what people didn't know was that she was harassed on social media after her pageant success—with more than one person telling her to kill herself. People weren't aware that at work she had overwhelming imposter syndrome, struggled with perfectionism, and felt the weight of representing all Black people in her on-camera job. And at home she was in a relationship with a partner who allegedly cheated on her. There was a perpetual inner voice that berated her for being "never enough."[4] Kryst is one of the first public figures to be labeled as having High-Functioning Depression. When the ups and downs of her life became too much to manage, she died by suicide on January 30, 2022. The following day, I met with a patient who kept talking about Kryst's passing. "I can relate to that feeling of just wanting to be relieved of it all," said this Ivy League graduate of color. "At least she can finally relax." That's how serious High-Functioning Depression can become.

THE FIVE V'S

Upon discovering that there was zero research on High-Functioning Depression, I decided to do studies myself in my laboratory in midtown Manhattan. Then I thought, why stop there? I decided to write a book about it (the one you're holding in your hands right now). If that sounds high-functioning AF, that's because it is. I'm the first clinical researcher to study HFD. And everything I found through my scientific investigation, online research, and years of experience with patients is in this book. I even developed three questionnaires (see pages 27, 68, and 90) that will help you figure out what degree of High-Functioning Depression you have—if you have it at all.

What my research brought to light was that High-Functioning Depression is almost always the result of trauma—whether we realize it or not. Trauma isn't always a life-shattering event. Yes, it could be big-T trauma, like being abused as a child or surviving a car accident, but it could also be little-T trauma, like having an overly critical parent or being betrayed by a close friend.

High-Functioning Depression also always shows up with two distinct symptoms that doctors have stopped talking about even as they become more common: anhedonia (a reduced ability to experience joy in life, which makes you feel meh or blah all the time) and masochism (a propensity for people-pleasing, self-sacrificing, and self-sabotaging behavior that can lead to imbalanced relationships and poor quality of life). I know these terms sound intimidating, but I'm going to help you get to know them better because they're the key to your cure. They're the building blocks of High-Functioning Depression, and to overcome HFD, I'm going to teach you how to knock them down.

When I started, there was no known treatment for High-Functioning Depression. Now there's actually therapy for it—because I created it. It's a framework I call the Five V's, and I'll walk you through all of them in this book. I've filled this book with surprising patient stories, actionable tools, fun exercises, and eye-opening questionnaires that will help you understand High-Functioning Depression and recover from it. The Five V's are not just evidence-based and derived from my work treating various age groups. This approach is also a result of government-funded research that led me to more than thirty countries. While High-Functioning Depression is an international phenomenon that crosses all cultures, you do see it more in groups who are considered to be "model minorities" in the United States, like East Asians and South Asians—people who have absorbed the message that you're not supposed to have happiness today; rather, you're supposed to work hard now and be happy later, once you've accumulated wealth and contributed to your society.

HOW TO USE THIS BOOK

While it might be tempting to fast-forward to Part Two of this book and start on your journey to recovery, I highly encourage you to start with Part One, where I discuss the roots of High-Functioning Depression. You have to understand the key roles that trauma, anhedonia, and masochism play in your condition before you can take the three of them out of commission. Only then will you be able to uncover joys you didn't realize you were missing, the passions you didn't know you'd put on hold, and potentially an entirely new life you never imagined you could live. Which is exactly what happened to me.

During the pandemic, I went through a painful divorce. The end of a marriage isn't within anyone's control, but because I am a high-functioning person, it made me feel like a failure. I was holding on to a core belief that I had to be perfect. That if I made a mistake, I wouldn't be as valuable or lovable. Through therapy and a lot of self-work, I turned that period of my life into a point of reckoning. For the first time, I began to realize—and believe—that I didn't have to be perfect in order to be happy. I stopped doing things just to check boxes and instead started doing things to bring meaning to my life. I started leaning into those Five V's that I told you about. For as long as I can remember, my calendar had been overcommitted. But once I started probing my core values and realized that self-care was every bit as important as my many other responsibilities, I started enjoying the luxury of doing nothing. No one has to be on the go *all the time*. The idea of intentional relaxation isn't even in the vocabulary of a person with High-Functioning Depression, so I knew I was healing. I started spending far more time with my daughter than I had before, which was a comfort to both of us, especially as our family underwent a stressful custody battle. I even got a hobby.

I decided to start focusing on doing something fun just for myself. I thought back to my childhood, when my siblings and I would put on skits and plays at our father's church. Working on scripts, putting on costumes, pretending to be someone else: it was all so fun back then. Wouldn't it be the same now? I hadn't had a creative outlet like that in decades, so I decided to try it out.

Once the divorce was final and custody was resolved, on the days when my daughter wasn't with me, I started recording video skits about mental health to post to social media. It felt good to do good. But I was also having a blast. I'd put a baseball cap on backward and use a filter to give myself a mustache and beard so that I could play both the man and the woman in a relationship with attachment issues. Or I'd switch up my outfits, hair, and makeup to show what different personality disorders look like. Not everyone loved it. Plenty of my colleagues questioned me. Apparently psychiatrists aren't supposed to wear pink and get glammed up to create funny social media reels. I forced myself to keep doing it and be myself anyway. Who says there's one way to be a psychiatrist? And why should I let them steal my joy? I also started teaching media and social media to young doctors at New York University, which led to a partnership with the World Health Organization's Fides health influencer community. My joy became infectious, and my students started to follow suit.

I've worked hard over the years to acquire traditional training from very prestigious institutions. But I knew all along that most of the evidence-based research we were taught about didn't include minorities or women. It didn't take into account cultural identity or background. My work is for everyone. The research I do, the way I show up on social media, the book that you have in your hands, and the work I do with my patients—all of it takes diversity into consideration.

In private practice, I help one person at a time. I love that I can educate that one patient in my office with a probing question or a funny story. But I quickly realized that when I told that same story as a skit and posted it on TikTok and Instagram, I could reach millions of people around the world. So much traditional media had shut down during the pandemic that people were turning to social media for information and for entertainment—and pretty soon they were clicking on my profile in the millions.

If not for the twin traumas of the pandemic and my divorce, you wouldn't be reading this book now. I wouldn't have stopped trying to distract myself from the emptiness I felt by doing more, more, more of what I thought I was "supposed" to be doing in life. I wouldn't have gone searching for (and found) answers about a condition that affects so many of us. I wouldn't have dreamed the formula for the science of your happiness. And I certainly wouldn't have created a new life for myself: a life full of joy that outshines the old one.

What could overcoming High-Functioning Depression make possible for you? You're about to find out.

PART ONE

The Roots of High-Functioning Depression

CHAPTER 1

Are You Ready to Meet the Real You?

High-Functioning Depression is a sneaky mental health epidemic that we see everywhere without realizing it.

We see it in the woman who is crushing it at work—never taking a break for lunch, responding to emails on the treadmill, and only going to happy hour if the boss will be there. She never asks for help because she secretly thinks that no one can do the job as well as she can. Her job is her identity. So much so that she even volunteered for a new project because she felt guilty for taking a sick day recently. So much so that she's in a hurry to get sex over with at night so that she can sneak another look at her work email after her boyfriend goes to sleep. So badly does she want to please, she brings donuts in for her co-workers even though she never eats any. She has a laundry list of people at work and home who depend on her, so she doesn't think she can slow down. But that's not the real reason she's at it nonstop. It's because deep down, she also believes that if she doesn't succeed, she's not lovable. It's a thought left over from a painful childhood in which she always tried to be extra good to avoid the wrath of abusive parents. But if you asked her if she was depressed, she'd tell you, "It's just a super-busy time right now."

We see it in first-generation minority college students at the top of their class. They have been told that they are lucky to even be here, and they have a fear of failing in the new, foreign land. That fear pushes them to excel academically even if it means working two jobs, shrugging off microaggressions at school, helping that friend who is about to fail chemistry, and then staying up all night to study for their own exam. They're too busy studying for the next test to celebrate the A they just got. If they're not pulling all-nighters and skipping showers to get it all done in a day, they're playing video games at 3 a.m. or borrowing some Xanax from a friend to try to wind down their anxiety. They may not realize they're depressed, and if they do, they don't say anything. They don't want to burden other people with their problems. After they graduate—with honors, of course—they take a job that's lucrative but unfulfilling. They start creating their American dream as a "model minority." But they're existing in a dull, black-and-white world instead of living in full color.

We see High-Functioning Depression in the dad who works eighty-hour weeks at his finance job to provide for his family because he remembers what it was like to struggle as a kid in a single-parent household after his father walked out. He'd rather miss tucking his kids in at night than come up short for their private school tuition or not be able to afford their ice hockey camp. But he doesn't see how unhappy his children are at the dinner table and he doesn't realize his wife's browser history is full of searches for divorce lawyers. The pressure that he feels has caused him to pick angry fights with his wife and drink more than he knows he should. But he doesn't think he's depressed. He thinks he just needs to manage his anger better. He brings his wife flowers and gifts because he loves her and because he secretly doesn't think he's worthy of her affection. He's sure everything will be better once he gets that promotion and can buy his wife a bigger house and get his kids front-row seats to a Taylor Swift concert.

High-Functioning Depression knows no boundaries when it comes to age, finances, geography, gender, or relationship status. We see it in the family matriarch who had every negative card dealt to her in life, from abuse to poverty, but is still the rock for every generation of her family. This woman can stretch a dollar all the way to an elaborate Thanksgiving meal, she can multitask all day long for her church or community, and she can raise successful kids. She can't spare a moment, though, to take care of herself. Even as a grandmother, she gives to everyone except herself until she ends up with an ailment like diabetes or heart disease that forces her to slow down. When she does, she sees that the people she's put all that hard work into caring for have moved on with their lives, and she struggles to find something to make her feel content in her golden years alone.

Surprisingly, what we don't see with High-Functioning Depression is an awareness of depression. Having done countless research studies on depression and seen hundreds of patients with the disorder, I know people with High-Functioning Depression don't usually think of themselves as depressed. In fact, the majority of my patients aren't coming to meet with me because they're depressed. Yes, some have exhibited the clinical symptoms of depression (like not being able to get a good night's sleep, feeling exhausted throughout the day, not having an appetite, or not being able to concentrate) at one point in their lives, or maybe they even currently do. But most of them come in because their marriage isn't working and they can't figure out why. Or they've had a health crisis (like inexplicable panic attacks or a substance use disorder) that they need to get under control. Sometimes their kids have stopped connecting with them and they are trying to get them to open up. Or they're tired of being the one person keeping their family together but they don't know how to lighten their load. Depression isn't what gets high-functioning people on my couch. The fallout from their High-Functioning Depression is.

DEFINING HIGH-FUNCTIONING DEPRESSION

As the only doctor who (at the time of writing) has studied this condition and published research on it, I'm able to define it in a way that reflects how patients are truly experiencing it. High-Functioning Depression is a mental health disorder triggered by trauma (things such as a painful childhood, declaring bankruptcy, or physical assault) that can lead to a lack of pleasure in life (anhedonia) and masochistic behaviors (in which you sacrifice your well-being for others).

You may be thinking, "Dr. Judith, trauma is for the people I see on the news who have been sexually assaulted or are desperately trying to survive life in a war-torn country. Trauma is that thing that happened to my cousin. It's not me. I've had tough times, but

I haven't been through any kind of serious trauma." Remember, there is both big-T trauma and little-T trauma, and either one can be at the core of High-Functioning Depression. Some people react to trauma by self-medicating with drugs and alcohol. Others (consciously or not) seek out more trauma by engaging in high-risk situations, like a combat veteran signing up for another tour. People with High-Functioning Depression channel the emotional struggles from their trauma into productivity. They're pathologically productive. That's how their post-traumatic stress is showing up. They appear content, strong, "put-together," and successful on the outside, but in reality, they're attempting (unsuccessfully) to use their hard work and high achievements to try to outsmart and outrun that trauma.

When this happens, work becomes like a substance you're addicted to. Except no one gets worried when they walk in on you sending work emails in the ladies' bathroom, the way they would if they caught you doing cocaine in the stall. And no one gets concerned about you staying up until 3 a.m. to sew your kids' Halloween costumes by hand, like they would if you were out at a bar. Instead, you're *rewarded* for getting so much done and always being available. This makes it harder to break the cycle of addiction. Your boss loves that you're on call 24/7, but your body and your brain do not.

You might also be thinking, "What you're saying about anhedonia is interesting, Dr. Judith, but that's not me. Life isn't about being happy all the time anyway." And I am sure I can guess what you're thinking when you see the word "masochism." But stay with me.

I estimate that approximately 75 percent of people with High-Functioning Depression have anhedonia, a reduced ability to experience joy in life. They're just going through the motions, feeling meh or blah all the time. *What do you want for dinner?* Doesn't matter. *Should we catch that movie?* I don't care, whatever you want. *How about a trip to Tahiti?* I guess that could be nice.

After a certain point, not even the work we commit ourselves to doing brings us joy. We get addicted to the achievements and accolades, but they no longer make us high. What's more, my soon-to-be-published research shows that the more trauma someone has experienced, the more anhedonia they're likely to experience and the worse their High-Functioning Depression will be. I factored this into a questionnaire I developed that you can use to assess how severe your HFD is. (See page 27.)

Uncover Your Superpower

Anecdotally, I've noticed that people with High-Functioning Depression often have a superpower that can be both a blessing and a curse. They might have an enormous capacity for love, but the amount of care they give to others drains them of energy. Or they have a tremendous tolerance for pain and can tolerate really difficult situations, so they put themselves in the line of fire too often. Or perhaps they're so extraordinarily patient that they delay gratification or even resign themselves to no gratification at all.

Set aside time to do some journaling, where you put your life under a magnifying glass to figure out what that thing is that makes you special — and how it slips into masochism or people-pleasing when you go overboard with it. You might try journaling about what you project to others that makes them think you have everything on lockdown. Or try to connect the dots by writing a few sentences about what others see in you and what you actually feel. The disconnect could reveal to you your strengths and your superpowers. For example, my colleagues think I have everything figured out. In reality, I feel like I barely have time to answer emails. And although I delegate, I have a hard time asking for help, so I can get overwhelmed. Unpacking the perils of your superpower might feel like looking at yourself for the first time because you didn't recognize how the source of your strength can also be your Achilles' heel. By the end of this book, you'll learn how to channel your superpowers into behaviors you value that enhance your well-being rather than sacrifice it.

THE DANGERS OF HIGH-FUNCTIONING DEPRESSION

Doctors don't treat a health concern unless it causes impairment. If you're able to get out of bed in the morning, show up for work, and take care of your family, no one is going to dig deeper. People will pat you on the back and say, "Congrats on the promotion!" On the outside, it seems like you're thriving. But on the inside, you're barely surviving.

People with High-Functioning Depression are impaired in ways that can be invisible to the naked eye. They can go an entire day without satisfying the basic needs any person has: food, water, human connection. They may be so hyperfocused on their goals that they ignore their body's signals that it's time to eat dinner, or don't realize that it's been several days since they had a meaningful conversation. They may organize elaborate bachelorette parties and agree to be every relative's emergency contact, but the reciprocity isn't there. Their romantic relationships may be on the brink, and they might not have a single friend to pick up the phone at 2 a.m. when they're the one in need.

Years of self-neglect eventually take a toll. You can feel buried alive under the weight of your responsibilities. You may end up with health conditions tied to poor nutrition, stress, or burnout. Your strained relationships may result in isolation, anxiety, and sadness. If you don't end up in your primary care provider's office with a serious health problem, you end up on my couch with low-functioning depression or another serious mental health issue—just like my patient Rebecca.

Rebecca, a beautiful thirty-year-old woman in a wheelchair, came to me because she was suffering from anxiety that was hampering her productivity at her seventy-hour-a-week software engineering job. She wanted to know if I could prescribe her some sleeping meds so that she could get more than three hours of rest at night—or at least make up the lost sleep on the weekends. Her job was seriously impressive. She admitted that most people would kill to work at the company she did—and to have the luxurious perks that came with the job—even though her boss was a narcissist and the hours were obscene. When Rebecca was able to claw away enough time to date, she ended up going from one toxic boyfriend to another.

Rebecca usually sat stiffly in my office and showed little emotion during our sessions; mostly she just seemed exhausted. But one day, after recounting her latest date with a guy who showed up three-quarters of an hour late and snuck off in the middle of the night after they'd had sex, she broke down crying. I was shocked. After those floodgates opened, Rebecca cried in every single session, letting the tears flow for most of our forty-five minutes together. It's like she'd been waiting for years to let all her feelings out.

She was tired of being completely self-sufficient. She wanted someone she could depend on the way people depended on her. She was sick of feeling like she wasn't enough in any aspect of her life — not enough for a guy to spend the night, or for her boss to stop playing mind games with her about the quality of her work. Over our months of working together, it became clear to me that Rebecca was still devastated by the trauma of the car accident that had put her in a wheelchair. We unpacked how, since the accident, she'd started caring less about going on vacation with friends or even listening to her favorite music on the car ride home. It was all work and not a single hour of play for her.

In one session Rebecca told me that she was quitting her job — without having another one lined up — and taking some time off to figure out what she wanted to do next. She basically had to get off the nonstop roller coaster of her work life in order to find the space and time she needed to heal. Within six months, she had found a new job in a different industry that had more normal hours and allowed her to delve into her passion for writing. She also had met a great new guy who was different from all the others she'd dated. "Who knows if we'll get married or even last the whole year," she told me. "I am just loving the connection we have right now and can't wait to see where this goes." Now that her every waking hour wasn't devoted to work, she had picked up an old hobby (painting) from her teenage years and reconnected with some friends from high school. They were even planning a visit to come see her. She finally felt like she was living the right life for her.

CAN I INTRODUCE YOU TO THE REAL YOU?

People with High-Functioning Depression think of success as the only path to happiness. Healing can help a person realize they're worthy of joy in life just as they are. Overcoming High-Functioning Depression can help you realize that in focusing on work and achievement, you've built the wrong life for yourself. Doing the work gives you a chance to uncover a new identity and create a new life for a new you. My clients have gone on to quit crazy jobs and toxic relationships in order to uncover their real passion, meet the love of their life, start a family, and more. They no longer worry about waking up one day feeling empty and exhausted, asking themselves, "Was it worth it? Is this how I wanted my life to be?" They know that the new lives they're building now bring them joy today, and will do so tomorrow.

When researching High-Functioning Depression, I asked myself, "What if this condition could work *for* us instead of *against* us?" If all the patients I was meeting with had the power to do it all at home and at work in spite of their symptoms, couldn't they harness the same strength, ability, and energy to change their lives for the better? In the pages of this book, I'm going to ask you to do exactly that. By the time you finish Part One, you'll be able to identify and understand the roots of your High-Functioning Depression. In Part Two, you'll learn how to take that knowledge and use it to honor your needs, find pleasure in all of your relationships, and fill your life with joy. You'll stop walking through your days on autopilot. You'll be too busy fully living.

DO YOU HAVE HIGH-FUNCTIONING DEPRESSION?

I designed this High-Functioning Depression scale for my professional research and adapted it for this book. Tally up how many times you answer yes to the following questions to see whether you have HFD and how complicated a case it might be.

1. Have you felt emotionally numb or detached for a period lasting more than two weeks?
2. In the past, have you experienced significant changes in your sleep patterns, sleeping either too much or too little?
3. Have you noticed a change in your appetite, eating either more or less than usual?
4. Do you often feel inadequate or overwhelmed by guilt, even when others assure you otherwise?
5. Have you experienced persistent low energy or feelings of burnout that make daily tasks challenging?
6. Have you struggled with feelings of hopelessness about the future or your current situation?
7. Do you find it difficult to concentrate or to complete tasks that you previously handled with ease?
8. Have you felt restless or stuck, unable to find satisfaction in activities you used to enjoy?
9. Have you had persistent thoughts about life's pointlessness, or increased thoughts of death or suicide?
10. Have you felt unusually sluggish or slow-moving, to the extent that it impacts your daily activities?

11. Have you lost interest in hobbies or activities that once brought you joy?
12. Do you often avoid seeking help for your problems to avoid burdening others?

SCORE YOURSELF

0–3:

If you answered yes three times or fewer, that's great. You either don't have HFD (0) or have a very mild case (1–3). You may already be practicing some of the techniques that I talk about in Part Two of the book, but you'll probably learn additional ways to bring down your score.

4–7:

If you answered yes between four and seven times, you have moderate High-Functioning Depression. You'll need all of the Five V's that I discuss in Part Two of the book, but you may not need the additional support I discuss, such as therapy.

8–12:

If you answered yes to eight or more questions, you have severe High-Functioning Depression, and you're at high risk for tipping into low-functioning depression. You need to keep reading so that you can start implementing the Five V's right away. You might also want to look at getting some of the additional support I recommend in Chapter 10.

CHAPTER 2

Trauma: The Weight We Carry

We don't talk enough about trauma.

To be fair, of course, if you're in therapy you probably talk a lot about trauma. Or if you're "doing the work" on your own, you probably journal about it or confide in a friend. However, the majority of the time, we try to magically make those excruciating moments of life disappear. We try to force all our trauma into a suitcase, lock it up, and store it away. We climb up on a rickety chair, lift that heavy suitcase up over our heads, and precariously attempt to shove it onto a high shelf, out of sight. Sometimes we get it up on that shelf. Sometimes we lose our balance and fall.

Instead of hiding it away, what we really need to do with this suitcase is unpack it. Trauma is the number one trigger for High-Functioning Depression. Of course, there are biological sources of depression, too. In fact, some research shows that when it comes to the risk of major depression, as much as 50 percent may be correlated with genetics, and thus be heritable — passed down to you through your genes.[1] Hormones and other chemicals in our brains can also play a significant role. However, my research has shown that psychological and social trauma can have significant power to push you into High-Functioning Depression.

Now, not everyone who has experienced trauma has High-Functioning Depression. But if you have High-Functioning Depression, my research has shown that it's very likely that you have experienced trauma. It's also very likely that your traumatic experiences have resulted in your HFD. But instead of acknowledging the trauma, we run from it. We keep pushing ourselves toward the next accomplishment, the next win, the next promotion, the next big event. Until we've pushed ourselves too far.

One of the symptoms of post-traumatic stress disorder (PTSD) is feeling like you're not good enough. You have overly negative thoughts about yourself and the world. You internalize guilt, shame, and blame as a result of your trauma. Those are also factors in High-Functioning Depression. We give too much at work, in friendships, and within our families because of those feelings of not-enough-ness. Subconsciously or consciously, we don't think ourselves worthy of unconditional love, uninterrupted rest, or unapologetic experience of joy in life.

WHAT EXACTLY IS TRAUMA?

One reason we don't talk about trauma is that we don't know exactly what it is. So let's start with a definition. The *DSM-5*, the diagnostic tool that medical professionals use, defines trauma as exposure to actual or threatened death, serious injury, or sexual violence. Exposure counts as directly experiencing the event yourself, witnessing the event happening to someone else, or even learning of a traumatic event that happened to someone close to you. Trauma is being physically assaulted while on a walk through a park in the evening. It's ending up in the hospital on a ventilator after getting Covid at the beginning of the pandemic, before we had treatments. It's having a gun shoved in your face by a police officer simply because you didn't do what they requested the first time.

These are examples of big-T trauma. Though the opinion is controversial, many experts believe the *DSM-5* was too limited when defining trauma. They, like me, talk about both big-T traumas (like those outlined in the *DSM-5*) and little-T traumas (like finding out your partner has been cheating on you, being dragged through a lengthy legal battle, or getting groped by your boss's boss at work). Emotional traumas don't get the attention that physical ones (like having a heart attack or losing a limb) do. In my research, big-T traumas lead to higher scores on assessments of High-Functioning Depression, but both kinds of trauma contribute to the condition. You get a lot of sympathy and empathy for big traumas like surviving a robbery at gunpoint, but when it comes to other traumas, people can be dismissive. For example, if you have given up all your possessions to come to a new country with nothing and start from scratch, people might say, "You're lucky to be in this country." Or if you had a basketball coach who held you to unrealistic standards of perfection, to the point of emotional abuse? People might tell you, "He's the best. You're lucky to train with him."

Almost everyone has trauma, but to different degrees. In my experience there are four types of trauma that lead to High-Functioning Depression. Let's unpack each of them now so that you can see if they resonate. I'm willing to bet that if you're reading this book, more than one will stand out to you.

THE FOUR TYPES OF TRAUMA

Childhood Trauma

By the age of sixteen, Eric, the oldest of three sons, was on a fast track to becoming the black sheep of his family. Extraordinarily bright, he attended an elite prep school on the Upper West Side of Manhattan and consistently brought home A's in all of his subjects. He played tennis competitively and he'd gotten involved in Student Congress—extracurriculars that were attractive to the colleges he was interested in. On the outside, things looked perfect. But on the inside, there were problems. It all started a year earlier when Eric became increasingly disrespectful at home: slamming the door to his room, playing his music a little too loud, not doing a single one of his chores, and even calling his mom the b-word once. His mom, Celeste, worried about Eric and about his brothers, who struggled to know how to respond to Eric's behavior. She and her husband were swift with punishments, but those never really seemed to do the trick.

School seemed to be the one place where Eric maintained appearances, but he never had a circle of friends he wanted to invite for a birthday party or a weekend away with the family. He never seemed to do anything fun—just schoolwork, extracurriculars, and video games in his completely darkened room until Celeste insisted he go to sleep. The worst was when she woke up in the middle of the night once to the sound of Eric vomiting in the downstairs bathroom. By the time she got there, he was passed out on the floor and she was in a panic. She could smell alcohol on his breath and found a bottle of vodka in his room. Celeste was very concerned, but she wasn't exactly surprised. These behaviors hadn't come out of nowhere. She and her husband had been going through a nasty divorce for the past year, during which Eric's acting out had escalated. But she couldn't figure out how to stop it. So she called me.

Divorce is one of the most common childhood traumas I see in my practice. Even with the most amicable of divorces, children can still undergo trauma because divorce hits everyone's emotions, financial security, and physical safety. I'm not suggesting that unhappy couples should stay together. A lot of the time people stay in marriages for their children and the kids end up experiencing more trauma than if the parents had separated. That's definitely the case in domestic violence situations, for example, or volatile environments where the parents argue all the time. But even when divorce is the better of two bad options, it is still going to be a traumatic transition for everyone involved. Divorce is the trauma that keeps on giving — and it happens in almost half of marriages. In South Asian families, like Eric's, divorce is less common and even considered taboo, which added to his trauma.

Eric was scared because suddenly his future was unknown, and the unknown feels terrifying to all of us. Which parent would he live with? Would he and his brothers be split up? How much time would he get with his parents? Would they be able to pay for the college he wanted? The divorce shook his identity. He was no longer a part of an idyllic two-parent family. He was embarrassed at school because, he told me, he had a broken family.

The childhood trauma of divorce kicked Eric's High-Functioning Depression into gear. Had we not started working on it when I met him, he probably would have headed down a dangerous path. Distracting ourselves from our trauma by hyperfocusing on achievements like becoming a star athlete or the school valedictorian might look positive, but it prevents us from fully shaping our identity. When we let ourselves be defined by our achievements, especially at an early age, we don't develop personalities or passions or unique defining traits that set us apart from what we have accomplished. This is why onstage or in public we seem to be exceptional, but offstage and in our families or at home we are empty and dissatisfied and even sometimes dysfunctional. Many of my patients with High-Functioning Depression are stunted in their emotional and personality development due to a childhood trauma.

A lot of the work Eric and I did in therapy was aimed at understanding why couples break up and why his parents had to get divorced. And we explored why acting out was his way of expressing his anger, a way to avoid using his words to talk to them both about how he was feeling. Before we started our work, Eric might do something like "lose" an expensive new jacket that his father had just bought him; after we worked together, he was able to say, "I'm angry with you, Dad, because you told Mom you wanted a divorce."

Divorce is just one of the childhood traumas that stay with us throughout our adult lives. In the late 1990s, a groundbreaking study on adverse childhood experiences (ACEs) was released.[2] By collecting data on thousands of patients, it was able to identify ten types of adverse childhood experiences that predict vulnerability to negative physical and mental health outcomes, like growing up with someone who was a problem drinker, having a parent who ever hit you so hard that it left a mark, or not having had enough food to eat. In the updated 2020 version of the research, experiences like being treated unfairly because of your race or your ethnicity, living in foster care, or witnessing violence were added to the list.[3] All of these traumatic events can trigger negative ripple effects that last into adulthood. According to countless peer-reviewed studies, the more ACEs you have, the more likely you are to have health problems ranging from weight gain and heart disease to depression, anxiety, and substance use disorder.[4] If any of this is making you uncomfortable, take that as a sign that it's time to get help healing from your childhood trauma.

Adult Trauma

As you make your way through adult life, you can have traumatic experiences that bring you to your knees. One interesting twist is that you may choose a profession that can expose you to trauma, putting you at increased risk of High-Functioning Depression. This includes any job that puts you in contact with life-and-death situations, any career where you're constantly being asked to put the well-being of others ahead of your own, and any profession where you are expected to push your body to its limits:

- Police officers, firefighters, EMTs, and other first responders, who run toward danger instead of away from it to save other people

- People in the armed forces, who may risk their lives half a world away to keep their country safe
- Teachers who work in unsupportive or toxic environments, or who are paid so little they experience significant debt while educating the children who are the future of our country
- Professional athletes—from football players to gymnasts—who push their bodies to the point of physical injury in order to perform at the expected level
- Governmental leaders who in office must deal with the pressures of carrying a country through (or trying to avert) wars or other horrors
- Doctors, nurses, and other healthcare workers who witness deaths and serious injuries or illnesses even as they work double or triple shifts

Some people pick these fields and, rather than leave, stay in them and become retraumatized repeatedly. Others have experienced trauma in the past and choose these fields for a false sense of control over their lives. I was the former—until I decided to switch from anesthesiology to psychiatry.

I remember my first day as a medical resident in the intensive care unit. A twenty-year-old patient with HIV and hepatitis C started crashing and needed chest compressions. I jumped into action, doing the chest compressions of CPR even as I felt her ribs crack beneath my hands and she vomited all over me. We were unable to save her, and after they called time of death, no one pulled me aside to ask if I was all right, reassure me or acknowledge how hard I had tried, or even hand me a towel. The faculty physician just looked at me and said, "Okay, let's talk about what we did right and what we did wrong." Every moment of that experience had been traumatic, but not a second was spent helping me process it in a healthy way.

Adults can also find themselves stuck in the cycle of High-Functioning Depression in the wake of a gut-wrenching failure like having to shut down the small business you founded that never took off, forcing you to fire employees who depended on you—and sending you into tremendous debt yourself. Having your livelihood threatened and not knowing if you'll be able to feed yourself or your family or even pay next month's rent is traumatizing. It also can be traumatic to survive a life-threatening health crisis, like a cancer diagnosis or an injury that makes you feel like your body failed you. It can be traumatic to drag yourself out of bed every day and show up to a job where you face an abusive supervisor who trashes your work, insults your intelligence, and barely pays you what you're worth. It can be traumatic to go through a public scandal or humiliation, like having naked pictures of yourself spread on the Internet.

Someone with High-Functioning Depression reacts to these situations by thinking, "I have to do better" or "I can never hit rock bottom ever again." They're haunted by their perceived failure and are constantly trying to polish what was tarnished in the past. It took me two years to realize that my divorce wasn't a personal failing or something that I could control. Instead, it was a major trauma that was forcing me to drastically change my life. That's exactly what happened with my client Ximena, a hardworking thirty-four-year-old elementary schoolteacher.

"I'm ready to find love again," Ximena told me as she nervously crossed and uncrossed her legs while sitting on the edge of my office couch. Two years earlier, Ximena had met a green-eyed IT worker named James in a coffee shop, and she thought that after a decade of searching it was finally her turn to fall in love.

At first her relationship with James felt like the kind that she had witnessed in her parents, who had been married for over forty years. But then, a few months into the relationship, things started to change. James started asking Ximena if he could borrow money for rent or to pay back a friend. If she said no, he'd stop calling or making plans. Eventually she'd give him the money just so that things would go back to "normal." They'd gone from having sex every time they were together to only once a month—he never initiated, and when she wanted to be intimate, he always had an excuse. He seemed to be on edge more often, insulting her with loud comments about her dress not being appropriate for her because she was overweight, or her makeup making her look a little "street."

His temper was worse when they were at her house together. A few times she wondered if he'd get angry enough to hit her. "Everything he did made me feel…smaller," she said. "I have incredible parents, I'm smart, I work on myself—how did I let this happen? I knew that a real relationship didn't work like this. But I took way too long to break up with him."

Ximena maintained top performance at work, but she felt terribly inadequate when she was with James. She didn't dare tell any of her friends because she was so embarrassed about allowing herself to be treated so poorly. But after a hard talk with her gynecologist, whom she had gone to see for a sexually transmitted infection she got from James, she finally realized that it was time to let go of the idea of "what could've been" with him because she needed to keep herself safe.

It is traumatic when people we trust end up being predators: the type of people who target those among us who are generous, vulnerable, kind, or sheltered. I think James was one of those people, picking out a kind, bighearted schoolteacher to take advantage of. It is also an adult trauma to be in a physically, mentally, or emotionally abusive romantic relationship that convinces you you're not good enough and don't deserve a happy life. The trauma of that relationship had destroyed Ximena's self-esteem. She and I worked on building her self-confidence, creating healthy boundaries, and identifying red flags in men so that she would never get walked all over again.

Intergenerational Trauma

Ask anyone who has ever been to my office and they'll confirm the following statement: I have the best pens. In my waiting area you will never see a basic Bic or a cheap promotional pen that came a thousand to a box. I only have collectibles. The first two times Kadene, a client of mine in her forties, asked if she could keep the pen she used to fill out her intake forms, I said yes. But the third time, we almost got into it. Having worked with her, I knew that Kadene had a lucrative and stable career as a data scientist. Crunching numbers didn't thrill her, but it allowed her to live a very comfortable life here in the States and send money back home to her family in the Caribbean. And she certainly could afford to buy all the pens she wanted.

Kadene's parents had grown up without basic needs like three meals a day or clean clothes without holes in them. That childhood trauma then got passed on to their daughter, who never went hungry but watched her parents stockpile food. She never went around wearing clothes with holes in them, but she certainly always had hand-me-downs even though her parents could've bought her new outfits. Her mother and father had passed down what we call scarcity trauma: the experience of having basic needs unfulfilled. As an adult, Kadene could order out every night of the week if she wanted. But she never did, because her inherited trauma made her always worry about losing resources the way her parents had.

I understood this phenomenon well. My mother was the second-to-last of fourteen children who survived childbirth. (My grandmother actually birthed sixteen children.) Because my grandmother had to stretch money so far to support them all, she often withheld food—even when there was enough—just in case. That scarcity mentality was passed along to my mother and then to me, in the form of pressure to excel so that resources would never be scarce again.

Some people react to scarcity trauma from their childhood by forcing themselves into scarcity situations as adults: they go on shopping sprees and max out their credit cards because deep down they're uncomfortable with the amount of money in their bank accounts. Having resources is unfamiliar to them. They can't stop overspending because their brains and their bodies are used to living on the edge of poverty. They were born into debt, so now that they have resources, overspending brings them back to that familiar and comfortable baseline.

Other people react to scarcity trauma by shifting into survival mode. They hoard the plastic containers their takeout comes in because it's basically free Tupperware. They keep the tags on dresses they bought five years ago so they can return them in case they never get around to wearing them. They consider the expiration date on food from the grocery store a suggestion at best and at worst a flat-out lie by food companies to get you to buy more food. Kadene was in the shifting-into-survival-mode category.

"I just take free things," she admitted to me after we talked about all the food missing from the waiting area for my office. I put snacks out because it's impossible to focus on your mental health if your basic needs for food and water aren't being met—which Kadene took as an invitation to bring home breakfast for the rest of the week. "I'm worried one day the money won't be there," she admitted.

Scarcity trauma passed on to her by her parents made her hyper-focused on working hard to have plenty of money in her savings account, keep a fully stocked fridge, and, yes, hoard items that she didn't even need, like the pens from my office. It also triggered her High-Functioning Depression.

Kadene came to me because she was miserable at her job. It paid well, but she often had to work on the weekends, and her boss was horrible to her. Quite often, other people can pick up on the fact that you're a quiet, hardworking employee who can be taken advantage of—and Kadene was a prime example. But she felt stuck.

"I hate it there, but it's a good job, I'm making more money than I ever have, and I'm helping my family," she said to me.

"All right," I replied. "But when are you going to start living for *you?*"

"I don't know," she said, sounding surprised. "I've never thought about that."

Kadene and I spent our time together fleshing out her dreams for her own life as opposed to what others had envisioned for her. We worked together to challenge her fears around her scarcity mindset, and we talked about where she really needed to be frugal and what she might splurge on. She told me about her love of photography and decided to start investing in expensive cameras and taking classes on the weekends. In a few months, she turned that hobby into a side hustle, taking portrait shots of people in her neighborhood on weekends. When it became lucrative enough, after fourteen months, she began working as a full-time photographer. I'd love to tell you she didn't have to take a pay cut, but she did. Still, what's more important is that she looked forward to working every single day, which helped to quiet that paralyzing fear of losing everything. She had time to spend with friends. She was so much happier than she had been in years—and my pens stopped disappearing.

Financial stress is the number one stress in America, and particularly for people with scarcity trauma, so managing it is a big deal. If you're neurodivergent or have ADHD, spending is also an area of weakness and vulnerability; you can have more impulsive behaviors and more stress around money than others. Either way, if you don't have a therapist who is inquiring about your spending habits, bring it up with them or seek out a trusted source to talk to. Even if you don't experience financial hardships, storms your parents had to weather can leave you standing in the rain, soaking wet. Research has shown that historical traumas rooted in racial discrimination and the aftermath of war (like the Holocaust, the Civil War, slavery, the forced relocation of Native Americans, Jim Crow, and the financial impact of World War II on the United Kingdom) can have silent, negative health impacts on the descendants of those who experienced them.[5] In short, our ancestors pass along trauma because trauma impacts our DNA; this is called intergenerational trauma. Passed-down trauma can have an impact not just in the next generation but also in later generations. Intergenerational trauma can impact you if your parents or grandparents were the survivors of genocide or were refugees.

In fact, all the childhood and adulthood traumas I mentioned earlier in this chapter can get passed down to the children of people who experience them. For example, if one or both of your parents have one of those dangerous, trauma-inducing professions (like being a firefighter or a police officer), you and your children could inherit the trauma, becoming exceedingly worried about safety and extra fearful of danger. As another example, coming from a group of people who have been discriminated against—such as immigrants, people of color, and religious minorities—can lead to what's called survivor's guilt. You feel fortunate to live in a place and time that provides more opportunities, but that also means that everyone is counting on you to succeed. You feel the pressure of being a "token minority" or a "model minority." You can never take a break, you can never make a mistake, and unless you heal from your trauma, you may never find happiness or get to know the real you. And the trauma may recur if you feel like you are treated badly or unfairly as a result of your race, ethnicity, or religion.

Drawing Your Trauma Tree

Because we don't talk about trauma, you might not even be aware of some of the trauma that your family members have experienced—and thus the intergenerational trauma you inherited. One of the ways to unpack this is by creating a Trauma Tree. See Appendix A for a comprehensive list of the types of traumatic experiences people with High-Functioning Depression may have lived through. Use it to create a family tree and see how your relatives' experiences may be impacting you — and how your traumas might go on to impact your children. Start with what your family has told you of their experience over the years, but also use this as an opportunity to ask them questions and share what you've learned in this book about what trauma is. Here's an example of my Trauma Tree to help you envision yours.

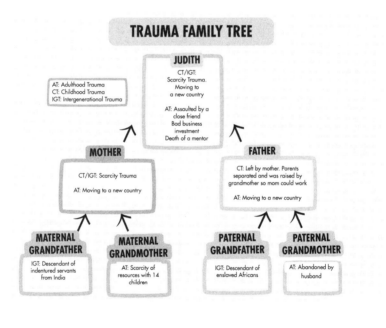

TRAUMA FAMILY TREE

AT: Adulthood Trauma
CT: Childhood Trauma
IGT: Intergenerational Trauma

JUDITH
CT/IGT:
Scarcity Trauma.
Moving to
a new country

AT: Assaulted by a
close friend
Bad business
investment
Death of a mentor

MOTHER
CT/IGT: Scarcity Trauma
AT: Moving to a new country

FATHER
CT: Left by mother. Parents
separated and was raised by
grandmother so mom could work
AT: Moving to a new country

MATERNAL GRANDFATHER
IGT: Descendant of
indentured servants
from India

MATERNAL GRANDMOTHER
AT: Scarcity of
resources with 14
children

PATERNAL GRANDFATHER
IGT: Descendant of
enslaved Africans

PATERNAL GRANDMOTHER
AT: Abandoned by
husband

Collective Trauma

When Hurricane Katrina slammed into the South in 2005, it killed nearly two thousand people, destroyed almost a million homes, and left the people of New Orleans without food, safe water, and shelter.[6]

Bernie Madoff's Ponzi scheme not only siphoned billions from Hollywood A-listers but also drained the life savings of ordinary people hoping to retire comfortably, leaving tens of thousands of people financially devastated.[7]

Nearly three thousand people were killed as a result of the September 11 attacks on the World Trade Center and the Pentagon. The deadliest terrorist event on American soil shook New Yorkers in particular, but also sent shock waves throughout the rest of the nation. Even if you weren't in New York, you felt like it had happened to you. You worried that it could happen again, maybe this time in your city.[8]

Covid-19 killed millions of people across the globe and put half of the world in economic peril. People actually wondered, "Is this how it all ends?"[9] As a minority female business owner who ran a lab and had a thriving practice during the pandemic, I'm not fully over the collective trauma of Covid.

The impact of these types of collective traumas is so immense, it has an entire field devoted to it: disaster psychiatry. But unlike the other types of trauma that I've discussed, collective trauma may be easier to heal from because you're not singled out and alone; instead, you're going through it with other people. You're not the target. Everyone is suffering. There's community in collective trauma. And usually there are more resources available to help people deal with the fallout.

At the same time, people with HFD that has been triggered by a collective trauma feel like they have to carry the weight of the world on their shoulders — like they can't let their team, family, or community down. Everyone wants a part of them. Even though they've suffered the same trauma as everyone else, they don't give themselves a break. Even though there are times when these people want to give up, they don't because they can't disappoint others. That's certainly what happened to me and, I'm sure, countless others.

I liken what we're experiencing today to an ocean of trauma. The waves keep coming, one after another, so we can never recover. We're trying to swim back to shore, but wave upon wave of trauma is taking us back out to sea. Some waves feel rough but manageable. Others are so large that we struggle to catch our breath. (See the diagram below.) While some of us can be overwhelmed by the waves, those of us who have processed our trauma in therapy and learned tools for managing it are able to navigate those waves like a professional surfer. We watch a wave coming in, get on our board, and ride the wave until the waters become calm again.

WHY WE IGNORE TRAUMA

Regardless of how big or small a particular trauma was, it's trauma, and it's all emotionally, physically, and psychologically shattering — which is a big reason we don't talk about it. Let's say you survived witnessing your mother physically assaulted by your father, or you were able to walk away from a car crash despite seeing your life flash before your eyes. Who wants to relive that kind of event? Trauma is like a horror movie that scared the living daylights out of you or a roller-coaster ride you had to shut your eyes to make it through. You just want it to be over. Another way to think of it is like an onion that you're afraid to start peeling and chopping. You know it's going to make your eyes water, but you don't realize that once you get through the crying and the stinging, you'll be able to wipe away the tears and see clearly again. Another reason we shy away from talking about trauma is that one of the lesser-known symptoms of both trauma and depression is guilt, and the feeling of guilt, which often leads to shame, forces us to ignore and bury trauma.

What feels more comfortable or easier than talking about our trauma is imagining that the horrible thing didn't happen at all. Avoiding people, places, situations, and reminders of trauma is a well-documented symptom of PTSD. We often essentially gaslight ourselves as a coping mechanism to avoid the uncomfortable truth about our trauma. However, pretending that thing from our past didn't occur or doesn't matter is the worst type of magical thinking. You imagine, "If I don't talk about it, it didn't happen." Or "It was bad, but it wasn't that bad. So I can just move on." Without acknowledging the truth, we can't get validation from others about how terrible the experience was, or support from qualified people who can help us heal.

There are other reasons some people don't talk about trauma, including something as simple as not having the words for it. Maybe we don't know how to share what happened, or we're afraid of what others might say to us when we open up to them. It could be that from a cultural point of view, you don't have the language for talking about trauma. Perhaps your culture condones or looks the other way regarding practices that others would consider traumatic—female genital mutilation, which is a part of cultures in some areas of Africa, Asia, and the Middle East; honor killings, which have roots in some cultures in Asia, the Middle East, and North Africa; corporal punishment, which is still tolerated in some schools; dangerous hazing rituals, which still take place in some military environments.[10] Finding culturally competent care (so the person helping you understands you better) may be critical for processing your trauma. When I attend Caribbean mental health fairs, people come to my booth but then pretend they are just there for the food because there's so much stigma around therapy. I work hard to show attendees that mental health is actually part of our Caribbean values. Other times, it may take an outsider (so the person helping you is unbiased) to help you feel heard. Figure out what works best for you. Attempting to ignore, diminish, or compartmentalize your trauma forever can have serious consequences.

WHY WE THINK WE ACTUALLY DESERVE TRAUMA

Have you ever heard of the "just world" hypothesis? It's the idea that good things happen to good people and bad things happen to bad people. For example, when a woman walking in the park in the evening gets physically assaulted at knifepoint, many people think, "She shouldn't have been there. She should have known she'd attract unwanted attention." Or during the pandemic, when people came down with Covid and ended up in the hospital, many people thought, "They probably weren't wearing a mask" or "They went ahead and attended an indoor party, so that's what they get." Or if someone is a victim of police violence, there are those who think, "They probably gave the cops a hard time" or "They shouldn't have been in that area late at night." Too often, we don't show compassion for people who go through certain types of trauma because we think they must've done something to deserve what happened to them. Even if you're able to catch yourself before saying these things out loud, such negative thoughts often get to live in our minds for a few seconds before we squash them.

Instead of blindly accepting the "just world" hypothesis, let's look at some cases where it's wrong. After all, bad things happen to good people every single day. Someone who eats healthfully and exercises on a regular basis gets cancer. Someone who is a devoted caregiver to their elderly parents gets fired for missing too much work and needs to file for bankruptcy. A generous person who volunteers at a homeless shelter is robbed and killed on the way home from a dinner shift. Not to mention that good things happen to bad people every day. Abusive people can build billion-dollar businesses by taking advantage of their employees while they vacation on their mega-yachts. Violent criminals escape jail time because there's not enough evidence against them for a conviction. That guy who cut you off on the freeway will calmly get to his destination on time while you arrive late and still brimming with road rage.

While we might recognize that the "just world" hypothesis is false when it comes to others, those of us with High-Functioning Depression often don't recognize that the hypothesis is false when it comes to *our own trauma*. We don't realize that we didn't do anything to deserve what happened to us. We don't give ourselves compassion, take time to acknowledge our pain, and learn how to move forward in our lives in a healthy way. We do the opposite. We walk around thinking that the bad thing happened to us because we were careless or irresponsible, or we come to think that we just might be a bad person. One of the most common symptoms of trauma is internalized blame and shame. We think we must've done something wrong, something to make us deserve what happened to us. So we stop caring that we're feeling meh about everything because we suspect we might not be worthy of happiness. That meh feeling is yet another sign that it's time to take steps to break the cycle.

CHAPTER 3

Anhedonia: Did You Know You're Unhappy?

I love Batman. If we ever meet, feel free to debate me on who wore the black cape best. Without hesitation, I will tell you that Michael Keaton was my favorite Batman and the 1989 film with Jack Nicholson as the Joker was my favorite Batman movie.

You had billionaire Bruce Wayne, a poster child for High-Functioning Depression triggered by childhood trauma. Both his parents were murdered in front of him when he was just a boy, which led him directly to the adult traumas of constantly putting himself in harm's way, fighting crime, and running toward danger, like police officers and other first responders. (One of the lesser-known symptoms of trauma is putting yourself into risky situations to trick your brain into thinking you have a sense of control over danger.) Batman always puts the needs of Gotham's people ahead of his own — and he doesn't even get paid for it. Add on top of that the collective trauma of living in Gotham, a city constantly on the brink of disaster. That's a lot of trauma — and Bruce Wayne/Batman pushed through all of it, working around the clock to track criminals, build sophisticated crime-busting gadgets, and be the hero Gotham needs.

The Joker was just as determined as Batman, but you know what the difference was between the two of them? The Joker had fun. Batman had a cold stare, kept his jaw squared, and had a black suit on when he descended into a room. The Joker wore brightly colored outfits, had a perpetual smile, and left behind exploding gifts. Batman sat in his cave alone, brooding and plotting his next move. The Joker and his crew gleefully danced their way through a museum while intentionally knocking over priceless statues and scrawling graffiti on iconic paintings. "Jack is dead," the Joker says to his former boss after the accident at a chemical factory that led to his chalk-white face and exaggerated smile. "You can call me the Joker. And as you can see, I'm a lot happier."

Don't get me wrong. The Joker had some serious mental health issues. But our hero, Batman, wasn't much better off—and many of us are walking around like Batman. We're trying to distract ourselves from our trauma by trying to be the hero. We do, do, do. We go, go, go. But we never feel, feel, feel. That goes for both happiness and sadness. We don't end up necessarily feeling depressed or sad. We end up with anhedonia, which is feeling nothing.

ANHE-WHAT?

Have you heard the saying "Not all who wander are lost"? Well, not all who are depressed feel sad. Some feel nothing or empty. They feel blah or numb. Some even feel constantly restless. Those people are experiencing what is called anhedonia. And chances are that if you're experiencing it, you probably don't even realize it.

"Anhedonia" is a word that has been in the medical literature for over a century. The term was coined back in the late 1800s by French psychologist Théodule Ribot to describe the disappearance or absence of the ability to feel pleasure.[1] While anhedonia isn't new, it presents as a new beast in the 2020s compared to the 1890s. The *DSM-5* defines it specifically as "markedly diminished interest or pleasure in all, or almost all, activities." It manifests in two ways: first, you stop seeking out fun things that used to bring you joy, and second, even when you participate in them, they don't bring you joy.[2] An easy way to remember what it means is to break down the word into its Greek roots: *an-* means "without" and *hedone* is "pleasure," so it literally translates as "without pleasure" or "lack of joy."[3]

When you're experiencing anhedonia, your daily goal is just getting through the day—not trying something new at that delicious Italian restaurant you're going to with friends after work, or perfecting your form on that dumbbell press at the gym, or checking in the morning to see if that beauty serum is starting to take effect. Even the joy of achieving a task like successfully executing a new recipe for a family dinner or wrapping up a report at work is robbed from us. There's no excitement from expecting, no joy from experiencing, and no pride for executing those goals. Only self-doubt: "Should I have seasoned the pork chop differently?" "Was the PowerPoint engaging enough?" And once we're past that, we don't celebrate it. Instead, we're on to the next goal. And the next. And the next.

I believe anhedonia is something that we all experience at one point or another. I estimate that at least 95 percent of us have felt this feeling at some moment in time: our favorite song just doesn't uplift us the way it usually does, or getting to sit down with a pair of knitting needles for an hour is not as satisfying as usual. Anhedonia quietly sneaks up on you — seemingly out of nowhere — and starts stealing all of the joy out of your life. You're killing it at work and you're a pillar of strength at home, but when you reach inbox zero while everyone is out on a Saturday night, leaving you home alone, you're not satisfied with a job well done. Instead, you feel empty. For many, anhedonia can pass as quickly as it came, and it's not an issue. It's a problem, however, when you experience it for long stretches of time. And because people with High-Functioning Depression are very good at adapting to uncomfortable circumstances, we can feel this way for long periods of time without even realizing it.

I want to bring the term "anhedonia" into everyday language because there's power in naming something. The act of identifying and naming how you feel makes you feel better and less scared. It's called "affect labeling," and it's a process of emotional regulation that research shows can help you feel less stressed.[4] I wanted that for my patients who, increasingly over the past few years, were telling me that they weren't enjoying things as much as they used to. They weren't processing their emotions, so they didn't really know how they felt. These people were busying themselves as a distraction or as a way to sublimate uncomfortable feelings. Anhedonia also helps numb those uncomfortable feelings. But not forever.

A patient of mine who was experiencing anhedonia told me a story about how she was vacuuming her living room and suddenly started screaming and crying. But as soon as she saw that her behavior was terrifying her three-year-old daughter, who had been playing on her iPad but then started pulling on her mother's skirt to see what was wrong, she immediately stopped crying, comforted her daughter, put away the vacuum, started making dinner for the family, and went right on with her day. She never told a soul what happened until she eventually came to me for treatment of her postpartum depression and HFD. We can run from these symptoms and conditions, but we can't hide from them forever.

It's important to note that anhedonia itself isn't a condition or a disease. It's a symptom of a condition. Anhedonia is to depression, for example, what a dry cough and sneezing are to a cold. It's also just as contagious, in a way. We've all had that angry professor, micromanaging boss, or impossible-to-please relative who overworked themselves, projected their issues onto others, and was inherently joyless. I've even been guilty of this in my own family. Not only was I overextended, but I signed my grade-school daughter up for so many activities (ballet, swimming, soccer) that she was overextended as well. "Are you having fun?" I asked her once. "I'm okay," she said, without any emotion in her voice. That lack of feeling can so easily be spread to the family members, colleagues, or friends who constantly interact with the anhedonic person. They normalize "blahness" with every interaction they have. After my daughter gave me that ambivalent response, I decided that if she's not passionate about an activity, we put a pause on it and instead focus on ones she does feel passionate about. The treatment for anhedonia is to be present and do things you once loved with full attention. As it turned out, a few months after I pulled her out of swimming, she mentioned that she wanted to go back to the pool and that she missed her teacher. That's how I knew it was time to sign her up again.

Not to scare you, but some of the most common conditions associated with anhedonia range from psychiatric disorders (like schizophrenia) and neurodegenerative disorders (like Alzheimer's and Parkinson's) to substance use disorders.[5] When someone is dependent on a substance, for example, they eventually stop getting pleasure out of using it. It doesn't give them the same high that it did at first. So why do they keep going back to it? Because they are trying to get that feeling back. People in the autism community may display anhedonia because their decision-making processes are less influenced by rewards.[6] Anhedonia only gets addressed in loud, more visible conditions. But in the quiet, invisible conditions that fly under the radar, like High-Functioning Depression, it goes undetected. We need to start paying attention to the people who fly under the radar.

Anhedonia is symptomatic not only of High-Functioning Depression but also of post-traumatic stress disorder. That's one of the reasons I've spent so much time covering the impact that trauma has on people with High-Functioning Depression. It's all connected. When you try to think about when you started to feel anhedonic, try to locate the point in time when you first experienced trauma. That's probably when you stopped prioritizing play. That's when you went from being in your feelings to feeling nothing. And that's when you stopped filling your cup with joy. If you're wondering if you are experiencing anhedonia, there's a quiz at the end of this chapter (page 68) you can take to find the answer.

WHY HAVEN'T I HEARD ABOUT ANHEDONIA?

For one thing, it's a quiet symptom. Other symptoms of depression can be loud. Depression can show up as loved ones who are absent from family gatherings. It can manifest as crying and tearfulness. It can be overwhelming. Anhedonia is silent and sneaky. It's not glaring. It's not obvious.

The term "anhedonia" also sounds awkward. There's not a lot of love for medical jargon in popular culture. In science and medicine, we use polysyllabic words with Greek and Latin roots all the time, but in everyday speech they're rare and frustrating to people.

Another reason you may not have heard of anhedonia is that doctors aren't really looking for it, so it floats under the radar. They make note when someone has no sex drive, has a loss of energy, has a lack of appetite, or talks about not wanting to live. They don't notice when eating doesn't give you pleasure or you're having sex just to make your partner happy. They're about keeping you alive, not helping you get the most out of life. If you're experiencing it, you might not even say anything to your doctor because the feeling has become so normal to you that you no longer notice it, or because you imagine everyone else has the same meh feeling you do. It's easy to explain away not having a good time at the movies because you were so tired from a long day of cleaning the house and prepping meals. Or to think that the reason you couldn't savor sitting quietly with your latte at the café is that you were so distracted by work. If you don't bring it up, chances are your primary care provider might not notice your anhedonia, much less take action.

In medicine, we've traditionally been focused on fixing problems. If a patient is sad, we want to help them become happier. If they're on the road to burnout, we want to help them ramp up their self-care and slow their pace. But if the patient is feeling meh? That problem isn't often recognized. We don't focus enough on cultivating joy in my profession. We focus on what's wrong with people, rather than what could be right with them.

One last reason you don't hear much about anhedonia is that our culture doesn't encourage talking about our feelings. It's actually the opposite; our culture actively discourages feeling our feelings. Think of all the times that people ask you "How are you?" and you give them a generic "Fine" instead of a thoughtful answer, something like "I'm exhausted" or "I'm feeling exhilarated" or even "You know what? I'm not sure." How often are you at a party and someone checks in, asking, "Are you having a good time?" and you reflexively tell them, "Yeah!" But in reality you can't find someone to talk to and could use an intro. Or you're feeling pretty meh today and in all honesty even a party couldn't snap you out of it. Or your feet are killing you and there aren't enough seats. We don't want to be rude or take up too much of another person's time with our feelings and needs. But it might also be that we don't want to take a good look at our feelings ourselves.

HOW ANHEDONIA IS TIED TO HFD

In medical school, future doctors learn to look at ailments through a biological, psychological, and social lens. It's called the biopsychosocial model.[7] Every physician is aware of this model, which helps them not only understand the cause of an illness but also identify all of the potential solutions for treating it. Here I want to walk you through a biopsychosocial model for High-Functioning Depression in a post-Covid world where rates of anhedonia have skyrocketed (one out of two people worldwide is at risk of experiencing a mental health disorder by the time they reach age seventy-five, and during the pandemic rates of depression increased 25 percent globally).[8] You

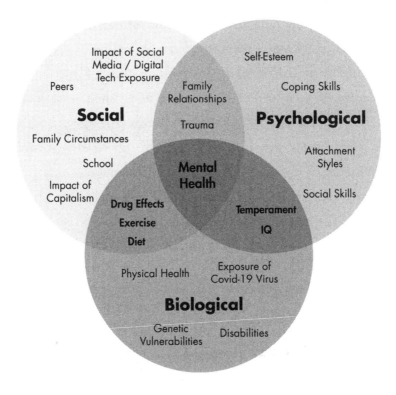

can use three lenses to look at (and ideally list out) the root causes of your High-Functioning Depression. They'll also help you start to uncover the science of your happiness.

Biological Factors

When a patient presents with High-Functioning Depression, I first consider their biology. Do they have a history of depression, anhedonia, or any other mental health condition that might be impacting their mood? I look at genetics. Does any family member have a history of depression or another mental health condition? Has the patient ever noticed that a parent or sibling seemed to struggle to enjoy life?

The biological part of an ailment includes not just the disease itself but also other factors that affect the human body. These days, our bodies are exposed to extreme forms of pollution. We consume a lot of highly processed foods. We are fairly immobile compared to our predecessors, who hunted, foraged, and fished—we just click and food comes to our door in thirty minutes or less; we're not walking to work but hopping into an Uber. Not getting enough sunlight or exercise can definitely have a direct impact on your mood, as can poor nutrition.

Do One Thing: Make a Small Health Move

Research shows that even if you don't feel love toward yourself, if you behave in a way that shows yourself love, it can help you overcome the anhedonia, sadness, or depression that you are experiencing. You can use this knowledge to outsmart your biology in small ways. Ground yourself daily in just one self-care activity that can help you be more present in the moment, feel less stressed, and possibly experience more joy. A stressed brain, after all, can't experience joy. Going for a five-minute walk, for example, could help improve your mood — not to mention the benefits of getting some steps in and breathing fresh air. And while low vitamin D levels are tied to increased symptoms of anxiety and depression, it only takes between five and thirty minutes of sun exposure most days of the week for your body to produce the amount of vitamin D it needs.[9]

While mental health issues can't be cured in a day, any small step — from a journaling session to searching online for a free group therapy session — could provide the momentum you need to create bigger change.

Knowing how you scored on the anhedonia quiz (page 68) can help you find more experiences to create for yourself that will lead to you feeling more joy. Look at the questions you answered yes to and consider what you would need to do to turn that yes into a no. What would make taking a soak in the tub more enjoyable — maybe some candles or a bath bomb? How could you be more present during intimacy — maybe having a sexy getaway at a hotel? You are probably thinking, "Wait, Dr. Judith. Instead of just trying to boost joy in new ways, why not do more of the things I already enjoy?" Of course you can still enjoy things you find pleasure in now. But the goal is to increase your overall joy by creating new experiences you cherish, and by finding more joy in the places where it is lacking right now.

Psychological Factors

From our level of self-esteem to our attachment styles, psychological factors often come back to trauma, which we discussed in the last chapter. One of the biggest ones that we all experienced was the pandemic. Even though we are living in a post-pandemic period, Covid was a major collective trauma with ripple effects lasting until today—and beyond. Suddenly, one day in March 2020, we were told that other humans were dangerous, to maintain six feet of distance, and not to leave the house. When our own family members got sick, we had to quarantine them under the same roof. Suddenly the things that bring us joy became sources of fear and anxiety: family gatherings, birthday parties, just getting together indoors to go bowling or go to a museum. It's hard to look forward to having fun with other people when you're terrified of being infected by them.

In disaster psychiatry we learn that memorials are very important to processing and healing from collective trauma. In New York City, for example, we have the waterfall memorials to September 11 at the World Trade Center. In London, the Stairway to Heaven Memorial commemorates the worst civilian disaster of World War II.[10] Even on a smaller scale, the tombstones we purchase for loved ones in graveyards or the plaques we put on benches memorialize the love that we have lost. And many countries have designated special days to commemorate collective trauma, such as Martin Luther King Jr. Day and International Holocaust Remembrance Day. These things are important because they validate how we felt and what we went through. But there is currently no memorial or day of remembrance for Covid-19. We've just been told to move on, without acknowledging how tragic, difficult, and joyless those years were. We suffered collectively, but the onus is on us to heal individually. However, those of us who feel like we are *not* back to normal don't need to feel as though we're crazy. There is nothing wrong with us. Something bad happened to all of us, and we are still processing it without the help of society.

Do One Thing: Get Honest About Your Emotions

Remember how I said that culturally it's accepted to hide your feelings? Well, this is something we have the power to change, one conversation at a time. Every time we respond to someone who asks "How are you?" with a genuine response instead of a canned "Good, and you?" we're taking one step forward in breaking the taboo. But in order to do this, you might need some new vocabulary words.

Take a look online and search for a feelings wheel.[11] The words, which list an array of emotions, may include adjectives you haven't used in decades, so it's important to refamiliarize yourself with them. You might actually have to look up what some of them mean. Then, the next time someone asks you how you are feeling, instead of saying "Fine," think back to the wheel and offer a more thoughtful answer. If you're not comfortable doing this with the people around you, you can also do it with yourself in a journal. For example, are you tired of that chain restaurant always getting your order wrong, or are you angry about it? Are you just happy to be seeing your new baby niece, or are you elated? Are you annoyed with your boss, or do you feel betrayed by him? There is power in naming your feelings.

Social Factors

Your family, friend circles, school colleagues, and more have an impact on your High-Functioning Depression, but so does something that isn't a living, breathing thing: social media. During the pandemic, we were all isolated from each other. What did we use to feel connected? Social media. And how did we use it? In excess. There's still a lot we don't know about the long-term effects of social media on the brain, and especially on the developing brain. But we do know that in the short term it interrupts the reward pathways that control pleasure and joy—and that's a recipe for anhedonia. Recent data from the Centers for Disease Control show that people are affected by the constant images of perfection they see on social media and television. That if a young person is rejected by a peer or left out on social media, this emotional pain can feel worse to them than physical pain. Humans are designed to live in the world—not in front of a screen. During the pandemic we had no choice. Now we do. But many of us have not reentered the world and are still conducting our lives predominantly on screens.

Substance use disorders also fall under the umbrella of social factors. We are now seeing the worst substance use disorder epidemic in U.S. history, and it is directly tied to the pandemic. Some people who typically did not drink, for example, turned to binge drinking or drinking in excess. Other people who had never used dating apps started seeking out unhealthy sexual relationships online. And, of course, a lot of people started working way too hard. We were chasing releases of dopamine, a feel-good chemical in the brain, to make ourselves feel a burst of pleasure. As a result, we became more dependent on these things—alcohol, sex, work—to deliver that elusive high.

Social media algorithms impact your brain in a way that mimics substance use. The inconsistency of hits of pleasure along with the low lows you feel when you are rejected online set your brain up for anhedonia just like the highs and lows of drugs do. In the same day, I may see a teen patient who reports not feeling excited about anything, so he stays home on his phone all day, and a young adult patient who is four weeks sober and feels that nothing brings him joy the way alcohol did. And it is not just social media. Streaming makes it easy to create unhealthy habits: We don't patiently wait for an episode to come out in a week, we binge-watch a whole season or even a whole series in one night. Then we feel empty and meh when it is over.

Do One Thing: See No Evil, Hear No Evil, Speak No Evil

This exercise is about eliminating social factors that could be having a negative impact on your feelings and temperament. After all, if you're already experiencing anhedonia, you don't want experiences that could take you from feeling blah to feeling bad.

If you *see* things on social media that make you feel bad about yourself, for example, try unfollowing some negative accounts or limiting the time you spend scrolling. If you find yourself attracted to gossiping and *hearing* bad things about another person, stop. Gossip can sometimes feel like a form of connecting, but in reality it separates us from each other. It's not just sharing information; it's sharing information with the intention of taking delight in another person's misery. You don't have to watch TMZ or read celebrity mags or talk to your auntie about which relative is doing what shady thing this week.

Finally, if you find yourself tempted to *speak* ill of other people, don't. Ever notice that the people in your life who say the most negative things are inherently unhappy? It's hard to start speaking positively about yourself until you stop speaking negatively about others. Changing any behavior isn't easy, but give it at least a week to see how your mood has shifted.

I've given you a few ideas to get you started on the road to being happier and experiencing more joy in life. There are far more exercises in the second part of this book, when you dive into the Five V's, but for now just keep in mind that the goal is not to be *happy;* it's to be *happier.* The first is an ideal we may never reach. The second is completely obtainable on an hourly basis. You may not be the most joyful person you know, but you can increase your joy points every day simply by hugging a loved one, letting yourself take a break from work to eat lunch on a park bench, or sitting at your kitchen table to drink a cup of coffee in peace—no phone scrolling, no doing the dishes really quickly while you're in there, just sitting.

Looping back around to the way I began this chapter, I should point out that at the end of the day, neither our hero, Batman, nor our antihero, the Joker, got it right. When we experience trauma, we may go into one of two modes: all logical / not feeling anything (like Batman) or all emotional / acting on fear and grief (like the Joker). But none of us truly wants to be Batman or the Joker. When you process trauma, you learn to have a balance of both logic and emotion, which we call Wise Mind in Dialectical Behavioral Therapy. What I wish for you is that hybrid. I wish for you to have Batman's logical, good intentions paired with the Joker's emotional capacity for joy. Sure, you can save the world. But make sure you're having as much fun as possible while doing it.

ARE YOU EXPERIENCING ANHEDONIA?

If you're wondering whether you fit the criteria for experiencing anhedonia, there's a test for that right here. There are already scales for anhedonia related specifically to food, sex, or hobbies in the medical literature, but I developed a new one that addresses the overall lack of pleasure that you might have related to High-Functioning Depression. Keep track of your yes and no responses to the following questions. If you're ever uncertain about how to answer, choose the response that feels most authentic. There is no middle ground.

One thing you may notice about the test is that it is sensory in nature. This is why I want to be clear in the definition of what "joy" really is. I want to be sure that you aren't expecting to be smiling or exploding with happiness with every action. Engaging in the acts described in these questions means that you are pleasing your senses. You are able to feel pampered or proud. You can luxuriate in one moment and feel fulfilled in another. All of these feelings are joyful. "Happy" is not necessarily the only feeling that we are addressing in anhedonia. Anhedonia is lack of joy, all these other feelings, and more.

Ideally, you'll take this quiz twice: once now and again when you're finished reading the book to see how your answers may have changed.[12]

1. Do you often make delayed future happiness statements instead of feeling gratitude in the moment?

   These sound like "When I get this job, then I will finally be happy" or "When I fall in love one day, then I will finally be happy."

2. Do you find it hard to feel fulfilled by resting or taking breaks because, instead, you feel restless and empty when you're not busy?

3. Do you almost never take the time to savor your meals?

   This might be because you're multitasking by eating while working, mindlessly munching in front of the TV at night, or scarfing down food in the evening because you forgot to eat all day.

4. Do you seldom enjoy the curiosity of reading for leisure?

5. When you take naps, do you wake up feeling tired instead of refreshed?

6. When you watch TV or movies (streaming included), are you doing something else or distracted from the program?

7. When you make an effort to dress up, do you hardly ever luxuriate in the experience?

8. When others compliment you, do you have a hard time feeling pride at the praise?

   This might sound like you saying, "Oh, I got this on sale" or "This hairstyle is pretty much wash and go."

9. Do you have a difficult time feeling connected to others during social interactions with friends and/or family members?

10. Is it challenging for you to relax on vacations and/or holidays?

    This might be because you bring your laptop with you for work or you overpack the family itinerary with too much to do.

11. Do you find it difficult to enjoy your expertise with your favorite hobbies or activities?

12. Do you find it hard to feel delight in listening to music?

13. Do you have a difficult time enjoying sensuality during physical intimacy or sexual behavior?

14. Do you struggle to feel present during self-care activities?

    Self-care activities could be anything from a warm bath, massage, or mani-pedi to journaling, doing yoga, or coloring in an adult coloring book.

15. Do you find it difficult to be present while experiencing simple pleasures?

    Examples of simple pleasures might be sipping a nice cup of coffee, putting lotion on your body, or smelling cupcakes baking at a bakery.

16. Do you have a hard time feeling skillful or in flow while working?

    This could be because you often feel your work is not good enough or you could have done better.

SCORE YOURSELF

0–3:

If you have three or fewer yes answers, that's great. You either don't have anhedonia or are experiencing it very mildly. That means you're likely engaging in activities that are giving you purpose, meaning, and joy. Whatever those things are, keep it up. What you're doing is working. The only thing you may want to focus on is adding to your calendar even more enjoyable things to look forward to, both in the short term and in the long term.

4–11:

If you have four to eleven yes answers, you likely have mild to moderate anhedonia. Your attempts at joy might be lopsided efforts. For example, you might be making time for joy, but you're too stressed to experience it. Perhaps you book vacations to relax, but you end up working through them. Or maybe you make plans to see concerts with your friends, but you're gone before the final set because you feel guilty missing your kids' bedtime. Maybe you're dashboard dining on your drive to work, or you pride yourself on having not taken any personal time off in years. If this sounds like you, don't worry—there are plenty of techniques and exercises later in this book to help you.

12–16:

If you answered yes more than eleven times, you likely have severe anhedonia and may need extra support in addition to this book, like group therapy, one-on-one therapy, or a prescription medication.

(I've included more information on this in Chapter 10.) You need a higher level of care because your lack of joy puts you at an increased risk for slipping into low-functioning depression or acquiring a substance use disorder. This is especially true if your relationships are faltering, because this can mean that you don't have a support system of friends and relatives to listen to you, validate your feelings, and keep an eye on you. Happiness researchers have shown that unhappy people are at increased risk for poor work performance, getting divorced, and even experiencing a heart attack, so it's important to take severe anhedonia seriously.[13]

CHAPTER 4

Masochism: Why Do I Self-Sabotage?

I never thought I'd end up in therapy. But I spent three years see-ing a therapist who charged $450 per session—and I didn't truly take advantage of his help until the last few months. Can you believe that? Let me explain.

On my way to becoming a psychiatrist, I was in training at Columbia University, where they paired psychiatry residents with highly sought-after analytic psychiatrists for therapy sessions. We were residents, though, so instead of being charged what would be the equivalent of $450 now, we paid a tenth of that for forty-five minutes with the brilliant minds who saw high-profile clients from addresses on New York's posh Upper East Side.

The goal was to make sure that we examined ourselves before examining other patients. Our teachers wanted to make sure we had unpacked our own trauma and our own issues that could get in the way of successfully treating others. Basically, it's putting on that pro-verbial oxygen mask first—a pretty brilliant idea. So once a week, I'd lug an excruciatingly heavy purse filled with two laptops and whatever textbooks I was studying at the time over to my fancy therapist's office. I'd sit in a luxuriously decorated waiting room with an expensive Persian rug on the floor, which I'd stare at until the therapist called me into his office. And when I left, I'd always pass by the same guy in a well-tailored suit and slicked-back hair. Probably a Wall Street guy, I thought. He smelled of money and, for reasons I wouldn't discover until later, he always looked at me a little strangely as I passed him in the waiting room on my way out.

To tell you the truth, I was skeptical of the process for a while. I even skipped sessions in the beginning. I thought I didn't need therapy. "I'm doing fine," I said to myself. "This is a waste of my time." I wanted to get to the real work. I believed being a psychiatrist would mean focusing on people with major mental health issues, like schizophrenia. I didn't have a major mental health issue like that, so what did I need therapy for? I didn't realize—and you might not yet, either—that those kinds of acute disorders are not the majority of mental health problems in the world. Think about it: How many people do you know with schizophrenia? Now how many people do you know who probably have High-Functioning Depression? The majority of people who need a therapist's help think they're doing all right but they actually aren't. The majority of people who need a therapist's help, as my high-priced psychiatrist was about to reveal, were like me.

What my therapist saw that I couldn't was that I was completely burned out. I had given myself an insanely punishing schedule without realizing it. For starters, I was in a highly competitive program at an Ivy League institution in one of the fastest-paced cities in the world. I had begun my career in medicine thinking I would go into anesthesiology, and that training required waking up at 5 a.m. to get to the hospital in go-go-go mode, where I'd hear bloodcurdling screams for epidurals from women in labor and be confronted with death almost every single day. It was all so intense. I'd go home, go to sleep, and do it all over again the next day.

After two years in anesthesiology, I decided to leave the program. I was having severe anxiety about the extreme nature of the field. And I was being drawn in a different direction. In my last year of medical school I'd spent a life-changing month leading trauma clinics in South Africa at an orphanage for HIV-infected girls. That was the kind of impact I wanted to have. So I decided I wanted to transition from anesthesiology to psychiatry. I got the last spot available in Columbia's program. After my first year in the program, I got to research cultural competency, which meant traveling across the globe to understand how different cultures approached mental health. To date, I've traveled to thirty different countries. Anytime I had a break from school, I would travel abroad. But not for vacation. I would work in other countries, presenting and learning about how psychiatry is practiced abroad and how mental health issues are treated through a cultural lens. I even created a program so that my fellow residents could learn Spanish and increase our cultural competency here at home. It felt so normal to me to work this hard that I didn't even realize I was risking my health in the process.

After about five sessions — most of which I showed up late for — my therapist looked me in the eyes and said something he shouldn't have. "We're not supposed to use the term 'masochism' in therapy, but it applies to you," he said. "You're a masochist."

It wasn't until we unpacked that diagnosis and I learned what masochism truly was that I started to understand why I had been running myself ragged trying to do all the things. So let me explain it to you here, and maybe you'll have the same experience.

NO, NOT THAT TYPE OF MASOCHISM

When most people hear the word "masochism," they think about whips and chains. That's not the type of masochism that we're talking about. This isn't about sexual preferences. In fact, it's not about sex at all. Masochism, as defined by the *DSM-III* beginning in 1980, is a personality disorder characterized by a pervasive pattern of self-defeating, people-pleasing behavior.[1] Like me choosing work over vacation, lugging around two laptops in my purse, skipping sessions with a high-priced therapist that I got to see for practically free — and waiting until one of our final meetings to tell him about a traumatic and toxic romantic relationship I'd been in.

Masochism is a form of self-sabotage. According to the *DSM-III,* when someone has masochistic tendencies, "the person may often avoid or undermine pleasurable experiences, be drawn to situations or relationships in which they will suffer, and prevent others from helping them."

But by 1994, when the next version of our medical bible, the *DSM-IV,* came out, this definition was nowhere to be found. This volume included a disorder called "sexual masochism," but it had dropped any reference to the self-defeating behaviors mentioned in the previous version.[2] I remember being taught during my psychiatric training that masochism had been removed from the *DSM* because it was politically controversial. People were concerned it was seen as victim-blaming, particularly when it came to labeling survivors of domestic violence as masochistic. Some of the traits listed in the *DSM-III* included choosing people and situations that lead to disappointment, opting for failure or mistreatment when better options are clearly available, and inciting anger or rejection from others and then feeling hurt, defeated, or humiliated. Back then, the editors of the *DSM* worried that including masochism put the onus on women who were being abused, implying that they were "choosing" mistreatment and "inciting" hurt and humiliation. But looking at domestic violence decades later, we have a clearer understanding of what happens in such traumatic situations—what psychologists call the "trauma bond." Masochism, in my opinion, has a different but no less significant role in High-Functioning Depression. I'm not using the term to blame a victim. I'm using it to help you see what's happening so that you can take control of your happiness. Understanding your masochistic tendencies isn't about embarrassment; it's about empowerment.

WHAT DOES MASOCHISM LOOK LIKE?

I've included a quiz at the end of this chapter, on page 90, to help you figure out the degree to which masochism is at play in your High-Functioning Depression. But I'll also paint a picture for you here. We tend to see masochism in people who choose professions that put them in situations likely to lead to disappointment or failure, like healthcare workers neglecting their own health while caring for dying patients. We see masochism in public sector workers who choose a job that doesn't pay them what they are worth, and in teachers who work in environments that can incite anger from kids that can humiliate them. I've even seen it in caregivers, like Aurora, a fifty-four-year-old Filipino mom who would do anything for her family.

At age forty-three, after several failed cycles of IVF, and just as Aurora had given up on having children, she and her husband had a miracle pregnancy. She was so grateful to be starting a family, she quit her executive job to be a full-time mom. When her son was eleven, he was diagnosed with ADHD, which is when he started coming to see me. Every time Aurora brought her son in for appointments, I noticed her limp as they approached my door. She never complained about anything, but when I'd ask her how she was doing, she'd wave her hand casually as she mentioned the laundry list of responsibilities she had: running errands for her husband, keeping the house up, shuttling her son to appointments and practices, taking care of aging parents. When I'd ask about her limp, she'd say her swollen knee just needed a little rest, ice, and elevation, but that she'd been too busy to get to that. After weeks of pain, she finally got checked out by a physician and found out she'd actually torn a ligament in her knee and required surgery. Had she seen her doctor sooner, they might have been able to avoid surgery, but walking around with a torn ligament for weeks had worsened the injury to the point where surgery was inevitable.

As is true for many people with High-Functioning Depression, Aurora's whole identity was tied up in being the go-to person for her family. If you're the one keeping all the balls in the air, and suddenly you aren't able to do that because you're injured or in pain, you feel like you're letting people down. You feel ashamed, unworthy, or unlovable because you're not serving that one function. That's why Aurora ignored her pain for so long that she ended up having to step away from that role for even longer as she recovered after her surgery. On an unconscious level, she thought she had to be the rock. But in reality, her family would've loved her just the same if she had been taking better care of her own needs instead of running herself ragged trying to be the model matriarch. No surprise here: people who are parents or caregivers also have higher levels of anhedonia and High-Functioning Depression, according to my research.

WHERE MASOCHISM SHOWS UP MOST: RELATIONSHIPS

Self-sacrifice is usually an aspect of masochism, and patients with HFD are relentlessly sacrificing themselves. It often shows up in maladaptive and toxic relationships. When you're constantly in people-pleasing mode or living with a martyr complex, you will attract people who take advantage of you at work, in friendships, in romantic relationships, and even in family relationships. And if you're giving, other people are going to be taking. Because of the imbalance of give and take, masochism makes it difficult for you to have genuine, meaningful relationships with other people. You probably won't notice, though, because you spend so much time supporting other people that you don't stop to look around and think, "Who's supporting me?"

One of the reasons you fall into these unbalanced relationships is that you don't vet your relationships properly. With everything you put on your to-do list, you barely have any time to yourself, much less time for vetting relationships. You're so distracted with work that you may also miss or ignore relationship red flags entirely. It's important to note that busying yourself is likely a trauma response. Unprocessed trauma leads you to cope by distracting yourself, but you internalize feelings of low self-worth, blame, and shame. Just below the surface, you're thinking, "Maybe I don't deserve thoughtful friends or a loving partner." You routinely put joy and pleasure on the back burner everywhere else in life—why not with relationships? On top of that, if a relationship stops being pleasurable and starts being burdensome, your anhedonia makes you so accustomed to a lack of joy that you don't bother thinking you should end the relationship. You just fall deeper into the lack. In fact, my research into High-Functioning Depression showed that married people had higher rates of anhedonia than single people.

A masochistic relationship is one where you spend endless hours listening to a self-absorbed "friend" complain about their evil mother-in-law or the fabulous trip they just took—even though you've only gotten four hours of sleep because you have a big project at work and can barely stay awake. It's one where you tough it out with an unreasonable and demeaning boss even when you could easily find another job and free yourself of a tyrant. It's smiling silently at the older sibling who alternates between mercilessly making fun of you in front of family and asking to borrow money (which you give them) in private. It's not breaking up with the "partner" who isn't ready to commit but does want to move in together after quitting his job to take up playing the drums—so you can support both of you with your hard-earned salary. You've tied your self-worth to pleasing and uplifting others. But what about you? Ultimately, masochistic relationships are also terrible for your health. The stress and overwhelm of always being there to support other people while getting no support can be as bad for you as smoking.[3]

The Seesaw

Take out a piece of paper and write the name of someone in your life you have a significant relationship with. It could be a romantic partner, best friend, relative, or even very close coworker. Create two columns on the paper. In column 1, list all the things you did in the past week to maintain your relationship with this person. Think: forwarded them a funny meme on social media, invited them out for dinner, texted them to check in, sent them a review of a book or gadget that you think they'll love. Now, in column 2, list all the things they've done to maintain their relationship with you in the past week. Is one column, or side of the seesaw, heavier, or are they balanced? Are you the one putting in all the effort, or is there reciprocity? Later in the book, I'll explain how to shift (or in some cases move on from) unbalanced relationships. But for now, just take an inventory. Repeat this exercise to examine your three closest relationships. Notice any patterns?

THE THREE TYPES OF MASOCHISM

To identify—and ultimately let go of—the unbalanced relationships in your life, you need to understand the different ways masochism shows up. In my practice, I've noted three major types of masochism that consistently emerge in people with High-Functioning Depression.

Cultural Masochism

What it is: Self-sacrificing behaviors that are tied to (or even prescribed by) a person's ethnic traditions, religion, nationality, or family values. This type of masochism is for our beliefs.

How it manifests: Having studied cultural psychiatry across the globe, I've seen cultural masochism everywhere. It's in British culture, where people are taught to have a "stiff upper lip" and to avoid complaining about work. It's in Christian culture, which teaches followers to turn the other cheek when they have been wronged and promotes examples like the Good Samaritan and Job. It's in America's culture of capitalism, which doesn't offer nearly as much paid maternity leave, paternity leave, or vacation time as other countries (the average American clocks less than half the number of vacation days as the average European—eleven days versus four weeks). On top of the pressure cooker of the workplace, capitalism leads to a staggering economic gap where the rich get richer and the poor get frustratingly poorer. It's even built into the culture of some families, where older children are expected to give up portions of their own childhoods to help raise the younger kids.

Whom it benefits: Everyone at the top of the hierarchy, whether that's the nobility separating themselves from the commoners, one racial group trying to dominate another, religious leaders historically keeping acolytes in pews instead of active at rallies, or the CEO keeping you at your desk.

Relationship Masochism

What it is: Self-sacrificing behaviors that are tied to trying to please others: co-workers, friends, romantic partners. This type of masochism is for other people in our lives.

How it manifests: It probably won't surprise you to learn that relationship masochism usually shows up in women. This kind of masochism manifests in women taking on all of the household duties or parenting work in a romantic relationship. It's also when women take on the majority of the *emotional* labor in a relationship: being the one who always plays peacemaker so that your husband and his brother don't get into arguments at family gatherings, or pumping your partner up before she has to give a big presentation at work. I've seen it across the globe: for example, in some societies girls are expected to be polite and deferential, while boys are expected to speak up and assert what they want. These same roles then get reinforced in the workplace, where women may not always question making less than their male counterparts, or in society, where women may not speak out against double standards. And whom are we kidding—that person who brings in donuts to the morning meeting, volunteers to take notes, and straightens out the chairs after everyone leaves is almost always a woman. Relationship masochism can also be seen anytime someone takes on all the work of planning outings for a friendship circle or keeping them all in touch on the group text.

Whom it benefits: The patriarchy—and anyone in your life focused more on taking than giving.

Career Masochism

What it is: Self-sacrificing behaviors that are tied to a person's job (or unpaid volunteer work) or career-related accomplishments. This type of masochism is for accolades and advancement that we think are important or that we think will bring us happiness but in which we prioritize others.

How it manifests: You can see this type of masochism in any field where employees are overworked, are undervalued, and still don't feel like they're doing enough. Think public defenders with massive grad school debt and low pay to represent the people who need them the most. Or journalists reporting from war-torn countries, risking their lives to deliver truth to the world. Or agricultural workers, or employees at nonprofits, or people in the military, or people in the clergy. It can even be the entry-level employee at the finance firm who gets stuck with eighty-hour workweeks and sacrifices any semblance of a social life for the dream of someday making it to the corner office. If your job involves a significant physical, emotional, or financial burden for the good of something or someone else, then you're likely experiencing career masochism. It's also worth noting that career masochism can look like sacrificing yourself for career success. People with High-Functioning Depression can inextricably link their professional achievement to their personal self-worth.

Whom it benefits: Everyone except you. Often the greatest beneficiaries of someone's career masochism are those at the top of the financial hierarchy in a capitalist society.

* * *

One of my clients, a forty-year-old partner at a management consulting firm, is a perfect example of career masochism. Jacob came to me because he was overworked and struggling with burnout but couldn't figure out how to work less than sixty hours a week. From nine to five, his calendar was booked solid with client meetings and calls and recruiting lunches, so the only time he had to solve staffing problems, put out fires on projects gone sideways, and reply to an endless stream of emails and text messages was before and after hours. On weekends, he hatched plans for starting his own firm, networking with colleagues on the golf course or at courtside seats for a basketball game. He once took a work call at the ER when his daughter was being treated for a broken arm (he never took out his earbuds at the hospital—just muted himself while talking to her and the doctors).

One of the problems with masochism is that it's contagious. You can pass it on to friends, family, and of course co-workers. So not only did Jacob maintain these over-the-top hours, but the consultants who worked under him did, too, just to keep up with him. Meanwhile, all the other partners would regularly take two-week vacations, but Jacob never did. He thought he hadn't reached a point in his career where he had the clout to do so (in fact, the opposite was true). I managed to persuade him to take a weeklong vacation in the Maldives during the slowest month of the year. When he realized that nothing bad happened while he was unplugged and away—and that his body and brain felt so much better—there was a shift. He could see that he was working much harder than he needed to be. And after spending quality time with his family, he realized how much he was missing out on.

Three Easy Ways to Break the Masochistic Cycle

Ending a cycle of masochism can be difficult because there's always someone who benefits from it and who won't want to let go of those perks. In the next part of this book, I'll give you a proven set of tools for overcoming High-Functioning Depression and, in turn, leaving masochism in the dust. But for now, here are a few simple steps that you can take to start letting go of your masochistic traits.

Listen to your body. Remember Aurora and her swollen knee? You don't have to be in physical pain to get a clue from your body that you may be hurting yourself. You might notice that your heart is beating a little faster because you've been downing coffee all day in order to keep up with work, and you're overcaffeinated. I tell my friends that if my nails are chipped, that's a sure sign I'm overworked and need to slow down for some self-care. Speaking of which...

Listen to your friends. Sometimes the sacrifices that we make force others in our lives (like our lovers, friends, co-workers, neighbors, and kids) to make sacrifices as well. I take cues from my team at work, my friends, and even my daughter. If they're hinting that a project timeline is too ambitious or I've been staring at my emails all night instead of paying attention to them, I don't brush it off. I take it seriously and change my behavior. You can be proactive about this as well. Before you make a big decision about taking on a project at work or in your personal life, ask a trusted friend if they think you're putting too much on your plate.

Listen to your heart. Take a pause before you say yes or no to a task and ask yourself if you really want to do it. Very often, there's a small voice inside of us that realizes we're too burned out to work all weekend or that we don't want to do our partner's laundry today. That favor you twist yourself into a pretzel to execute may go unnoticed by the other person, and ultimately it doesn't increase your value or your worth — two things you have without needing to do anything.

MASOCHISM AND ATTACHMENT STYLES

If you think you might be masochistic, it's worth understanding your attachment style. "Attachment style" is a term that has become part of pop culture vernacular, but it does have roots in research. It's not a diagnosis or in the *DSM*, but it's generally accepted by experts. The phrase was originally defined by psychoanalyst John Bowlby and developmental psychologist Mary Ainsworth to describe how babies interacted with caregivers. Decades later, it was adapted by psychologists and psychiatrists to describe how we behave in romantic relationships — how comfortable we are depending on partners, and how close we allow people to get to us. There are four categories of attachment style: anxious, avoidant, secure, and combination.[4]

- **Anxious attachment.** About 20 percent of people fall into this category, marked by a fear of being abandoned by our partner. It can cause us to sacrifice our own needs to please our partner, to play manipulative games for our partner's attention, or to need more reassurance from our partner to feel safe in the relationship.
- **Avoidant attachment.** About 25 percent of the population falls into the avoidant attachment style. This is when we

have trouble getting close to someone because we value our independence more than intimacy. Someone with avoidant attachment might actually pull away from a partner they feel is getting too dependent upon them. This, too, is a form of masochism.

- **Secure attachment.** Roughly half of the population falls into this category of attachment, which embodies the ideal balance in a relationship. This balance means you can communicate your needs without playing manipulative games. You can react to the needs of your partner without sacrificing yourself. You can depend on others and let them depend on you.

- **Combination.** About 3 to 5 percent of the population displays an insecure combination of the other categories, like anxious-avoidant or secure-anxious or what some call fearful avoidant. These people want intimacy but push others away for fear of being hurt.

I'm not saying that all people who are masochistic have the same attachment style. Although people with anxious attachment tend to have higher rates of masochism in romantic relationships, masochists can have any attachment style. For example, you could have a secure attachment but experience some trauma in life that causes you to fall into masochistic relationships. Something happened along the way in life that made you feel you weren't worthy and that it was all right for people to treat you poorly. But understanding your attachment style can help you be more aware of what form your masochism might take.

In addition to your own style, I want you to think about a potential partner's attachment style. In my practice, what I have noticed is that people with masochistic tendencies tend to be attracted to partners with one attachment style in particular: avoidant. Seeking out partners with an avoidant attachment style puts you in a situation where you're not treated well by your partner, you're not rewarded for the hard work you do in your relationship, and you're working toward the impossible mission of getting that person to love you. Masochists gravitate toward people with avoidant attachment styles because it gives them a perpetual project to work on. That's exactly what happened with a patient of mine, Nykia, who had a cycle of dysfunctional relationships from childhood to adulthood.

It all started when Nykia was ten years old and her father was in a car accident that left him in a wheelchair, paralyzed from the waist down. Her mother turned to drinking after the accident, which forced Nykia to do a significant amount of the caretaking that her father (and her mother) needed. She learned to do it all—making dinners, cleaning the house, even taking checks to the landlord so the family wouldn't be late with the rent. While trying to hold her family together, Nykia became programmed from a young age to be a caretaker and picked up a questionable trait: self-sacrifice.

Fast-forward to her adulthood and career as a successful entrepreneur in the beauty industry. When Nykia wasn't in front of her laptop trying to get ten more sales or spending one more hour perfecting promotional materials, she was constantly catering to her circle of friends. Nykia was the bestie who remembered everyone's birthday and planned a brunch to celebrate it. She was always the one who started the email chain when it was time for the gang to plan a vacation. Nykia was the friend everyone knew would answer the phone at 1 a.m. when they needed to talk to someone about having their heart broken. She was everything to everyone. But no one in the circle did any of those things for Nykia.

What brought Nykia to therapy with me was wanting a family. She wanted to meet a partner, get married, and have children. So far she'd only been a booty call for a string of men she'd met online, or the girlfriend who was consistently cheated on. She kept ending up in relationships with men who didn't treat her well, because she was convinced that she could win them over. She always answered "You up?" text messages and constantly made excuses for men who didn't put in any effort to be with her. Her anxious attachment style and masochistic behaviors led her like a heat-seeking missile toward men with an avoidant attachment style. But rather than begin by tackling her romantic relationships, Nykia and I started working on her maladaptive friendships. If the so-called friends in her circle couldn't be bothered to pick up the phone when she called, they certainly weren't going to introduce her to a nice guy or throw a baby shower for her. She needed to develop a healthier model of attachment with everyone around her—which was absolutely possible.

So many people worry that they're stuck with their attachment style and there's nothing they can do. But here's the good news: attachment styles aren't like blood types or fingerprints. You can change them over time. It takes work (through therapy and real-life practice), but it is possible. And just realizing that you may be drawn to an avoidant style can save you a lot of heartbreak in the long run.

ARE YOU MASOCHISTIC?

Let's face it: there's nothing sexy about wearing a five-pound golden crown of masochism. But once you take a look in the mirror and recognize the people-pleasing pressure you've put on your head, you can take it off, relax your shoulders, and stand taller. I've brought the *DSM-III*'s list of criteria for masochistic personality disorder into a new era to help you more easily understand if you might have this symptom.[5] Keep a tally of your yes and no answers. The more yeses you have, the more likely it is that you suffer from masochism.

1. My identity is tied to what I can do for others. I bend over backward to help people even though they may not have asked me to. I can't help but self-sacrifice in order to show up for others.

   I stay up all night working on projects for my child's school so that I am accepted by other parents. I wait in line for hours to get tickets to a show for someone I've only been dating for a short period of time in order to gain their approval.

2. People are always coming to me for favors. They ask me for things because I rarely say no and/or rarely reject them.

   Parents may repeatedly ask me to pick up their kids from school, and I agree even though it is very inconvenient. People expect me to pay the bill/tab even though we ate/drank the same amount. Co-workers asks me to take on some of their duties even when I have more than enough work on my plate. My boss frequently asks me to stay late or to take on more work even though I am clearly burned out.

3. I often find myself in situations that are not in my best interest and that frequently lead to disappointment, failure, or mistreatment.

   I put myself in situations that are not in my best interest, like being in a relationship with someone who is married, pledging a sorority or fraternity where abuse is rampant, not setting boundaries with a hypercritical parent, trying out for a team with a notoriously brutal coach, or dating someone I need to fix or rescue.

4. I frequently turn down opportunities for pleasure or enjoyment and instead work or engage in acts of duty.

   I skip the office happy hour to tie up extra work or clean the house while everyone else in the family is relaxing or watching a movie. During the holidays, while everyone else is opening presents, I am the one cleaning up the wrapping paper.

5. When people offer to help me, I turn them down or tell them I can do it without their help.

   I clean the house before the housekeeper comes over. I throw a party/event on my own and turn down other people's offers to plan it. I struggle with carrying luggage, and when a stranger offers assistance, I turn them away.

6. I feel uncomfortable when people do kind things for me, compliment me, or treat me well.

   Receiving compliments is awkward for me. When getting an honor, I may joke and downplay it. When invited to an exclusive event, I may turn down the invitation because I believe I do not belong with that special crowd.

7. I have a hard time celebrating wins.

   I work hard for promotions, and when I get them, I don't tell anyone because I do not want to be celebrated. If my job were to offer to honor me with a public award, I'd ask to accept the award privately. If I did receive an award publicly, I may trip and fall getting on the stage because on a deeper level I do not believe I should be praised.

After my therapist explained what masochism was and why he thought I was a textbook case, he also shared something else. "When you're late for our sessions, it makes me late to meet with all the other patients after you," he said. Suddenly I knew why the Wall Street guy in the fancy suits always looked at me strangely on my way out. I was showing up late because my masochism made me feel like I wasn't worthy of my therapist's attention or the support that he was offering. But by not taking my therapy seriously, I wasn't just hurting myself; I was also impacting the patients who came after me.

That wake-up call with my therapist changed how we interacted moving forward. I started prioritizing our sessions and doing the work to understand myself better. Hopefully, now that I've explained High-Functioning Depression and the anhedonia and masochism that can go with it, you understand yourself a lot better as well. You can see the ways in which High-Functioning Depression has caused you to lose your sense of self—and you're probably eager to figure out how to get yourself back! In the next part of this book, I'll introduce you to the Five V's: the exact steps you need to take to overcome High-Functioning Depression and reclaim the joy-filled life you deserve.

PART TWO

Healing with the Five V's

CHAPTER 5

Validation

Whenever Sofia walked out of my office after a therapy session, she always left something behind: A compact black umbrella that she'd placed on the floor next to her and forgotten on her way out. Her cell phone, which had gotten tucked in between the cushions of my office couch and was easily overlooked. A ring she'd been nervously twisting all session and then slammed down on a table next to her in frustration. But she wasn't just forgetful. Subconsciously, she wanted to come back to my office for these things — she wanted to come back for more therapy. She knew she needed help.

Sofia was an extremely hardworking writer from a very poor, rural part of the Midwest. She'd made her way to Los Angeles, determined to go to film school and become a famous screenwriter. But in her first few months in California, she was sexually assaulted by a potential mentor and agent who invited her to his office after hours. Immediately after he attacked her, all she could think about was getting out of that office. Once she got home, all she wanted to do was to pretend it hadn't happened. Sofia didn't want anything to get in the way of her success in the industry.

As a result, when she wasn't throwing herself into her schoolwork or the paralegal job that paid her tuition bills, Sofia was feverishly trying to write the next indie sensation. "I'll be happy once I graduate," she told herself, justifying her four hours of sleep a night with the praise she got from her instructors, who thought she was the next Wes Anderson. "I'll be happy once I get a job in the industry," she told herself whenever she pushed through her fears to network with anyone who might be able to help her find a job.

It worked. After graduating, Sofia got a job on a show in New York and moved there (in hindsight, she realized she moved as far from California as she could without leaving the country). But her High-Functioning Depression didn't stay behind; in fact, it plummeted into low-functioning depression soon after she arrived. The psychological stress and the pandemic had pulled her from high to low. Sofia struggled to get out of bed in the morning and stopped going to the writers' room via Zoom to pitch ideas for the next episodes of the show. She found she couldn't stop thinking about the assault. By the time she reached me, she couldn't write at all, had taken a leave of absence from the show, and was struggling to pay her bills.

"What's wrong with me?" Sofia asked, sitting on the couch with her legs tightly crossed and her fingers laced over her knees. "I thought I was so strong and resilient, but I let one encounter ruin my life."

High-functioning individuals tend to not acknowledge negative experiences because we're taught that no one wants to see negativity. Sometimes we don't even reveal them to the people who are here to help us, like therapists. Women, and women of color in particular, are taught to push through trauma. Our pain is poorly understood—and, worse, our pain is poorly treated. That's why I put in extra effort with my patients.

I took Sofia through an assessment for PTSD called the Clinician-Administered PTSD Scale for *DSM-5* (or, as psychiatrists call it for short, the CAPS-5).[1] It was originally developed for veterans, but it works for any person who has gone through a trauma. The vast majority of psychiatrists don't know how to do a CAPS-5 assessment, but I use it all the time because it lets you quantify the impact that a trauma has had on someone. You have an actual number, not just an impression or an idea. The CAPS-5 asks questions like "In the past month, have you had any unwanted memories of your assault while you were awake?" and "Are you able to put your assault out of your mind and think about something else?"

At the end of the assessment, I was floored. Sofia had the highest CAPS-5 score I'd ever seen. More important, that number was shocking for Sofia as well. Just like seeing that your blood pressure had skyrocketed to 200/90 or that your BMI had landed you in the obese category, seeing her CAPS-5 score was a wake-up call for her. It allowed her to see how severe her trauma was—especially compared to what others go through. It enabled her to realize that there was nothing wrong *with* her, but that something wrong had happened *to* her. It empowered her to go from blaming herself and living in shame to pressing charges against that agent and getting back to writing again. No, it didn't happen overnight. But it did happen over our future sessions.

Her CAPS-5 score was the irrefutable validation of her experience that she needed to give herself grace and begin to overcome her depression.

ARE YOU READY FOR TAKEOFF?

In aviation, someone in the cockpit calls out "V1" when a plane is going so fast down the runway that takeoff can't be aborted. The pilot has to commit to fly. Now that you've read about all the signs that you're experiencing High-Functioning Depression, we're about to hit our own V1 here with the first of the Five V's. This is the part where you leave the runway and take flight to reach bluer skies.

Validation is one of the most complex of the Five V's I'm going to be sharing with you in this book. But if you can master validation, the other V's will be a breeze.

When it comes to healing from High-Functioning Depression, validation is a two-step process of acknowledging traumatic experiences that you've had and accepting your emotions around those experiences. Remember, a traumatic experience could be anything from the emotional trauma of having an abusive boss who berates you at work to the physical trauma of being robbed at gunpoint or attacked with a knife. What's more, the emotions that you have around that experience can also run the gamut, from overcompensating and overworking to feeling crippled by overwhelming fears and anxiety. Through the validation provided by her CAPS-5 score, Sofia was able to acknowledge how traumatic the experience of her sexual assault had been. She was also able to accept that feelings of listlessness and sadness and an inability to derive joy from the creative work she once loved would be the outcome of an experience like that.

Pen a Path to Recovery (Part I)

Now that you understand that trauma has many different faces, take a moment to pick a trauma from your childhood that you want to work through. Why your childhood? Because having some distance from the event can help you unpack it a little more easily without judging yourself or feeling ashamed of anything that happened. Next, pull out a pen and paper and write a full page about what you experienced. What happened? Who was involved? Why did it happen? How did you feel? What would you say to your younger self? Get it all down on the page. Don't stop writing, don't judge your thoughts, and don't reread what you've written. Once you're done, hold on to that page until you finish reading this chapter.

WHY VALIDATION IS SO HARD FOR PEOPLE WITH HFD

It's hard for most of us to spend time thinking about experiences we likely want to forget or move past. It's doubly hard for people with High-Functioning Depression, for multiple reasons.

- **We don't stop to think about feelings.** We spend so much time in "go mode," checking things off our to-do lists and finding ways to help others, that we spend very little time thinking about ourselves and getting in touch with our emotions. What's more, some people with depression have a symptom called alexithymia, which makes it difficult for them to recognize their emotions—and emotions in others. But you have to be able to name your emotions to face them.

- **We don't want to seem weak.** People with High-Functioning Depression have all-or-nothing thinking. We think that someone is powerful or they're weak—nothing in between. We don't want to appear needy or vulnerable, so we don't ask for help or validation. There are other complicating factors, as well, that cast a cloud over the feelings we need to see more clearly.

- **Our emergency defenses have been triggered.** People with HFD often detach or disassociate from their feelings around traumatic events. That's our body trying to protect us so that we can get to work, care for our families, pay our bills on time, and make it through the day. We don't have time to feel sad or anxious when we have to get everyone out of the house on time in the morning. As a result, we have a hard time identifying and tolerating negative emotions.

- **Our culture looks down on it.** Many of us have been discouraged from exploring our emotions. For example, validation can be more difficult for men because they are often raised to hide their feelings. Even women, who are usually more culturally acclimated to talking about their emotions, can worry about getting labeled as "overreacting," "hysterical," or even "crazy." Difficulty expressing emotions isn't only dictated by gender. It's also impacted by faith, culture, race, and identity. For example, British culture is notorious for requiring a pronounced stoicism. Asian cultures can sometimes value tradition and duty more than feelings and emotions. How you see yourself based on any of these identities can make validation easier or harder for you.

- **Our family didn't model it.** Your family plays a large part in your ability to name and express emotions. If you were raised by parental figures who were uncomfortable showing emotion ("Everything is fine!") or didn't create a space for your negative emotions ("Don't get so upset about it!"), this is going to be tougher for you. They may have even struggled with a mental illness that made it hard for them to model emotions.
- **Our instinct told us to avoid it.** Maybe you witnessed a time when showing emotions made someone around you seem less lovable or less favored in your social circle. So you decided to push your own emotions way down before they got you into trouble.

No matter what your instinct is telling you, there's no skipping this step in your healing. We have to be able to understand, express, and obtain some level of control over our emotions to overcome HFD.

WHY DO WE HAVE TO FEEL TO HEAL?

Imagine someone has pushed you into a pitch-black room and locked the door behind you. Then you hear the terrifying sound of something or someone running toward you at full speed. Chances are you start swinging in every direction to protect yourself. Right? But now let's say you get locked in that same room with the lights on and you can see the threat coming toward you. You can also see what tools you have in the room to defend yourself from this person or thing running toward you. You can even tell if what's running toward you is a threat at all. Maybe it's headed for the door you just came through.

That room is a metaphor for life. And the sound of something running toward you at full speed? Those are your feelings. When you're not able to identify and name your negative emotions, you can feel scared and helpless in the face of them.

Human beings don't like not knowing things. Not knowing can threaten our sense of safety. Knowledge, on the other hand, feels good and is empowering. Knowing the difference between poison ivy and a four-leaf clover is the difference between a pleasant walk through the woods and a world of pain. Knowing the difference between a scarlet king snake and a coral snake is the difference between life and death. Knowing the difference between anger and sadness is the difference between an unfulfilling life and one that brings you joy. We often mistake sadness for anger, and when we do, we may act impulsively or ragefully. We may start swinging at the air to defend ourselves—and we may end up hurting people that we care about.

When I work with patients who have a lot of rage-filled mood swings—like a hotheaded CEO who is stressed about the company's bottom line, for example—they're surprised to learn from me that their anger could be a manifestation of their unidentified anxiety. They're in that dark room swinging at the air and hitting their direct reports and co-workers with angry comments because they're worried about Q4 earnings.

If you think you have anger issues but actually have anxiety, trying to manage your temper isn't going to get you your desired outcome. You need to turn on the lights in that dark room and see what you're really facing. Only when you see those negative emotions for what they are and validate them will you be able to pick the appropriate tool and take appropriate action to heal from them. To quell your anger, you might need to see that anger for what it may be: anxiety, sadness, guilt, embarrassment, or fear masquerading as anger. If you don't name and validate your feelings, you can't create a plan to give yourself the support you need.

MASTERING THE "FEEL TO HEAL" TRIANGLE

Cognitive behavioral therapy (CBT) uses something called the cognitive triangle to visually represent how our thoughts, feelings, and behaviors are perpetually intertwined. While each corner of the triangle can impact the others, it's generally believed that our thoughts belong at the top of the triangle, and that they impact our emotions and, subsequently, our behaviors, which are the remaining corners. So if we can change our thoughts for the better, we can change our emotions and then our behaviors for the better as well.

For example, if I think, "As an immigrant, I have to work twice as hard to get half as far," then my emotions will reflect that in the form of self-doubt, depression, overwhelm, and sadness. My actions might be to overcompensate and overexert myself to prove my worth, or to seclude myself and give up. However, CBT holds that if I change my thought to "People will value what I bring to the table," then my emotions are more positive: hope, trust, and self-confidence.

In turn, my actions will be more confident and I won't feel the need to overpromise and overdeliver.

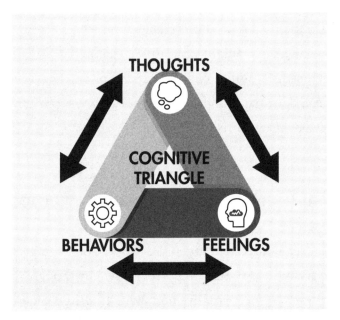

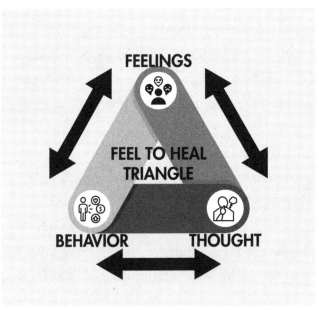

People with High-Functioning Depression need to turn the CBT model on its side so that feelings are at the top of the cognitive triangle, for three reasons. First, suffering from HFD means that you don't sufficiently value your feelings. That's why it's so important for you to focus on them primarily, then let everything flow from there.

Second, a lot of our thoughts are just plain wrong. When we can shift to our feelings, we can push back on these erroneous thoughts and get clarity faster. For example, if you start with the thought "It's my fault I was assaulted," you might arrive at the feeling of shame and a behavior of avoiding relationships. But if you start with the feeling "I felt powerless," you can arrive at the thought "I was targeted and didn't deserve that" and the behavior of seeking therapy or taking a self-defense class. This is how starting with your feelings can help you overcome the internalized blame so many trauma survivors have.

Third, when our thoughts are wrong, the resulting actions are often wrong. If your heart is racing and your hands are shaking while you're giving a presentation at work, your thought might be "I'm doing a terrible job," and you might feel overwhelmed; then you might push yourself to work really hard for the next five hours to overcome that. But if you can start with your emotions and realize that you're *feeling* anxious because you have imposter syndrome and don't *think* you're qualified for your job, then you can *challenge the thought and change the behavior* around it by remembering that your team wants and needs you there. And, hey, didn't you get a promotion last month? Eventually you might even get to a point where your behavior is not to stay late at work but to leave fifteen minutes early so you have time to get to a yoga class. But more on getting you to that dream life later.

Sometimes clients have a hard time moving past their thoughts. Instead, they ruminate on them. People with HFD want to keep busy thinking they're fixing a situation by focusing on their thoughts, but really they're just making themselves sick. Rather than tackle the problem, I sometimes encourage them to notice it and just let it be in the background; this is the principle behind metacognitive therapy (MCT), one of the newer therapeutic approaches. With metacognition, you can train your brain to think differently about thinking. There may be an elephant of a problem in the room, but you can still take a deep breath, relax your shoulders, and enjoy the smell, taste, and warmth of a cup of tea. We don't say the thought isn't there, but we don't focus on trying to change the thought. I use metacognition with myself all the time. I might be thinking, "I have a looming deadline." But I don't try to change my thoughts about the deadline. I just eat my dinner and play with my daughter knowing nothing catastrophic will happen. When feelings of anxiety and stress come along, you can try noticing but not focusing on your thoughts.

Now that you understand how focusing on feelings (instead of dismissing them) can help you overcome false thoughts and core beliefs, the trick is to sharpen your focus. One way to do that is by naming, acknowledging, and validating your feelings, instead of ignoring them, dismissing them, or busying yourself to avoid them. No one ever teaches us how to get the validation we need, or how to give it to others. So I'm here to show you that now.

THE THREE TYPES OF VALIDATION

To begin to acknowledge the upsetting or traumatic experiences that you've had and accept your emotions around them, there are three validation tools you can use: self-validation, verbal validation, and factual validation. You only need one of them to start down your path of healing from High-Functioning Depression. But the more tools you can use, the easier that journey will be.

Self-Validation of Experiences: Did Something Happen to You?
This is one of the most powerful types of validation because it strengthens you from within. Self-validation is the practice of acknowledging and accepting indisputable facts about traumas that you have experienced in your life. This is validation you can give to yourself without needing the aid of a therapist, a parental figure, a best friend, or any other person. You're reinforcing the reality of a trauma on your own. That trauma could include being raised by a narcissistic parent, surviving a natural disaster, being bullied in school, being bullied in the workplace, a health scare, surviving a car accident, losing a loved one, escaping a school shooting, or some other occurrence that could overwhelm your body and mind. All of these are experiences that people with High-Functioning Depression might think we can get through if we just grit our teeth or toughen up. But the reality is that we need to acknowledge them for what they are: traumatic events that can shake even the strongest human being to the core.

As someone with High-Functioning Depression, you may find it difficult to identify the traumas you've experienced over the course of your life and acknowledge that they have left a lasting scar. Even though I called many types of them out in the beginning of the book, you might still be reluctant to believe that being pulled over by the cops at 1 a.m. on a desolate road or losing your job while living paycheck to paycheck had that big an impact on you. We often have to see it to believe it, which is why I'd like you to practice self-validation by taking the time to listen to and witness how other people have reacted to traumas that you've experienced.

Award-winning television producer, author, and screenwriter Shonda Rhimes once said, "Any time you allow someone to see themselves reflected in another person on screen, there's validation there."[2] That's exactly why I prescribe some of my patients a unique homework assignment: to watch a movie with a theme that reflects their life, mirrors how they're feeling, or explores a trauma similar to the one they've gone through. If you were bullied as a child, try watching *Wonder, Moonlight,* or *Bully.* If you're dealing with a painful divorce, consider getting under the covers and watching *Marriage Story, The Squid and the Whale, A Separation,* or *Scenes from a Marriage.*

Whatever your traumatic experience, head to Google, search for movies that reflect it back to you, and start witnessing your experience. Find the character in the story who mirrors you and accept them as your alter ego. Let yourself be moved by the similar events of their life. Witnessing someone else explore the range of emotions and the real impact associated with that event could help you tap into the validity of your own experience with it. As you watch the plots unfold, you'll realize the universal truths about how these difficult moments can push people to the edge.

Can't imagine how you'll find two full hours for this exercise? Worried that watching someone be abused might be too triggering?

That's fine. You don't have to watch a whole feature-length film to get the impact of this exercise. Instead, you could read a poem, a short story, or an article about an experience you share with another person. You might listen to a song or a podcast episode related to it. Whatever medium you choose, pay attention to how you feel while you're letting a writer, director, musician, or actor put a spotlight on and validate your experience.

Self-Validation of Emotions: How Do You Feel?

If you were to step inside my office, you'd notice that I have mirrors everywhere: on my desk, on the wall, on shelves. It's not because I need to put on makeup in my office or because I'm checking myself out before meeting with clients. It's because mirrors are an incredibly powerful tool for self-validation. There's something very powerful about making sustained eye contact with yourself. Your reflection doesn't lie.

I want you to start looking at yourself in the mirror more often and silently asking yourself how you feel. This isn't about judging your appearance. This is about evaluating your mood. The more you do this, the easier it will be to tap into your emotions. You'll be able to read what your bright eyes or slightly closed ones are telling you. What your half-smile or your raised eyebrows are getting at. Then, after about fifteen seconds of staring at yourself, I want you to admit aloud how you're feeling. Name it and claim it. Look at yourself and say, "I feel sad" or "I'm excited" or "I'm feeling afraid" or "I'm pretty happy today."

You can do this at home, but you can also do it anytime you pass by a mirror or catch your reflection in a store window. Give yourself a few seconds to stare into your own eyes and tap into your own emotions. This practice of self-validation is easier if you're well versed in the range of emotions you could be expressing. In my practice, when I work with children, I show them a chart of different smiley faces that range from afraid to excited and ask them to pick which one they're feeling today. It helps children who might not be used to expressing emotions find a way to do so. What follows is an adult version that you can refer to if you need some help expanding your emotional vocabulary.

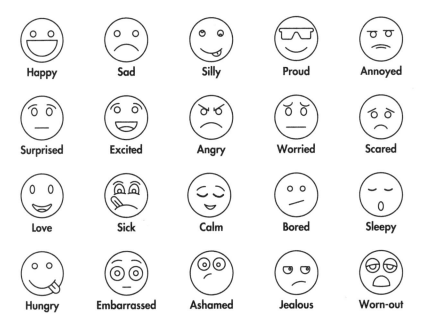

The goal of the mirror exercise is not to sit in negative emotions. I'm not trying to get you to wallow in a sea of sadness or regret. I would like you to acknowledge those difficult emotions so that you are aware of how they impact your emotions and thoughts. For example, after validating your feelings, you could then repeat a positive affirmation that acknowledges them but lifts you up. Try something like:

I can forgive myself for not being perfect.
I am brave despite my emotions and I know I can get
    through this.
I am getting stronger every single day.
This feeling won't last forever.
I'm better today than I was yesterday.
It's okay to feel what I'm feeling right now.
I choose to let go of negative thoughts and invite in
    happiness.

Sometimes when we take that last glance in the mirror before leaving the house, we see someone who didn't take the necessary steps to look like we care about ourselves in public. Maybe your hair is disheveled or your clothes are wrinkled. You may have even left the house with socks that are different colors or pants that don't fit you well. All of those signs speak volumes about how you're feeling: frazzled, overworked, unconfident, distracted. My team always jokes that if my hair is in a bun at work, that means I'm going to be working hard today. You might bun up when you know it's time to get down to business at work, and leave your hair down to cue yourself that it's time to relax. That's why I encourage my clients to pay attention to those passive clues, but also to use style to actively express their feelings as well.

Style is an expression of culture, and expressing our culture is important for mental health. Black people, for example, tend to have distinctive and artistic styles when it comes to hair, nails, and clothing. Early in my psychiatry training, I was told to dampen those cultural expressions and to conform to the norm of how everyone around me appeared. I didn't realize it at the time, but this was a way of killing Black joy and invalidating my emotions. (More on this later in the chapter.) Whether it's natural hair, braids, or locs being considered inappropriate or nails being thought of as too long and loud, African Americans and any people part of the African diaspora are often muted in these spaces, where we are conditioned to believe that we're not allowed to enjoy expressing ourselves. Instead of lowering your volume, I want everyone reading this to increase it — even if it's as simple as letting your hair down.

You can also use your clothing choices as a form of self-care — maybe by wearing soft, soothing fabrics, like a cashmere sweater that caresses you, or a flowing skirt instead of a pencil one that is more constricting. You might choose a color to uplift you, like a yellow dress that makes you feel energized and motivated even when you're tired, or a red top that makes you feel fierce and unstoppable even when you're insecure. Putting on a sharp suit or freshly polished shoes might make you feel more confident even on your most unconfident days. Fashion can be the reflection of how you feel and how you want to heal.

Verbal Validation: What Did You Say?

When Camille came to in her ICU bed, the first thing she let out was a disappointed sigh. "Ugh, I'm alive," the thirteen-year-old said, closing her eyes again and shaking her head. It was almost one o'clock in the morning, and I had been on call at the hospital when she came in to be treated for an overdose. She'd taken an entire bottle of Prozac and her heart had almost stopped beating. Her twin brother had gone into her room to yell at her for not doing her half of the chores and found her just in time to call 911 and have doctors pump her stomach and save her life. Now Camille was facing the fact that her attempted suicide had been unsuccessful. She was no longer in acute physical danger, but we had a long way to go from there.

As I was leaving the ICU, I bumped into her parents, who had been on a weekend getaway upstate. "I'm so sorry," I said to them. "I can't imagine what you must be going through."

"We've been at the hospital for over an hour," the mother replied, taking in my verbal validation. "No one has said they were sorry for us the entire time we've been here. It's all been questions, paper-work, and next steps."

Verbal validations are affirmations that you get from trusted sources around your emotions and your experiences. My verbal validation of the parents' feelings—without even naming them—created a connection between us. Someone had acknowledged their emotions, or at least that they were going through an intense emotional event. It made them feel seen and understood. It would also be the key to helping their daughter, whom they insisted I start meeting with for treatment. It was through those sessions that I realized Camille desperately needed verbal validation as well.

Camille's parents were extremely wealthy and able to send both of their children to prestigious private schools in Manhattan. While her twin brother was the captain of the boys' varsity volleyball team and dating the class president, Camille struggled socially in the shadow of her sibling's success. She was painfully shy, didn't care at all about the latest trends, and found it almost impossible to make friends.

"Don't worry," her parents would say—the exact opposite of validation. Like telling a frantic person to calm down or a depressed person that life isn't that bad, telling a thirteen-year-old not to worry is invalidating. This was a house where people didn't talk about their feelings. So instead of acknowledging her struggle, Camille's parents bought her gifts to make her feel better. They sent her to therapy, where she wasn't heard, either; she was just given a bottle of pills. Everyone wanted to fix the problem, not listen to it—and they had no idea how serious it was. For someone Camille's age, being socially rejected at school feels worse than being stabbed to death. Social rejection lights up the same part of the brain as being physically harmed does. After months of feeling isolated at school and unheard at home, Camille just wanted to end that pain. That's when she started emptying the bottle of Prozac into her hand.

In the months that I worked with Camille, I took her off Prozac and, among other things, started doing some intense listening and validation. "Wow, it must be really hard when all the kids in your class go on spring break together but you're left out," I'd say. "How does it feel when your parents don't listen to you telling them about the hard time you're having at school?" It wasn't enough for me to validate Camille's emotions for an hour every week. I had to teach her parents how to do it, too. When you're a therapist treating high-risk children, you also have meetings with their parental figures.

I brought it to both parents' attention that they had essentially been ignoring their daughter. Not intentionally; with her dad it was because he was so obsessed with work, and with her mom it was because she felt her kids had it so easy financially that they couldn't possibly have anything to complain about. During those sessions, I taught Camille's parents how to avoid talking over their daughter, to reflect back what they were hearing her say, and to make nonjudgmental, empathetic statements. That's the difference between saying "Every time you don't get what you want, you yell at me" and saying "It seems like you're angry because we're not going to Ibiza this year." You might be thinking, "Maybe adults can talk like this. But kids? No way." Here's the thing: Kids are better at learning than adults, and they pick up on effective communication techniques like this very easily. It's adults who struggle with thinking before we speak so that we can get our desired outcomes.

Verbal validation can come from any reliable source: a friend, a partner, a therapist, a faith leader, or even commiserating strangers on social media. I call the comments section on my Instagram feed "group therapy" because when someone shares a painful experience there, total strangers will chime in with "That sounds so difficult, but I know you'll get through this" or "You're not alone. My mom was abusive and she did that, too."

Even public policy has the ability to offer verbal validation. Mandating paid maternity leave, for example, is validation for women that they deserve time off after going through childbirth, which often can be physically traumatic. It affirms that bringing a new life into this world on Friday means you can't hop back to work on Monday because of all of the physical, emotional, financial, and mental shifts that are taking place. The inclusion of all-gender bathrooms in public spaces is validation of people who may be gender-nonconforming or who don't identify as male or female. Workplaces that permit mental health days validate that every single one of us needs a break from the overwhelm at times — and that we're entitled to take such a break.

One of the reasons it's so important for you to work on self-validation is that we don't always get it elsewhere. For example, we don't live in a society where women get menopause health days or where men get significant paternity leave. And whereas countries like Belgium and the United Kingdom have either legislated a four-day workweek or run successful pilot programs to encourage employers to provide it, other cultures encourage their workers to toil into the weekend.[3]

When it comes to verbal validation, it should be noted that (like love) if you want it, you should learn how to give it — and there is a learning curve.

Verbal Validation: How to Know What to Say

As someone with High-Functioning Depression, you're used to ignoring your own needs while showing up for the people around you. But validation is different, and in many ways more nuanced, than the support you're probably used to giving. So I'm going to cover some of the most common mistakes people make when it comes to verbal validation:

- **You're talking too much.** Validation requires a lot of listening. You know how everyone talks about the difference between "taking up space" and "creating space"? Well, this is it. Validation is not about chiming in every two minutes to say, "If I ever see your scumbag ex walking down the street, I swear . . ." or "Girl, you know you should've left that job years ago." It's about giving someone the space to be reflective. When someone is sitting with you and telling you what they're going through, the very act of allowing them to do this shows them that their emotions and experiences are worthy of your time and attention.

- **You're fixing the problem instead of finding the feeling.** We have a tendency to show support through action. When someone tells us their problems, we instinctively want to solve them. But verbal validation is better served by listening than by problem-solving. This isn't the time to suggest your friend tell her mom that the jokes about her weight hurt her feelings. This is the time for you to give her your full attention and tell her you understand how those comments make her feel. One of my colleagues actually tells her clients to sit with their hands under their thighs as a reminder to not jump into these kinds of conversations with a solution.

- **You're asking closed-ended, judgmental questions.** Questions like "Isn't that cruel?" or "Aren't you angry with her?" don't allow the other person space for reflection. Instead, you want to lean into open-ended, nonjudgmental questions, like "How did you feel about that?" or "What was going through your mind when that happened?" or "Can you help me understand what happened a little better?"

- **You're taking "I don't know" for an answer.** As you're aware, we can struggle with naming our feelings for a variety of reasons. You might ask someone to tell you how they felt about something and get a blank stare or a shake of the head. Instead of focusing on the emotional impact of an event, try to get them to share the physical impact. When they tell you their stomach hurts or they got a headache after an awkward conversation, that could help them figure out if it made them anxious. (In some cases, you can't really ask questions. For example, let's say someone posts on social media sharing a traumatic experience that happened to them. You don't need to dialogue with them about their feelings. You could simply state, "Thank you for sharing your story. That must've been so hard" or "I went through something similar and no one listened to me, either. I'm so sorry this happened to you." In a situation such as this, a simple like can be validating.)

- **You're enabling them.** Beware of people who trauma-dump. If you have someone in your life who is always complaining about something to you, it's time to stop them from making you their emotional landfill. You have to speak up for yourself. You might say something like, "I hear how you feel and this seems to happen a lot. Is there a reason you're in this situation repeatedly? Is there something you can pinpoint?" When you cross the line from validating to enabling, it's time to create a boundary.

Factual Validation: Who's the Expert in This?

This last type of validation is based in science and data. It can come from healthcare professionals, and it can include tests, like the

CAPS-5 assessment that I shared with my patient Sofia, described at the beginning of this chapter. It should be noted that factual validation is slightly different from the other two forms of validation in that we're not validating someone's feelings. Instead, we're validating the impact an experience had on them in a quantitative way. For Sofia, being able to quantify the trauma that she had gone through validated her experience and put everything into perspective for her.

Healthcare professionals have countless ways to factually validate a patient. Another way I do this is by running blood work. Low iron means someone is low on energy and might not be getting the exercise they need to boost their mood. A vitamin B_{12} deficiency could lead to impaired cognition, which could explain why someone is not functioning as well at work as they used to and is getting frustrated. A vitamin D deficiency can cause someone to feel depressed; while some people aren't in a place where they can say "I'm depressed" or "I'm sad," when they can see that their vitamin D levels are at 5 nmol/L when they need to be at 50 nmol/L, that is factual validation that something is wrong. It's not uncommon to see abnormal blood work in a person with High-Functioning Depression. We don't just ignore our feelings; we ignore our health, too. We're too busy taking care of everyone else's well-being to worry about our own.

Physical ailments are another form of factual validation. In some cultures it's less acceptable to tell someone that you're feeling overwhelmed or down than it is to say that you have a headache or lower back pain. Overwhelm would be a weakness or a moral failure, but a physical ailment is morally neutral. That's how patients with HFD end up in their doctor's office with the physical manifestations of their emotional struggle. You don't realize that you're anxious; you just think that you have gastrointestinal issues, constipation, or neck pain that you need a pill for. I have jet-black hair now, but when I was in my twenties, I started going prematurely gray and my hair started falling out. I didn't need a visit to my PCP to figure out why; I knew it was the unrelenting stress from my residency.

Factual validation is when you head to your dentist for a mouth guard so you can stop grinding your teeth, and your dentist tells you to focus on your stress levels as well. It's when you go to the cardiologist because your heart has been oddly racing at times, and she explains that you've been having panic attacks. It's when thousands of people went to my website and crashed it trying to take the anhedonia quiz I developed. They wanted proof of what they were feeling.

Western medicine doesn't have a monopoly on factual validation. When your massage therapist is able to tell you what you do for a living based on where you carry muscle tension, that's factual validation. When an acupuncturist is able to help you get a good night's sleep or increase your chances of pregnancy, that's factual validation of what stress is doing to your body. There are multiple ways to listen to your body, receive the message it's sending, and get validation of your experience. In turn, you'll be able to give yourself some grace, access the help you need, and get out of the cycle of HFD.

All that being said, sometimes all the validation in the world isn't enough. I once had a patient, Malcolm, who worked in the music industry for a big-name artist—the kind of musician who notoriously wrecks hotel rooms and ends up recording their album six months after the due date. He absolutely loved being in a creative industry but hated how he was treated by the talent and his co-workers: 3 a.m. calls for immediate assistance, vicious jockeying for promotions, constant flights across the country to venues, never being able to take a vacation.

I saw Malcolm for five years, and every single year he'd be hospitalized for some mysterious illness—passing out in public, crippling pain down one side of his body, sudden blindness in one eye. It was all factual validation that he ignored. He'd be in the hospital for a couple of days, then he'd be right back at work the next day. "It's just a busy time right now," he'd tell me. "The album is about to drop, so it's stressful."

After his most recent hospitalization, for a seizure that had no known cause, I had to give Malcolm some tough love. "This job will kill you," I told him.

"That's what I'm in therapy for," he replied. "Even when I have a meeting in L.A. the night before and a concert in London the next day, I still make time for these sessions."

Even the best of us can think that just by going to therapy we are going to get better. In reality, we may be merely checking a box rather than practicing the techniques we're being taught—promising inside our therapist's office that we'll change, but not doing anything once we walk out that door. Malcolm needed more than just validation; he needed someone to call him out on his actions.

"It's important that you're making time for therapy," I said. "But an hour in here isn't going to help you overcome traveling across eight time zones every week. We have to figure out a way for you to pay more attention to your body so that you're not having a health crisis every year." I eventually persuaded Malcolm to start networking and find another creative job. He did—and his ER visits came to a screeching halt.

Self-Validation Exercise: Calm Yourself

Because people with High-Functioning Depression (especially doctors and nurses) are constantly in "go mode," they tend to have high heart rates. If this sounds like you, try this exercise, which will give you factual validation, help you understand your body better, and (hopefully) relax you. If you wear a watch with a heart rate monitor, stop and notice when your beats per minute go above 100. If you don't have a heart rate monitor, just check your pulse at your wrist, count the number of beats in 15 seconds, and multiply by 4 for beats per minute. When your pulse spikes, ask yourself how you feel (emotion: "I'm feeling stressed") and why you feel that way (thoughts). You'll be able to work the High-Functioning Depression Triangle to avoid negative thoughts and behaviors ("My kid hates me after our argument. I feel like smashing my phone on the floor") and lean into more positive ones ("Our talk didn't end the way I wanted it to. I'll try again tonight"). When you land on the positive thoughts and behaviors, watch to see if your heart rate comes down.

A WARNING ABOUT INVALIDATION

"God doesn't give us more than we can bear." This classic saying invalidates your pain and encourages you to push past it rather than acknowledge it.

"You're so lucky your parents are rich. I had nothing growing up." Here's a case where comparison is the thief of validation.

"Tough break. But I guess that's why you get paid the big bucks!" Invalidation like this teaches you that you must make sacrifices to be virtuous.

Are you seeing the trend here? Invalidation is anything that causes you to diminish what you're feeling or avoid acknowledging what has happened. For example, if you were abused as a child, it could be a parent gaslighting you into believing that the abuse never happened. Or it could be a friend telling you that what you went through wasn't that bad, because they experienced much worse. It can be someone glossing over or even ignoring what you've shared about your emotions or experiences, instead of acknowledging what you're going through: "That sounds terrible," a friend might say in reaction to you sharing bad news. "Do you still want to grab dinner?"

One of the first social media reels I ever created was about the Freudian stance we are taught to take as therapists: no reactions on our faces, no emotions coming through. But what I found is that my sessions were way more effective when my patients saw a reaction from me. They didn't want their pain ignored; they wanted a reaction to show that it was recognized. With invalidation, you don't just miss out on the benefits of validation; you fall deeper into the spiral of shame, because your fears—that you're overreacting, that you aren't being tough enough—have been confirmed. If you are constantly being invalidated by the people in your life, you may find that you turn to drugs or alcohol for help coping with the painful experiences you've endured.

Invalidation comes from other people and from environments. Your workplace might run rampant with invalidation if you're a frontline worker with what feels like perpetual double shifts, a public school teacher who has to fight for supplies and staff to do your job, a lawyer who works around the clock because one mistake could end the career you spent years building.

I have to admit that I created an invalidating environment at my office back when I was in the midst of my High-Functioning Depression. My employees would say, "We need to slow down. The pace we're going at is not sustainable." Instead of acknowledging the reality that everything was not fine, I'd ask them, "Couldn't we just do a little bit more?" I was telling them and myself that this wasn't that bad, that we could push harder, that we could do more, that everything was fine. But in reality, we were all struggling, and I should have found another way for us to move forward without pretending it would be easy.

I once had a social media follower leave a deep message in the comments section of one of my posts. He was a state trooper who had been deployed by the governor to work border patrol. The work conditions were horrific, the living spaces were horrendous, and no matter how much he and his co-workers complained to their superiors, nothing ever changed. That level of invalidation resulted in ten suicides on that job in less than a year.

It doesn't take a migrant crisis to create deadly invalidation. You could be in a highly competitive medical residency program where the environment normalizes mainlining coffee, only getting four hours of sleep per night, and never complaining about the conditions. In fact, medical residents are often blacklisted if they complain about their schedules. It is not a coincidence that medical residents have the highest suicide ideation rates in any profession.

Most of us can't go toe-to-toe with our boss, or just pick up and quit a job. But we can all recognize invalidation when it's happening and try to set up boundaries to prevent us from experiencing its negative effects. You can set a firm cutoff time for when your workday ends, reach out to allies inside and outside your workplace for emotional support, continue advocating for yourself in the workplace, and start making a plan to find a new job.

Pen a Path to Recovery (Part II)

Think back on that traumatic experience from your childhood that you wrote about. Then pull out another piece of paper and a pen and write a letter to your younger self. Reassure that younger version of you that what they experienced really did happen — no matter how much it seems like something out of a movie and no matter how many people around them deny it. Tell your younger self that what they experienced was not their fault. They didn't cause this terrible thing to happen and they certainly had no ability to stop it. Tell them that you know how they felt — and name those emotions. Then assure them that those feelings are real and valid. Finish the letter by thanking your younger self for being so strong and assuring them that things will get better when they grow up; in fact, you're working hard on that right now.

If you don't want to write a letter, there are other ways to do this exercise. You can create a video for social media that follows the #youngerself trend. You could record a voice note that you play back for yourself. You could write a poem for your younger self or focus a stream-of-consciousness journal entry on your inner child. This can be a really uncomfortable exercise, so do it whatever way feels most comfortable to you.

One of the reasons I ask my patients to do this exercise is that in changing the way you look at the past, you're changing the way your brain thinks and processes information about the present and future, too. If you can stop shaming, blaming, or judging your childhood self for your parents' divorce, or for the time the family dog got out of the house and ran away, you can also find it within you to stop shaming and judging your adult self for getting a sexually transmitted infection last year or losing money to a scam artist this month.

People with HFD often lose their voice because they let other people walk all over them. Self-validation allows you to find your voice again. The more you self-validate your experiences, the faster you'll be able to do it and the less time you'll have to wait to feel the relief that comes with it. Eventually you'll be able to self-validate in real time — shifting to positive self-talk as soon as you begin the negative self-talk, switching to a positive behavior right when you're about to slide into a negative behavior.

Now that you've read through the chapter, chances are your letter to your younger self is more understanding, validating, and empathetic than what you originally wrote about your experience in the earlier version of this exercise (page 99). It probably uses fewer judgmental statements and more positive language. Congratulations on taking those positive steps toward healing. You've got factual proof of it in your hands.

CHAPTER 6

Venting

Hands down, one of the best and worst things about social media is the comments section. If you're bold enough to show up on Instagram, TikTok, or YouTube, then you've definitely felt the ice-cold chill of an anonymous person trolling you. You probably also got this timeless piece of advice after moaning to a friend about it: never read the comments.

But I disagree. If I never read my comments, I would never get to see that my social media feed is filled with messages hundreds of lines deep from followers who are sharing their hurt, their trauma, their overwhelm, their everything. "At age twenty-seven, I felt burnout and completely exhausted," one follower wrote. "Resented my family for their failure to give me any credit for all that I've done and for them demanding more. No way am I subjecting myself to a sixty-hour/week high-paying job just so my parents can brag. No way."

"My stepmom did a trauma dump about my dad's infidelity," another wrote. "Now I have blocked my dad and the rest of his family because interacting with them causes anxiety. Also, one little argument or intense conversation with my partner leaves me in an anxiety shock."

"I was so high-functioning to the point there was a period in my life the only way my brain could stop me from pushing and pushing through work, friends, family was by fainting...literally fainting every morning. In the end, it was a very huge problem of depression. I was working from 7 a.m. to 2 p.m. at one place and after that from 2 p.m. to 11 p.m. It wasn't for the need of money. It was because I felt I wasn't doing enough."

Why would people post their most intimate and painful secrets for the world to see? Because we need to vent if we want to shake off the sadness of what's bothering us and obtain that ever-elusive inner peace that everyone else seems to claim with ease. Human beings are social creatures who need and crave connection and communication. Just like shelter and food, feeling heard is a basic need that we all have. Whether you are sharing your feelings or concerns with another person (or, in the case of social media, with millions of people) or reflecting on them in your journal, venting is the process of letting your frustrations out, rather than keeping them bottled up. It's also something that people with High-Functioning Depression rarely do.

As high-functioning individuals, we are often silent about our pain because we are taught that no one wants to hear negativity. We don't acknowledge our negative emotions because we think they mean we're less than perfect—and that's not acceptable. We also feel guilty because we equate venting with complaining. And how dare we complain? We're not the only one to have come from a traumatic background. And isn't where we are now far better than where we once were? Sadly, silence traps us in a cycle of overwhelm that may eventually be the end of us. It reminds me of a famous Alice Walker quote from her novel *Possessing the Secret of Joy*. "If you lie to yourself about your own pain," the book's African heroine writes on a sign, "you will be killed by those who will claim you enjoyed it."

On my social media posts, you'll see scores of people venting about family, but in my practice, romantic relationships are the number one thing that people come to me to vent about. They aren't feeling validated by their partner, so they come to therapy to ask: "Why is he like that?" "What am I doing wrong?" "Why don't they make me feel loved?" Venting about work (like the toxic co-worker who has been bad-mouthing you to the boss) and kids (like the child who keeps getting sent to detention) come in second and third.

Honestly, your imagination is the only limit to the things you could be venting about, so have at it. The upsides of having some-place to download your feelings—and hopefully have them vali-dated—make venting not only worthwhile but also essential to your recovery from High-Functioning Depression.

THE BENEFITS OF VENTING

It's healing to have a place to talk about how painful it is when your sister sneakily fat-shames you on brunch dates, how much your back hurts from spending all weekend helping a friend move, or how your boyfriend is a seven-year-old kid masquerading as a forty-year-old man. The process isn't so much about slamming someone as it is about having a release for the emotions building up inside you. It's also critical for people who suffer from HFD, for four specific reasons: you're under enough stress already, you never slow down long enough to understand what's really bothering you, you're putting your health at risk by staying silent, and it helps end the cycle of intergenerational pain. Let's unpack each of these.

You're Under Enough Stress Already

People with High-Functioning Depression race through their day on anxious energy from the moment they wake up (usually before their alarm goes off in the morning) until the second they crawl into bed at night (and doom-scroll social media because their brain is too busy to let them sleep). Venting relieves some of this excess emotional energy.

One of the problems is that, culturally, we're taught not to vent. Though this is slowly beginning to change, for a long time the norm in American society has been to keep your feelings inside and deal with difficulties privately. We look down on negativity and we claim that everyone should toughen up and stop complaining.

We should think of venting, however, as complaining's savvy older sister. The one who still wears glasses instead of contacts but unpinned that tight bun and let down her hair so you can see her curls. Venting isn't about blurting out how much you hate someone or something to anyone who will listen. It's an intentional, emotional release that allows you to move forward with your life. And when done properly, it can free you from the heartache and pain you've been carrying. Not having an outlet for that stress can, quite frankly, be deadly.

"I'm finally happy," my mentor, psychiatrist Fadi Haddad, told me when he started meeting with a therapist who understood him. Haddad specialized in adoption psychiatry, helping traumatized children attach to their new parents. He essentially became a third parent in most of his cases, enmeshing himself in the lives of the families he helped. He also ran the first-of-its-kind child psychiatry emergency room in a New York City public hospital. He saw some of the most severe cases of child mental health emergencies in the world.

As someone who had High-Functioning Depression, Haddad worked extraordinarily long hours, and rarely took a day off; even when he did go on vacation, he was available by phone. But once he started meeting with a therapist, he finally had someone to vent to about all the traumas that he was witnessing. He also had someone he trusted and respected to validate his very real need to take time off—and someone who would hold him accountable for doing it.

You Never Slow Down Long Enough to Understand What's Really Bothering You

When you're venting, you're letting everything out, but you're also gaining insight. Venting forces you to slow down and get to the root of whatever is causing your stress—and potentially helps you figure out how to overcome it. It's much easier to do this when you have someone else listening to you. As an outsider looking in, they can connect the dots and get a better understanding of where your frustrations are coming from and how to address them.

When my patients feel an excessive need to vent, that's usually a sign that something is eating away at them. This was certainly the case for one patient, whose need came to light when a number I didn't recognize popped up on my phone one day. Plenty of women have gotten phone calls from "the other woman" their partner was seeing. But I'm the only person I know who has gotten a phone call from "the other therapist" their patient was seeing. "Why are you prescribing my patient Lexapro?" the voice on the other end asked me. She had been about to put in a prescription for the same drug when the pharmacy alerted her that it had already been prescribed by another doctor. So she dialed my number.

It took us a while to figure out what was happening, but it turned out that our patient was comfortable only in triangular relationships. He felt like he always needed a backup person to be with (or therapist to talk to) in case someone abandoned him. That way his excessive need to vent would always be catered to. He learned that behavior as a child and repeated that behavior as an adult—which is how he ended up coming to see both me and the other therapist.

You're Putting Your Health at Risk by Staying Silent

Research shows that being able to express your negative emotions in a healthy way—like venting—can do everything from decreasing your risk of heart disease to increasing the strength of your connection with others. On the other hand, if you isolate yourself in your pain, it can make you emotionally and physically ill. You may start snapping at your children or your parents. You may not sleep as well at night. You can develop mysterious headaches and back pain. All of that can lead to a decrease in efficiency at work and the breakdown of your relationships with your friends and family, which only worsens the damage all this stress is doing to your body.

I wish I could tell you that the story of my mentor, Fadi Haddad, has a perfectly happy ending, but it doesn't. At the exact moment that he was starting to live his life, he suddenly fell ill with cancer and soon died. He likely didn't notice that anything felt wrong in his body until it was too late. When you work extremely hard, your body releases endorphins so that you don't get too exhausted, and this can mask symptoms. And like so many people with High-Functioning Depression, he was so devoted to helping others that he ended up last on his own list of people to care for. I still miss him to this day.

When I was a resident, I once had a patient, Evan, who was suffering from paralysis on the right side of his body. We ran every single test on him that we could think of, from MRIs to a lumbar puncture. But we couldn't find a reason for Evan's inability to move his arms and legs, or even blink his right eye. He just went from being fully functional one day to having partial paralysis the next, and his very pregnant wife called 911 to have him brought in. While we were trying to figure out what to try next, Evan — thinking that his days were numbered — made a confession to his wife that I overheard. She knew that Evan's father had passed away when Evan was only six years old. What she didn't know was that he'd had a heart attack in front of Evan, who was terrified and didn't know how to help his dad after he dropped to the floor. He broke down in tears telling her the story while she held his left hand. When Evan woke up the next day, he was able to move his right side. You might call it a miracle. I call it the magic of venting. All that trauma that Evan had held inside over losing his father at a young age reemerged when Evan was on the cusp of becoming a father himself. His paralysis stemmed from anxiety over parenthood. Sharing his secret with his wife freed his body and his brain. After another day of monitoring, we sent Evan home—with a strong recommendation for therapy.

Venting Helps End the Cycle of Intergenerational Pain

Venting encourages you to be honest with yourself about what's bothering you, and to verbalize that with someone else. When we release the stress and frustration that people with High-Functioning Depression tend to keep bottled up inside, not only do we take some emotional weight off our own shoulders, but we are also less likely to try to manage our stress in unhealthy ways that harm our friends, family members, or co-workers, and we may even strengthen those relationships in the process.

Once I was working with a famous hockey player who was suffering from High-Functioning Depression while going through a nasty divorce. All his life, he had kept his feelings inside, which was one of the reasons he ended up cheating on his partner and destroying their marriage. He was overcome with regret, not just for losing his wife but also for destabilizing his family—especially their daughter, who was caught in the middle of this extremely messy and extremely expensive divorce proceeding. By the time he got to me, he had spent weeks alternating between emptying the contents of his home bar and crying. Yes, this was a huge guy who'd been slammed up against the boards by his opponents and hit with pucks flying eighty miles an hour—and he was reduced to tears over the breakdown of his family.

The work we did together enabled him to start functioning again. By learning how to vent with me, he was able to better notice and name his emotions, and express them to others. This ended up changing the way that he interacted with his daughter. She started remarking to him how much better a father he had become by talking about his feelings. He started hearing her say she loved him more. Because communication is the foundation of venting, venting helps us work toward the open communication that is essential for a family to thrive.

TOO TERRIBLE FOR WORDS?

There are times in life when we have a secret that seems so big, so awful, so unimaginable that we wouldn't want to give it the breath of life by saying it aloud. Therapy and counseling were designed for the secrets you can't imagine telling. A few years ago, one of my patients, just ten years old, came to me because she was forced into mandatory therapy—she had missed so many days of school and been so disruptive in class that a child-services agency got involved. Kids tend not to be the most accountable patients. They need a little help from their parents, who can better remember what happened when and articulate exactly what's going on. So when I work with children, part of the session is with the parent and the child, part of the session is just with the child, and part of the session is just with the parent.

Over a few weeks of working with this girl and her single mom, I realized that the daughter had ADHD and needed help with organizational skills and even medication for focus. But I could also see that a lot of the mom's anxiety and depression were being projected onto her daughter. The mom definitely had High-Functioning Depression and was imposing her demanding and perfectionist tendencies onto her kid by pushing her so hard to succeed. Whenever they arrived for a session, I could hear the mom yelling at her daughter through the door of my office. She was so hard on this little girl, for reasons that seemed to have little to do with her daughter's behavior. It wasn't until our last session that I understood what was going on in that family.

People often think HFD is found only in high-powered women in corporate environments. But it's also found in lots of other people — including in women working double shifts at fast-food restaurants and raising their kids all alone, like this mom. My colleagues at the clinic said I shouldn't offer her parenting classes or trauma services because that would overwhelm her, given all she had on her plate. Knowing she was high-functioning, however, I thought the opposite. If she could work hard and take care of her kid, she should at least get a chance to have access to these services.

When the mom came in alone to meet with me, she confessed to me that she hated her daughter. She then broke down crying while telling me that when she was a senior in high school, she had been sexually assaulted at a party, got pregnant with her daughter, and become so depressed that she dropped out of school. Her family was very religious and didn't believe in abortion, so she never told anyone she didn't want the baby. Unfortunately, months into her pregnancy, she was diagnosed with cervical insufficiency, which left her on bed rest for months so that she could safely bring the baby to term. Now it was just the two of them, and she felt trapped and alone with a daily reminder of the violation she had never told anyone about... until now. Then she picked up her purse and walked out of my office.

Sometimes we have stories and feelings that are so heavy, we feel we can't share them, even with our family members, because we fear that we're burdening them: a diagnosis of cancer that you don't want to worry your children with, a looming threat of bankruptcy after a bad investment, the knowledge that we've fallen out of love with our partner but aren't ready to part with them. But keeping these things to ourselves is a form of masochism: we're sacrificing our own need to get our trauma out in the open in order to shield other people from the emotions we're experiencing. Healing from High-Functioning Depression involves recognizing that we are worthy of care. It involves learning that it is not just all right but expected to lean on others who care about us when we need support.

The process of venting and sharing is like exercising a muscle. The more you work on it, the stronger it gets. Your first try at venting and communicating your feelings might not be incredibly eloquent. But your hundredth will be. So let's talk about all of the different ways that you can get started.

WHOM SHOULD I VENT TO?

A Therapist

Hands down, therapy is the best way to vent. When you're venting, ideally you want a trained ear listening to you. As a board-certified psychiatrist, I've been through four years of medical school, four years of residency, and two years of a fellowship. That's a lot of education to learn how to listen to someone else. Therapists have the formal training as well as the life experience to listen to all types of problems and recognize common interpersonal patterns and dynamics, in order to help our patients heal.

The problem is that finding the right therapist isn't easy, and the best ones are in high demand and can have long waiting lists. Luckily, thanks to telehealth options that sprang up during the pandemic, access to therapy is better now than it has been in decades. I often tell people to start their search at *Psychology Today*'s website, which lists licensed mental health professionals all across the country. But that can be hit-or-miss. Not to mention that some therapists aren't taking new clients or don't take insurance anymore because of how complicated the healthcare system has become. (See page 251 for additional ideas.) If you can't find a psychiatrist or psychologist, consider a licensed clinical social worker, a psychiatrist in a residency training program, or even a group therapy program led by a licensed professional. Group therapy can provide a sense of community while enabling you to share your story. You might also consider other types of therapy like equine therapy or music therapy.

When you're working to overcome High-Functioning Depression with a therapist, make sure the one you choose has experience and success working with people who have struggled with the condition. Ask them what their methodology is for helping someone like you—and how long it will take. Finally, make sure you're not breaking the bank to get the mental health support you need. That might prevent you from making future appointments and then disrupt your care.

Now here's the part where I admit that therapy isn't the answer for everyone—whether because you can't afford it, because you've tried it repeatedly without results, or because you don't like the idea of paying a stranger to listen to your secrets. If you can't or would rather not meet with a therapist, consider one of the other venting methods below.

A Faith Leader

While preachers, imams, rabbis, priests, and other clergy don't receive anywhere near the level of training that therapists do on how to counsel a person, they're still extremely valuable resources for venting. Doctors like me have medical case studies that we review to improve our knowledge; faith leaders have biblical case studies that they lean on. While I have experience with patients, faith leaders will have experience talking to other parishioners. And just like us, they've heard it all.

I know it was wrong, but when I was a little girl, I was incredibly curious and I used to eavesdrop on some of the churchgoing women who met with my father, an evangelical Christian preacher at a church near my childhood home. They would tell him modern-day Cinderella stories (but far worse and with no prince in sight) of how they had come to this country illegally only to be treated like slaves by the relatives who took them in. They would vent about how they worked long hours at jobs that their "auntie" found them only to have their paychecks taken by their host family. Or about how they were expected to cook and clean in the house they were staying in, and never went out.

You don't have to have a job with a salary in the high six figures to be suffering from High-Functioning Depression. You can be working around the clock and lacking joy in your life while making minimum wage or less. The people who told my father their stories were never able to save money. And they could never vent to anyone except for my father, the preacher, for fear of being deported. Church was literally a sanctuary for them. It was also a great equalizer. Everyone under that roof was valued, loved, and treated with kindness—unlike what they experienced everywhere else. By venting to my father and praying to God for help, they were able to get through each exhausting, painful day.

Whether you're meeting with a mental health professional or a faith leader, you want to make sure that that person is a good fit for you. Ask yourself: "Do you feel heard when you're meeting with them? Do you get a sense that you have their undivided attention? That they understand your struggle?" You'll also want to make sure that it's convenient for you to meet with them. If they're only available at 2 p.m. on Tuesdays and you're scrambling to move your lunch hour at work so you can make it, it's going to be more of a burden than a relief, and you won't get what you need out of the process.

A Trusted Friend

There's a golden rule when it comes to venting to a friend: Pick a person you can vent to, and who can also vent to you. That way you ensure reciprocity and build mutual trust with the process. When it comes to venting, you want to be more like a drinking fountain than a lawn sprinkler, letting out your troubles in short, intentional bursts rather than sprinkling them around indiscriminately and letting them rain down on everyone in your orbit. Talking to anyone and everyone who'll listen isn't effective venting. It's just dumping your emotions on other people, which can, in fact, make you feel worse.[1] Focus instead on venting with just one other person with the intent and purpose of resolution.

Because I see it happen all the time, I also want to make sure to call out the one person you should never vent to: anyone whom you're in a position of power over. That includes people at work whom you supervise, people whom you've hired to work in your home, and, yes, your children. I don't care how hilarious a disaster that date you went on was; don't share it with your kid. It doesn't matter how badly your ex-husband has been treating you; don't trash him to your babysitter. You're burdening these people with your problems. Even if you're laughing about what a cheap date the guy you met on Bumble was, your kid is still quietly worried about you. And even if she would never say so, your housekeeper might just want to listen to music instead of hearing you rant about your evil boss.

People Reading Deep Comments on Social Media

The reason people vent in the comments of social media posts is that it's a form of group therapy that's available to you anywhere, any time of day—and with complete anonymity if that's what you choose. And it works. Most of the time people just want to get something off their chest and have others chime in with validation: "You did the right thing." "Your mom sounds awful." "I can't believe he did that to you." "You're going to be all right." Sometimes they are trying to self-diagnose and find a community of other people with their mental health issue. When someone sounds like they might have some serious mental health concerns, I point them toward resources, but the majority of people who comment on my feed just want to voice a frustration and then move on. On the other hand, of course, we've all seen how angry backlash against an innocent tweet or Instagram post can leave someone emotionally threadbare. I don't like it when I occasionally get comments from people who think I should lose my license for posting fun videos. But I just delete or block them and move on.

The following list of dos and don'ts should help you get all of the benefits of unloading online, without any of the drawbacks.

THE DOS AND DON'TS OF SHARING IN THE COMMENTS SECTION

Do:

- Post from a non-work-related account. That way it's clear the content is personal and your opinions are your own.
- Comment with a goal. Make sure you genuinely want to get someone else's validation, feedback, or advice.
- Turn off notifications after you share. That way, if there are rude or disturbing responses, they won't ruin your peace of mind.
- Give support back. When you feel that you can help or support someone because you have or had a similar situation, share it.

Don't:

- Walk into a lion's den. Avoid sharing if the comments section is a full-on brawl or is already very hostile.
- Expect automatic validation. Be prepared for some people not to empathize or agree with your perspective.
- Keep refreshing for responses every thirty seconds after posting. Once you've shared something that is personal, try to limit how much you allow yourself to check the comment section responses so that you don't obsess about it.

THE NOT-SO-SUBTLE ART OF VENTING

Now that you know why venting is so important and where to do it, let's talk about *how* to do it. Because, believe it or not, there's an actual art to getting all of your emotions out. And if you don't do it properly, there can be repercussions.

One of the biggest misconceptions I've seen in my High-Functioning Depression clients is something I call the fantasy therapy session. They imagine they'll get to lie back on a couch and dump all the problems out, and those problems will magically disappear in a few sessions. Sorry, but no. That's not how it works. Therapy is not lying down on a couch so someone else can figure you out. It's a lot of work for you, the patient. You'll uncover some things that are traumatizing or triggering. You'll have to do the work to process and prevail over scarring memories or complicated relationships or negative thought patterns. I tell my patients that the brain is a stubborn organ. Reexamining yourself and getting to know your true self isn't fast, but it's deeply fulfilling. It isn't sexy, but it's significant. And it isn't easy, but it's completely rewarding.

Another mistake I've seen people make when trying to release their stress or frustrations is trauma dumping. To put it simply, trauma dumping is when you verbally vomit all your problems and leave the other person listening to you overwhelmed. The bad news is that the other person might be so visibly turned off by the experience that you both shut down. The good news is that it's an easy mistake to avoid. Just ask yourself the following four questions before, during, and after you vent to another person:

"Did I Pick the Right Person?"

I know people who trauma-dump all over the place. You have to pick one person — not an army — to vent to. You also need to be mindful that you're venting to someone who has the capacity to hear your complaints. Could there be emotional fallout if, for example, you vent about how small your bonus was this year to your artist friend on government assistance? Similarly, it's pretty insensitive to complain about how overwhelming your kids are to your friend who may be struggling with infertility.

"Did I Ask Permission?"

Whereas your therapist is a professional that you're paying to listen to you and group therapy has rules around sharing built in, in a friendship you need a green light to unload. You might say, "Do you have a moment to listen to what happened to me this morning?" or

"Please let me know if this becomes too much for you." You can also watch for clues that the other person may feel you're dumping on them. Perhaps they look uncomfortable or they're not offering any significant feedback or suggestions.

"Did I Learn Anything?"

To avoid trauma dumping, you have to hold space for getting feedback from the other person to help you gain insight into your situation. This isn't a one-way conversation. You should be listening to the other person's questions and receiving the feedback they have, especially if you're talking to a professional.

"Am I Always the One Venting?"

If you're venting with a friend or family member, reciprocity is key. You have to make sure that you're giving and getting when it comes to venting. Otherwise you run the risk of overwhelming the other person. So make sure that you've held space for your friend or family member to share what's going on with them.

SOLITARY WAYS TO VENT

Journaling

Research shows that journaling is a powerful tool for reducing symptoms of depression, managing stress, and increasing cognitive processing to help you better understand yourself.[2] And you don't need to go out and buy a special book for it. My adolescent clients love using journaling apps like Day One and Penzu because they don't have to worry about their privacy being violated. (Anyone else remember being completely mortified when someone found and read your diary?) Electronic journals might also be faster to write in and easier for you to reread down the line.

People with High-Functioning Depression love structure, so there are a few ways that I recommend using a journal for venting. The first is to write in the journal as if you're talking to another person. You could address your entries to "Dear Journal," or to a real person in your life who is no longer here. One of my patients lost her husband to a sudden heart attack and would write in her journal as if she were talking to him. It was a way to come home at the end of a hard day and tell him about what happened at work, or wake up in the morning and share with him what she was apprehensive about in the coming day.

Another way to use your journal is by "griping with gratitude." On one page, write down all of the things you're annoyed, frustrated, or worried about. That could be everything from an argument you had with your partner to frustrations with your manager at work to stress over the surprise birthday party you're orchestrating for friends. Then, on the next page, list three things you're grateful for. The first page gives you some reaffirming validation about the difficulties of what you're going through, while the second reminds you what you have in life that is working to your advantage.

No matter how you decide to vent in your journal, make sure to include a date with each entry. Because journaling is a one-way conversation, the best way to reflect on what you've experienced is by looking back on what you've written in the past. This is how you get the personal insight that I mentioned earlier. I tell my patients to wait at least a week and then reread their past entries. Hopefully, you'll be able to see some progress that you've made with an issue you were struggling with. But you also might notice that you're stuck in a cycle and need some help getting out of it.

Prayer

As a child, I saw how going to church and talking to God helped so many immigrants who felt trapped and abused by the people who had taken them in. Even if they didn't have access to my father or want to share with him what was going on, they could whisper it to God. They could work through it in Tuesday night Bible study sessions and Friday night prayer meetings. Prayer might be the only place where some people can vent their secret pain.

Even if you're not religious, thinking that there's a higher being who loves you, is listening to you, and understands your pain can help. There's a reason that having some sort of faith or belief is popular. And, best of all, it's free.

Crying

Crying is a great way to vent without even using words. That's because crying allows you to release stress hormones. It can decrease your heart rate and put you in a state of rest—which most of us high-functioning people are rarely in. And it's very therapeutic.

Artistic Self-Expression

Interestingly enough, venting doesn't even require you to open your mouth. It can be something that you do with your hands. Any type of creative passion that you have can become an outlet for venting.

Head to a local art studio, grab a paintbrush, and let your mood dictate the colors you use and the images you create. Sit down at a piano and start striking the chords that come to mind or play a song that resonates with you in that moment. Go on social media and create a digital video or post expressing exactly how you're feeling.

"I hadn't acted in months," a High-Functioning Depression patient of mine, Emma, told me in a moment of joy. She had taken a break from performing on the stage (her passion) to get a degree in economics (her practical career choice). She was getting straight A's and had a wonderful boyfriend but was not feeling any pleasure in life. "Last night, I randomly decided to do something unusual," she said. "I stood facing the mirror and recited Ophelia's monologue from *Hamlet*. It felt...good. I haven't enjoyed slipping into character in months."

I could completely relate. When I was younger, my parents made me and my siblings get onstage and act and sing for church events. We'd grumble about it, but we actually loved doing it. As an adult, no one pushed me to do anything like that, and I almost forgot how much I enjoyed it. Then came social media. Taking on different personas in the skits that I record for my social media channels is one of the best parts of my day. It taps into that childhood joy, and the fact that I get to reach and help millions of people by doing it gives me permission to lean into that joy.

Creative endeavors are healing, particularly when they tap into our passions. They're a form of pleasure and joy that helps break us out of the cycle of anhedonia. I gave my patient Emma some homework: reciting one monologue twice a week for the rest of the month. You can do the same for yourself with any artistic passion you have, whether it's gardening, photography, knitting, cooking, sculpture, film, or whatever else will bring you some much-needed joy.

Since this is another solo endeavor, it helps to look back on your creative work a week or so later to try to gain the insight an outside voice (like a therapist or friend) might have nudged you toward. For my patient Emma, such questions might include: "Was there a particular reason that you picked Ophelia's monologue? Did it have anything to do with your current romantic relationship?" For someone who chooses painting, a question might be "Why might you have chosen dark greens and blues for your painting instead of yellows or oranges?" For a photographer: "Why did you take a photograph of a deserted street instead of a nature scene?" Once you've created a work, you can transform from the creator into the observer. Look at what you've made and search for themes. Try to connect the dots yourself, linking them to the emotions you were trying to release.

Now that you've learned how important venting is to the healing process and how to do it, I want you to put your knowledge into action with the following exercises. Try doing one a week and noting in a journal how they've impacted you.

Share Your Secrets

My current therapist had no idea how close I was to the end of my marriage until I was already in the midst of a divorce. I was reenacting the same masochistic and people-pleasing behaviors with her that I had with that first therapist from my residency training days. I didn't want to worry her with the details of my split — or appear less than perfect to her. High-functioning people often keep secrets even from their therapists because they don't want to disappoint or burden them. You can be in therapy, but you may not be getting enough out of it due to core beliefs of being unworthy or living only to serve others. Like me, you can be preventing yourself from getting all of the joy and relief from therapy by not fully venting. I wasted time when I could've felt less stress and guilt, along with more validation and support. So if you have a therapist, I want you to pick a secret to share that you haven't told them yet. See how it feels to let go of the burden of carrying this weight all on your own.

Write a Letter to a Cemetery

Have you ever lost someone before you got the chance to tell them something important? That you're angry with them? That you don't forgive them? That you wish they could take back something they said to you? Sometimes people in our lives pass on before we've had the chance for closure or reconciliation. Writing a letter to them is an opportunity to change that. You can write an anonymous letter with no return address to a deceased loved one who hurt you or a loved one whom you never fully understood and have questions for. Vent on paper and then ask the cemetery where they're buried if they'll place the letter on the grave. You can also search for organizations that will accept letters written to people who have passed away.

Wear Your Feelings

You've got to get dressed every day. Why not use it as an opportunity to turn anhedonia into excitement? When I'm feeling particularly sad, I dress to the nines so that my look can transform me from fizzled-out to fierce. You can also choose to wear cozy things like a fuzzy sweater or stretchy leggings when you're feeling uncomfortable or on edge. Dressing for your feelings can be soothing and a healthy form of self-expression.

Color psychology research shows, for example, that looking at pink can help you find calm, while red helps to increase your feeling of strength; if you wear red, people will perceive you as more sexually attractive. Seeing green doesn't make you jealous; it makes you relaxed, like when you're in nature. Sports teams that wear black get the most penalties, so when you're ready to unleash your edgier side, pull out that black leather jacket. Colors can be very personal to our experiences of home (like having a grandmother you loved who always wore purple) and to our cultural backgrounds (for example, red often symbolizes love and passion in North America, but in China it frequently signifies luck, and in certain African cultures it symbolizes death and grief).[3]

Sing Your Heart Out

There's a reason karaoke is the international sensation everyone loves to love (and hate), and why movie musicals are making a huge comeback in Hollywood.[4] Singing brings us all joy. Whether you love the sound of your voice or can acknowledge that carrying a tune is a struggle, most of us will still sing when we're alone in the shower or folding clothes or getting dinner ready. When I'm working with adolescents, I'll ask them to show me a playlist from their phone. Then we'll Google the lyrics of a few songs, print them out, and look for themes. On an unconscious level, the messages in the songs are there, and I find them with my clients. You can do this with your therapist as well to try to understand yourself better. You can also just pick an angry or rebellious song from your playlist to belt out when no one is around as a pleasurable antidote to anhedonia. Not sure where to start? My patients love these artists, whose music tends to have very rich psychological themes: Taylor Swift, Rihanna, Demi Lovato, Ed Sheeran, Alanis Morissette, Katy Perry, Adele, Kendrick Lamar, Ariana Grande.

CHAPTER 7

Values

Milky Way bars. Cheetos. Now and Later candy. Hershey bars. For an entire year of elementary school, my friends and siblings got all sorts of free snacks from me. Not only am I a high-functioning adult, but I was also a high-functioning kid. So when my school announced a reading contest, ten-year-old me didn't care about the prize, which was a massive stash of snacks. I wanted the honor of doing something that I loved. (I also happened to be the fastest at it in my class.) I blazed through everything from Judy Blume to Emily Brontë to Maya Angelou. I got the most points for polishing off *Little Women*—all five-hundred-plus pages of it. And I won more snacks than I could ever eat.

Years later in college and graduate school, reading became less of an enjoyable activity and more of a survival skill—and there were definitely no more free snacks. I was perusing genetics, biology, and organic chemistry textbooks until I was bleary-eyed. I carefully combed through journal articles. Reading went from my greatest pleasure to my greatest fear when I started having nightmares about the tests that I was about to take. I lost the joy that I had found in something that I deeply valued: learning.

It wasn't until years later—after I had been married and then divorced—that I realized how much joy was missing from my life. That's when I turned back to my childhood to reclaim it. I knew I loved learning and reading, so I started back at it. This time I switched from fictional women to real ones and picked up Michelle Obama's *Becoming*. From the first pages, I started to remember that feeling of joy I'd once felt when immersed in the world of literature. I fell in love with reading again. It's been a few years since then, and I'm up to reading a book a week. No pressure like back in school. All pleasure.

What I had stumbled upon as I tried to (and successfully did) pull myself out of the depression around my divorce was the third step every person with High-Functioning Depression must take in recovery: reclaiming your values.

WHAT EXACTLY ARE VALUES?

Chances are you've heard people online or commentators on television talk about moral values, or executives at your job talk about corporate values, but you may not have stopped to fully consider what your personal values are. Or even why they matter.

Your values are what you believe is most important in life. Don't get that confused with hard work or perseverance. People with HFD often make that error. Your values aren't things that bring you success or approval. Values are about what you treasure and what brings you a sense of joy. But most important, your values give your life a purpose. Values are often shaped by your family or by your culture. For example, some Asian cultures place a heavy value on education, which leads to encouraging kids to study hard and to pursue advanced degrees. Some African cultures put an emphasis on respect for elders that fosters caring for the elderly and paying attention to their hard-won wisdom. When asked about their values, most Americans will mention family (which leads us to prioritize spending time with them and working hard for them) or community (which can make us become very invested in our neighbors and the environment we live in).

In the Joseph household, my parents taught me and my three siblings that faith, charity, and family were our most important values. With my father being a Pentecostal preacher, it made sense that there was an emphasis on religion and helping others. They made sure we knew what caring for others looked like and that we were aware of how important it was. Every Saturday, we would wake up early and our parents would drive us down to the local YMCA to do charity work. We'd see families and children who were so much less fortunate than we were. As a child I thought it was such a drag. As an adult I'm thankful that my parents taught me empathy. When I meet with patients who lack it, I almost always find out that their parents didn't model it for them like mine did.

But the story that I most love telling and that always brings a smile to my face is about how our family valued family. Every night before my siblings and I went to bed in our family's tiny apartment, we would turn to each other and say, "I'm sorry for everything I ever did to hurt you." We might actually be thinking about something specific we did that day, like a mean comment we made. Or we might not have any idea what we could've done to hurt our sibling.

But the point was that our parents didn't want us to ever go to bed angry with each other. Because we were family.

On top of the significant impact that our parents and our culture can have on our values, the values we hold dear are also shaped by who we are at our core and what we come to experience through life on our own. That's why learning and reading became so important to me in addition to the values my mother and father had instilled.

WHY WE SHOULD CARE ABOUT VALUES

Before I help you to start identifying what your values are—and it'll take some work—I want to explain why doing this work is so essential. Hands down, values are one of the most critical V's for you to master on your way out of High-Functioning Depression. They inform (or at least they should inform) all your choices in life. They are your motivation behind everything. And without them, you default to making bad choices that are out of alignment with what is truly important to you. Here's what happens when you're able to identify and prioritize your values in your life.

You'll Stop Working Yourself to Death

As you've learned by now, part of having High-Functioning Depression means constantly being in "go mode": figuring out how to stretch a dollar without snapping it, putting in extra hours at a job (or multiple jobs), getting kicked out of the library on campus because it's closing for the night. It's easy to figure out how to work harder in the pursuit of material wealth. It's harder to figure out how to work harder in pursuit of emotional health. If you've been pursuing a promotion, an A+, a bigger house, a larger diamond for your wife's ring, you've been chasing after fool's gold. Real, 24-karat gold is happiness, pleasure, and fulfillment, and these come from your values — not from being named employee of the month or from a year-end bonus that means that you can afford to break ground on that wave pool you want in the backyard. When we lean into our values, we get pleasure out of work. When we lean away from them, we get anhedonia and fall into a cycle of High-Functioning Depression.

You'll Break Free from Unsatisfying Relationships

Values impact not only what we hold in high regard but also *whom* we hold in high regard. People with High-Functioning Depression go overboard in their professional *and* personal relationships. But when we define our values and start to adhere to them, dysfunctional relationships naturally begin to disappear from our lives. We enter into healthy relationships and break free from the unsatisfying ones because we know what we need to feel full, fed, and content. We can avoid devastating dysfunctional relationships or even divorce by knowing what's most important to us in life and not straying from that.

I once had a patient named Dennis, a successful and in-demand professional dancer who came to me because he realized he was deeply unhappy. After several sessions, I could see why. When he was just ten years old, his mother had a secret relationship with another man and then abandoned Dennis, his two younger siblings, and their dad to start a new life. As a result, adult Dennis hopped from weeklong relationship to weeklong relationship desperately looking for the love and attention he never got from his mother, but also resenting these women because he was still angry with his mom.

Dennis valued love and safety. But he behaved in a masochistic fashion, working nonstop and never investing time in his relationships. That is, until he sprained his ankle. Being forced to take a break from work gave him more time to think about how he was living and what was important to him. For the first time in forever, he was in a relationship that lasted longer than a week. The woman he was seeing helped take care of him while he was on crutches. He leaned into the caregiving that he had lacked as a child and that feeling of safety and love. He was finally feeling full, fed, and content.

You'll Put an End to Your Masochism

As I mentioned earlier in the book, if you never identify your values, or if you lose sight of them, that also can lead to masochism. This propensity for self-sacrificing and self-sabotaging behavior makes you likely to accept treatment from others that is painful (emotionally or physically), disrespectful, or harmful. Some experts even think that it's a form of aggression that we turn inward, toward ourselves (instead of outward, toward others), because of feelings of guilt.

Perhaps you had a childhood in which you didn't receive the love you needed. You might grow up to feel unworthy of that same love as an adult and, as a result, find yourself in relationships that aren't reciprocal and allow people to take advantage of you. That's because masochism propelled you to that choice when you weren't in the best place in your life. You can make healthier romantic relationship choices as you start to focus less on pleasing others and more on prioritizing your values.

Masochism extends beyond partnerships in love and can include work relationships as well. We might choose condescending co-founders, apply to work in a glorified sweatshop, or convince ourselves that the brutal boss we interviewed with is a misunderstood genius. Once we start to uphold our values, however, it saves us from this self-destructive behavior. We make different, healthier choices in our work relationships as well.

Get ready, because practicing and upholding your values is about to become your new way of life. It's going to skyrocket your joy and completely transform your relationships. Let's get started by figuring out what matters most to you.

NAMING YOUR VALUES

Unlike naming your favorite color or where you'd go on vacation for a week if money were no object, coming up with a list of your values can be tough. To help you along, I've included a list of more than fifty different values at the end of this chapter, on page 179. But before you look at the list, it's best to try to name them yourself. Looking at the list might lead you to find values you *think* you should have rather than the ones you truly do hold dear. Or a value that you really care about might not even be on the list I share later.

You can start to identify your values by asking yourself some key questions. Use these to try to come up with a list of three to five values that are most important to you:

- **Whom do you admire and what is it that you love about them?** Think about that classic job interview question: "If you could have dinner with anyone, living or dead, who would it be?" Sure, if this were pure fantasy, it would be great to sit down with Beyoncé, or with Noah from the Bible because you want to know how he got all the animals on the ark. But to get to your values, think about this like a real interview question, where you're trying to communicate something about yourself to the hiring manager. Maybe you'd want a five-course meal with musical genius Prince and you realize it's because you value creativity or being bold. Or you'd love to get lunch with New York representative Alexandria Ocasio-Cortez because you, too, are passionate about making a difference or blazing a trail. Maybe it's your grandfather who passed away when you were young, and you realize how important a value family is to you.
- **What makes you feel excited to get out of bed in the morning?** This goes deeper than being able to cross more items off your to-do list or not panicking every time your kid opens the fridge just to see what's inside while you watch your electricity bill spike. I'm talking about those ideals that make you excited (not anxious) about getting out of bed in the morning. Maybe you look forward to spending time in nature every week because it gets you in touch with your spirituality and brings you closer to meaning in your life. Or perhaps you're

excited to volunteer at your local food bank or animal shelter because you care about moving the needle on environmental, social, or political problems in need of solutions. When we aren't in touch with our values, we're just doing things out of obligation, which runs people with High-Functioning Depression into the ground. Whereas obligations can deplete us, having a purpose energizes us and can even increase longevity, offer greater resilience, and improve cognition.[1]

- **When was the last time you felt full, fed, and content?** This is my favorite question for figuring out someone's values because people with High-Functioning Depression struggle so much to answer it. That means we've tapped into something important. Those of us with HFD don't remember the good because we're so often feeling down. We don't recall feeling content because we're always so busy trying to land one more account, wrap up one more project, or organize one more birthday party. It's never enough. When I ask my patients about the last time they were full, fed, and content, very often we have to go far back in time. "Oh, that was before my parents got divorced," they'll say. Or "It was right before I got into this terrible romantic relationship." Such comments could be a sign that the person values stability, security, or genuine affection. If you're reading this and time-traveling through your life, the next question might help you get to your destination.

- **What were you passionate about as a kid?** For me it was reading and learning, but for you it might have been going on adventures, expressing yourself through fashion, or being kind to others. One of the techniques I use with my patients to help them think back to childhood is called "sensory engagement." I basically ask them to become an archaeologist of their own pleasure. I get them to use all of their senses to think back to a time in their lives when they were very happy. I'll have them look at old photographs from that time, listen to the kind of music they listened to, eat foods they would eat back then, or even visit their childhood home so they can touch and smell that environment. A sensory journey like this can trigger that sense of excitement about life that people with anhedonia rarely experience. Your conscious brain may not remember what brought you joy, but your unconscious one will get triggered by your senses of taste, smell, sound, sight, and touch.

- **How do you want to be remembered?** In her bestselling book *The Top Five Regrets of the Dying,* author Bronnie Ware, a palliative care nurse, listed what people looked back on in their lives and wished when they were on their deathbed.[2] And guess what? It never had anything to do with a major deal that they closed or the highest salary they ever achieved. In fact, they actually wished they *hadn't* worked so hard. Instead, they wished they'd had the courage to live their true life and express their true feelings. They also wished they'd had stronger connections with friends and had let themselves be happier. Perhaps courage is a value for you, but you don't realize it yet. Or maybe connection is a value for you, but you're going about it in the wrong way.

VALUES

* * *

Don't be alarmed if these questions didn't get you closer to creating the list of your top three values just yet — or if you didn't like the answers you came up with. These are questions I can spend a whole session on with patients who have never thought about their values. Sometimes you need to sit with your surface answers and dig a little deeper. Basically, don't take your values at, well, face value. You've probably been living, unknowingly, with High-Functioning Depression for years or even decades and thinking that your values are what you've been doing or striving toward already, like hard work, sacrifice, power, or what one of my patients shared while thinking back to his golden years: being the best.

Tomas was a former Division I basketball player who transitioned to become an extremely successful executive recruiter. He had been high-functioning since he was a kid — studying hard so that his mother would let him go outside and play basketball on the park courts until almost bedtime. He got a full sports scholarship to college, had an incredible run with his team, and then transitioned into a career that allowed him to use his sports skills off the court. Tomas had a knack for identifying talent and being the super-connector who placed people in the right position at the right time. He'd just been poached by a top company and had gotten his second pay raise in six months — but he was feeling burned out. When I asked him about the last time he'd felt full, fed, and content, he immediately started talking about winning the national championship in college.

"I was exhausted and excited at the exact same time," he said. "I

163

don't think I've ever experienced anything like that feeling when the buzzer sounded, the crowd erupted, and I knew that we were number one! I felt full and fed knowing that I was the best."

"Was it really about being the best?" I asked him. "Because you're at the top of your game right now as a recruiter, and you're not feeling full and fed."

"Actually, it wasn't that *I* was the best," Tomas admitted. "It was that *we* were the best. My team. My chosen family. Us achieving that goal and celebrating together was when I felt the most fed."

Tomas started out thinking that excellence and winning were values for him. But when I asked him that one question, he realized that what he actually valued was being a part of something bigger, having a team experience, and working with others to reach a goal. Knowing how important collaboration was to him, I suggested he start going to some networking events to connect with other people in his industry. He ended up finding a circle of like-minded colleagues who wanted to do something more meaningful with their careers but didn't want to go it alone. With these colleagues, he was able to construct a team. They ended up building a business together, and Tomas ended up happily working toward a bigger goal with his new chosen family.

Validating Your Values

At this point, you've likely come up with a list of three to five values that floated to the surface when you asked yourself the questions earlier in this chapter. Or maybe you skipped to the list at the end of the chapter and picked out the ones that sounded closest. Now it's time to test them and make sure they're accurate. That's right — just because you loved to travel as a teenager doesn't mean you still have wanderlust as an adult. Or just because you used to love Will Ferrell doesn't necessarily mean you want to be remembered for your sense of humor.

Your values can change over time. Or you may pick values that are idealistic rather than realistic, or values that others approve of instead of ones that resonate with you. Either way, they need to be tested. It's been said that if you don't question your faith, you have to wonder if you really have faith. The same is true of your values: if you don't question them, you have to wonder if you really have them. The good news is that a values test is extremely easy and (ideally) fun to do.

First, take one of your values — let's say art — and then imagine the absolute smallest step you could take toward exploring and exposing yourself to that value. So you might spend fifteen minutes looking up (but not signing up for) painting classes you could take in your neighborhood. Or you might Google whether there are any TED Talks on the power of art — but not watching them just yet. Or you could just browse books about art on Amazon, or at your local bookstore, and create a wish list — but not buy anything.

Now, ask yourself the classic therapist question: "How did that make you feel?"

Did you get excited by your exploration? Great! Keep art on the list. Did you start to feel anxious and overwhelmed? Cross it off the list. If you found that you spent more than fifteen minutes on that online search without realizing it, that speaks volumes. If you were dreading the search and then got bored five minutes in, that tells you all you need to know as well.

WHAT IF I COME UP WITH A "BAD" VALUE?

Not everyone has the privilege of holding only "good" values—the kind society considers virtuous—in their heart. I say privilege because it truly is. If you don't have your basic needs (like food and shelter) met, it's extremely difficult to cultivate "good" values. For example, if you grew up in an environment where your parents were primarily concerned with keeping you safe from the gang violence in your neighborhood, or with making sure that there was food on the table, you may have learned to value survival or control. You may have experienced something similar in your work environment as an adult. Perhaps, as a financial advisor or lawyer, you ended up in an "every man for himself" workplace. As a result, you think your values are money or superiority.

While you may place a high value on money, survival, control, or superiority, they aren't things that give your life purpose or meaning. They bring you anxiety and stress. They might be what you're revered for, but they're not what you want to be remembered for. They don't bring you happiness; they most likely bring you headaches and heartache. There's always more money or control to strive for. And while you're making those efforts you're missing out on life. You may have stability, but you don't have satisfaction.

Rather than calling some values good and others bad, I think of some values as being rudimentary and others as being transcendent. In the diagram on page 169, you can see how they even mirror each other. It's understandable that you may have prioritized rudimentary values (like food, shelter, clothing, sex, and safety) because of the environment you're trying to survive in. Rudimentary values are at the bottom of the pyramid that makes up Maslow's hierarchy of needs. People can stay in that rudimentary mode, or they can evolve to a transcendent level. It's those transcendent values that I want you to focus on identifying. Remember Nykia and the caregiving trap she'd been placed into? Her rudimentary value was self-sacrifice. But as an adult she homed in on a transcendent value: family. The problem was that Nykia had convinced herself that in sacrificing her desires and her wishes for her family—then later her friends and romantic partners—she was living her values. It was only after she corrected herself and put the value of family back at the center that she was able to start to thrive. The point is, values exist on a spectrum. It's possible to value family without creating unhealthy dynamics with family members.

In my therapy sessions with children, I'm known as the doctor with the stickers. Anything you're into, I'll find a sticker that celebrates it. I give the stickers out at the end of my sessions as a small reward for doing a good job—maybe they engaged in playing a game with me, or named their feelings, or even just showed up for therapy. I can tell when a child is benefiting from therapy and growing emotionally when they forget to ask for the sticker at the end because the session was reward enough. They liked coming in and feeling full, fed, and content at the end, no sticker needed. The same is true for adults. If we're taking on another task for a gold star or a sticker, rather than because it makes us feel full, fed, and content, that means we probably have the wrong motivation and we're probably not in alignment with our values.

All rudimentary values can be converted to transcendent values that will bring you a healthier, happier, and more satisfying way of life. (See the diagram on page 169.) For example, obsessively seeking external recognition and wanting to be the best could be signs of a rudimentary value like superiority. But the same drive could result in a higher-level value, like the pursuit of excellence. Similarly, a rudimentary value like control might be reframed and taken to a transcendent level as impact. And even a "Don't mess with my money" or "Money is what's most important" attitude can have a more sincere version, as my client Aiko found out.

Aiko wasn't poor, but she came from very humble beginnings. She, her parents, and her three siblings lived in a two-bedroom apartment in what was considered the run-down part of their city. She remembers waking up in the middle of the night to hear her parents arguing about why there wasn't enough money for the electricity bill, or gas for the car at the end of the month. Not surprisingly, Aiko grew up never wanting to find herself in a situation of economic uncertainty, and she started to value money. She started reading everything that she could about finance, and in high school she sought out an internship at a local bank. As an adult, she pursued a career in investment banking, working ten-hour days for a high-profile firm, and by the time she was twenty-five she was able to buy her parents a much bigger house than the one she grew up in. But she was unhappy.

When Aiko walked into my office, she dripped with money, from her Chanel glasses to the Louboutin heels I could see the red soles of when she sat down and crossed her legs. She booked an appointment with me because she had begun to have anxiety attacks. We soon uncovered the source of her distress: at age thirty-two, she had no partner and no children, and her days (and nights) were consumed with clients and work. Like her fellow workaholic colleagues in finance, she had no time to date. Every minute was spent chasing dollars. Her other values (like the desire to find a partner and start a family) had taken a back seat to the single-minded goal of making money. But when your value gives you anxiety, not pleasure or purpose, that's when you know it's time to reevaluate.

I worked with Aiko to help her convert her rudimentary value of money to something higher-level that would give her more time to create the family she wanted. Over the next few years she left her investment banking job and started working for a nonprofit, growing the organization's endowment fund. She got to use her skills in finance to support a worthy cause. Making money morphed into a value of making change.

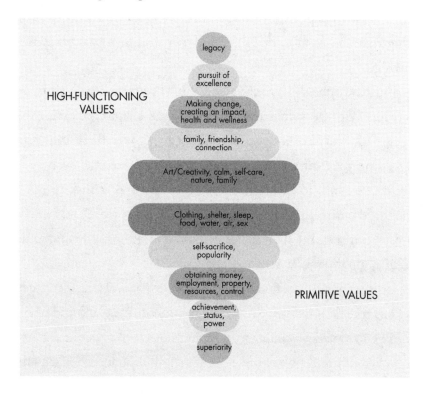

APPRECIATING YOUR VALUES

Now that you've got your list of tested values, it's time to start putting them into action. As you start to shift your time to investing in your authentic values — as opposed to spending inordinate hours on your job or sacrificing everything for your friends or your family — you'll begin to break from your High-Functioning Depression. But it's important for me to say up front that leaning into your values does not have to be hard work. I imagine some of you reading this book right now thinking, "Great, Dr. Judith helped me remember that I value faith, so now she's pushing me to go to church three times a week." Or "Yeah, I say volunteering is important to me, so I guess I have to sign up to work at a homeless shelter every weekend." As someone who had High-Functioning Depression, I know the last thing that you want to do is add another task to your already over-flowing to-do list.

Luckily, upholding your values doesn't require heroic efforts. In fact, just like the values test earlier in this chapter, it can involve very small, everyday actions. You have three goals. First, to practice upholding your values more frequently so they become a way of life for you. Second, to grow that practice over time. Third, to not go overboard with your values like you've done with work and relationships in the past. I don't want you crossing into the high-functioning realm again. So you'll need to pace yourself.

Let's say you're a coffee lover, like me, or a fan of tea. If this exercise has revealed that you deeply value community, you could opt out of going to a massive chain store to buy your tea or coffee and instead go to a mom-and-pop shop in your neighborhood. Or if equality is one of your core values, you could go to the chain and choose a fair-trade blend, meaning the growers and workers involved in making the coffee were treated fairly. Do you value generosity? You might make sure that you tip 20 percent to the barista who whips up your drink or leave some spare change in the "give a penny/take a penny" tray as you leave your local joint.

As you stride out of the coffee shop, head to work, and hop into an elevator, you can practice a mantra or affirmation in your head. If you value boldness, perhaps you're repeating to yourself "Fear does not control me" or "I will speak with self-confidence and conviction" or "I'm overcoming my fears and getting stronger every day." Maybe you value serenity and you say to yourself, "I'm calm and at peace" or "I let go of tension and invite peace."

You can even start putting your values into action when you do something as simple as getting dressed in the morning or commuting home from work in the evening. For example, you can stay true to a value of creativity or originality by putting together an outfit with surprising color contrasts or maybe wearing a beautiful pair of earrings that you got at an art fair. Whenever I have television appearances, I'm sure to wear outfits by my favorite Black female designer because I value culture and creativity.

Or let's say your core values include being present with family. On your way home after work, you might pick up your child from school, but instead of turning on the radio or making one last work call on speakerphone, you could devote that time in the car to your child: asking her about her day, telling her about how you're having her favorite meal for dinner, talking about a big trip that is coming up. As someone who specializes in child and adolescent psychiatry, I can tell you that even that small amount of time being present with kids makes a big difference.

Or what if the thing you value most in the world is connection? Maybe you slip a note into your partner's coat pocket telling him how much you care for him. Or maybe you remember that it's been months since you chimed in on your family's group text chat, so you drop in and share a funny story from the day to make everyone smile. Or you realize that it's been a while since you checked in with your college friends, so you shoot an email to your circle letting them know you'll be heading to the reunion this year and hope to see them. Later that night, if you value faith, you could say a prayer, read a Bible verse, or thank God for another day before falling asleep. Sounds pretty easy, right? Well, it is.

Create a Shrine

When I studied cultural psychiatry, I was always fascinated by how some cultures create shrines to the faith, traditions, people, and values that they hold dear, while others don't. Shrines are constant, visible reminders of the things and the people that give you meaning and purpose. One way to work on upholding your values is by having that constant, visible reminder of them. If your value is exploration, for example, you could have a shrine to travel, where you post pictures of all of the cities you've traveled to in the world or you color in on a map all the U.S. states you've visited. Want to lean into a value around inner peace? Maybe you create a meditation corner in your room with some cushions, a sound bowl, and a candle. Take a moment now to think about what kinds of shrines you could create in your home that are a visual reminder of your values.

A WARNING ABOUT VALUES

There is one thing I do need to caution you about. As you start to put your values into practice, you may find yourself getting pushback from friends and family. Your so-called best friend might be irritated that you've decided to donate money to Planned Parenthood this year instead of buying beauty products from their MLM side hustle again. Your sister may be upset that you're spending time at a pottery class when you could be watching her kids for her so that she can go on a date for the third time this week. Don't get discouraged. Their frustration is actually a good sign. It means you're doing something right.

I experienced this firsthand when I started making video skits on social media explaining the symptoms of different mental health disorders, ways childhood trauma can show up in adults, and what generational difference can look like in families. I was thrilled to see some of my videos going viral, but not everyone was happy for me.

"I have a very dynamic practice, but my patients wouldn't take me seriously if I showed up on social media the way you do," said one judgmental colleague.

"Oh, I see you out here trying to be an actress instead of a doctor," one colleague teased me.

In reality, I wasn't trying to get famous; I was succeeding in sharing information that could help people. But some of my colleagues were pretty stank about it. When you start to follow your heart and pursue your passions more, it's a bittersweet process. People will want to steal your joy. You'll grieve the loss of some people who you thought had your back. But you'll also feel freer, gain space for what you love, and invite into your circle new people who are holding true to *their* values. Over time it will get better. Don't give up your new joy for anything. Once you find the precious thing that makes you glow, protect it, invest in it, and surround yourself with like-minded people who also love it.

Unfortunately, chances are that as a person with High-Functioning Depression, you've probably been embroiled in a number of dysfunctional and masochistic relationships for quite some time. You may have to ask yourself if some of the people around you will get to keep their place in your circle — or if they need to get a one-way ticket out of your life. There may be no saving some of your connections. Remember, you want to feel full, fed, and content. You don't want to be around people who love to see you hungry, starved, and sad.

To figure out if a relationship with a friend or relative is worth preserving, try analyzing how they react to you prioritizing your values. Ask yourself which of these four categories most of their reactions fall into: jealousy, envy (people often equate jealousy and envy, but they are two different things), curiosity, or support. Let's say you've decided that one of your values is freedom and you're going to take a full three weeks of vacation this year to visit Australia.

"Good for you, Ms. Jet Setter, leaving us behind to travel the world," says your friend sarcastically. This is likely a comment rooted in jealousy. It's grounded in an inward feeling.

"Um, aren't you worried that your job will be upset about you taking all that time off?" says another friend. This person doesn't just want what you have. She doesn't want you to have it. That's envy. It's more outwardly aggressive and insidious. "Don't be surprised if you come back and there's someone else sitting in your office," she might say.

In contrast, a curious friend might say, "You've got to tell me: how did you pull this off? I'd love to do something like that. What cities are you visiting?"

And a supportive friend might respond by saying, "Way to go, girl. Travel is a really important value to me, so I visited Australia a few years back. I'd be happy to give you recommendations about the best hotels I stayed at. I even have some leftover cash I never converted back to U.S. dollars. I'll leave it on your desk at work tomorrow."

Let's also be clear that by putting yourself first and creating some boundaries, you're not trying to ruin your relationships with the people around you. You're actually trying to preserve and even strengthen them. You already know that putting friends and family first at the expense of yourself doesn't feed you, it bleeds you. When you set boundaries, some people may get upset because they'll realize they can't take advantage of you anymore. But the person who gets upset that you're no longer their personal ATM or assistant, or who texts a mutual acquaintance to complain about how you've become selfish, is not a real friend. Genuine friends would be curious and encouraging. They'd ask you to tell them about how you picked the charity you're donating to. They'd want you to text them a picture of the pottery that you make at next week's class. If you tell them that you're trying to spend more time prioritizing your value of health, they're not going to suggest you go to the fast-food restaurant for lunch today. Instead, they'll tell you about the new salad place that opened up a few blocks away and ask you if you want to run a 5K race with them in a few months. By holding fast to your boundaries, you're giving your jealous or envious friends a chance to change their ways, while also giving yourself a chance to discover what true support is.

It's not easy, though. And you may find yourself occasionally slipping back into your old behaviors. One easy way to hold yourself accountable to your values is to ask yourself a simple question before you sign up to manage your church's fundraising drive, agree to be Bridezilla's maid of honor, or take on one more project at work while your co-worker is out on sabbatical. The question is: "Am I doing this for a gold star, or am I doing this to feel full, fed, and content?"

Create a Time Capsule

Imagine pulling out a box every Thanksgiving or New Year's Eve that contains symbols of what everyone in your family values — and adding to it every year. It's a great way to celebrate your values. Maybe this year your son puts a bobblehead cartoon figure in because he values fun, while your daughter drops in a heart-shaped eraser because she values love. Or perhaps you'd rather create a vision board or a scrapbook together, where everyone can cut out magazine images and words tied to what's important to them and place them all on a piece of poster board or into a photo album. Part of the process is being playful together and devoting time to finding symbols of the things that you love. The other part is planning a day to look at and talk about what you found. Both are great ways to reinforce what you hold dear.

A LITTLE HELP, PLEASE?

If you're comfortable sharing your values with a few close, true, supportive friends, I absolutely encourage you to do so. Just make sure that they are like-minded people who are also focusing on what makes *them* happy and who will support you in your journey. In addition, you might seek out new people (at your art studio, in your church, from a networking event) who you already know hold the same values that you do. Once you know you have a trusted circle, you can lean on them to help you as you start prioritizing your values.

One way to do this is by asking for help directly. If the people in your circle know something is important to you, they'll help you prioritize it and they won't distract you from it. Another way to lean on a supportive circle is by getting feedback from them. You could ask something like, "Do I seem different around you these days compared to, say, two months ago?" They might say, "Yes, you seem happier and lighter these days." But they also might say no: "Actually, you still seem on edge a lot. I'm worried about you." Or "Honestly, it seems like you've swapped one drug for another. Instead of spending long hours at work, now you spend long hours at the animal shelter." That's a sign to you that it might be time to take another look at how you're leaning into your values.

Finally, you can just be a good listener when someone in your trusted circle is talking. I remember one evening I was rushing through my to-do list for the day and about to drag my daughter on an errand to go to the mall and return something. "Mommy, you're making me feel stressed," she said. All of a sudden I realized how unimportant the trip to the mall was. And, actually, wasn't I feeling tired and stressed, too? We put that errand off for another day.

There's one more person you can lean on to help you prioritize your values: your therapist. If you tell your therapist how important music is to you and that you used to play the guitar, they'll help you map out the baby steps to get you back on that road slowly. Your therapist can also be a great accountability partner, making sure that you actually do what you say you'll do and put it down in your calendar.

The Golden Locket Challenge

How will you remember to prioritize your goals every day? Every day this week, practice putting one of your values into a mental golden locket, and focus on doing one small thing to uphold that value at some point during the day. If you need some inspiration around setting a daily intention, try one of these ideas:

1. Plan to express your value as an act of kindness. (Be kind enough to give up your seat on the bus.)
2. Apply your value to the way you travel. (Be generous enough to pay the next person's toll.)
3. Change your space. (If you value calm, clear off your messy desk.)
4. Create a boundary tied to your value. (Decide you're leaving work on time to get to your kid's soccer game.)
5. Spend money on your value — even if it's only a dollar. (Time to tip bigger.)
6. Research something tied to your value. (Hop on Google and go wild.)

7. Mention your value in casual conversation. ("I love that picture of your kids on your desk, Marie. Family is so important!")
8. Ask AI. ("Hey, ChatGPT, I'm looking for small ways to be more courageous in my life. Can you give me five ideas that I can accomplish in five minutes?")

LIST OF VALUES

Accountability	Courage
Achievement	Creativity
Adaptability	Curiosity
Adventure	Dignity
Affection	Diversity
Altruism	Environment
Ambition	Equality
Art	Ethics
Authenticity	Excellence
Balance	Fairness
Beauty	Faith
Calm	Family
Collaboration	Forgiveness
Community	Freedom
Compassion	Friendship
Connection	Fun
Contentment	Generosity
Contribution	Giving back
Cooperation	Grace

Gratitude

Growth

Health

Hobbies

Honesty

Humor

Impact

Inclusion

Independence

Integrity

Intuition

Joy

Justice

Kindness

Knowledge

Leadership

Learning

Legacy

Love

Making a difference

Nature

Parenting

Patience

Patriotism

Peace

Perseverance

Political causes

Pride

Recognition

Resourcefulness

Respect

Security

Self-care

Self-expression

Self-respect

Serenity

Service

Spirituality

Teamwork

Time

Tradition

Travel

Trust

Understanding

Volunteerism

Vulnerability

Wisdom[3]

CHAPTER 8

Vitals

Earlier in the book, we talked about validating what you were feeling in terms of your emotional state. Now I want to talk about validating what you're feeling in your physical state. Too often, we're so busy working or checking things off our to-do list that we can't sense what's happening in our body. What's worse, we sometimes get messages from our body but we ignore them or even gaslight ourselves out of believing them. We tell ourselves, "You can get a drink of water after you finish this progress report" or "It's not that cold in here. You can go grab a sweater after you finish with the next client."

When we're suffering from High-Functioning Depression, we blow right past self-care ("I'm not tired; I don't need rest") all the way to self-harm ("I'll pull an all-nighter and get sleep on the weekend"). When you've transformed from a human being to a human doing, you don't even notice the pain in your lower back from sitting at your desk for so long. You don't realize that you have to go to the bathroom after studying overnight in the twenty-four-hour campus library. You're not aware that you haven't had anything to eat since you wolfed down a granola bar on the way to drop your kid off at school and now it's time for dinner. You don't realize that you're physically drained when your boss asks you to take on a new project and you smile and enthusiastically say yes.

With High-Functioning Depression, we run ourselves into the ground because we never stop for even ten seconds to consider how we're feeling. If we did, we might realize we're hurting. Worse, we might start to think about how much is missing from our lives. To start to change that, try this grounding exercise.

5, 4, 3, 2, 1: A Grounding Exercise

While sitting comfortably, shut your eyes, take several deep breaths, then look around the room and begin.

5. Name five things you can see beyond the page you are reading right now. Think about the vibrant colors that are all around you, the objects that you overlook every day, the people who are near you.
4. Next, name four things you can touch. Imagine stroking your own hair, feeling the cushioned chair you're sitting on, or rubbing the textured bracelet you're wearing. If you're holding this book in your hands, how do the cover and pages feel on your fingertips (or how does the e-reader feel in your hand)?
3. Then, think of three things you can hear. How often do we tune out the sounds of things we consider distracting? Cars passing on the street. The hum of your laptop. Birds singing. The white noise of a fan.
2. Now, name two things that you can smell. Your own perfume, deodorant, or skin? Someone cooking chicken next door? That garbage you should've taken out yesterday?

1. Finally, think of one thing that you can taste. Your mint toothpaste? The gum you're chewing? That sriracha you splashed on your lunch?

After you've done that, I want you to think about a muscle in your body — it could be a muscle in your forehead, your back, your core, or your shoulder. Focus on how it feels. Is it tense? Tight? Painful? If so, try to relax it.

After I do this grounding exercise with my patients, I ask them how it felt. Usually they're surprised. We don't realize how much tension we're carrying in our body until someone else suggests we relax our shoulders or points out that we're frowning and asks what's the matter. When I do social media posts on the physical ways that anxiety manifests itself, people say things like, "I used to give myself terrible migraines until I realized that I was clenching my jaw 24/7" and "I watched this while picking the skin on my fingers and didn't even notice I was doing it." We don't realize how anxious we are! But in just ten seconds, you can tell a lot about what's going on in your life by how your skin and hair look or how the muscles in your body feel.

Let me ask you another question. When you were focusing on being present, did you have time to think about anything else? If you were truly being mindful, the answer is no. In order to tune in to how hot, cold, tense, or relaxed you feel, you have to tune out thoughts and worries about which location you're picking for a friend's rapidly approaching birthday party, the midyear review with your supervisor in an hour, or whether or not your kid is going to pass biology this year. For ten whole seconds, you focused on your body — something people with High-Functioning Depression almost never do.

WHAT HAPPENS WHEN WE IGNORE OUR PHYSICAL STATE?

Think about what happens when the smoke alarm in your house goes off but you ignore it or even take the batteries out. Maybe you're in the middle of frying up some pork chops and you don't think there's a real fire anywhere. But what happens if next time it's not the smoke from the pan but an actual fire? You've ignored the warning sign of the alarm and your house is starting to burn down.

Now think about that scenario in terms of your body. Only this time, your constantly clenched jaw is the alarm being ignored and the emergency visit to the doctor for a chipped molar is the fire. Or nagging pain is the alarm and waking up unable to move your neck is the fire. Or exhaustion is the alarm and noticing more and more hair in the drain when you shower in the morning is the fire. Unfortunately, the more successful we become, the more opportunities there are for us to keep busy—and the easier it becomes to ignore our symptoms. Think of your favorite comedian canceling the next leg of their tour due to exhaustion—that's from ignoring their body in an effort to stay high-functioning. Your favorite singer sitting down for the whole show instead of doing the normal dance routine or your CEO getting up to address employees looking haggard and talking in a hoarse voice? That's a high-functioning person spiraling toward physical impairment and low-functioning depression.

Before I created work-life balance for myself, I used to get terrible upper respiratory infections all the time from working too hard. I'd get so sick with laryngitis that I couldn't talk to patients or present at speaking engagements no matter how badly my High-Functioning Depression pushed me to do them. I once had a patient who knew when she was overworked because she had a pseudoseizure. She literally had to have a non-epileptic seizure to realize that she had overloaded herself and it was time to create some space for rest.

With High-Functioning Depression, you stop only when your body shuts down—when low-functioning depression, trips to the ER, and health scares stop us in our tracks, long after our brains have sounded the alarm with warning signs. We need a therapist, prescription antibiotics, or a hospital bed to tell us that it's time to slow down—and even then we don't always listen. None of us want to acknowledge that our bodies fail us at times. In fact, they may fail us so badly at one point in time that it becomes the last time. Sorry to be morbid, but the reality is that if you work yourself to death or disability, the game is over.

So I want to reintroduce you to your inner thoughts to help you keep your body strong. When you're intentional about your well-being, you won't sacrifice your body for work because you'll know that without your body you can't do anything. I want you to prioritize your health because you're so much more than what you do. You have value beyond what you produce or how you support people. But if it makes things any easier for you, I'll tell you that prioritizing your health also means you'll avoid dropping out of the workforce prematurely from major health issues or low-functioning depression. If you can get grounded and be present in your body, you can stop sacrificing your health in the short term *and* improve your well-being for the long run. To do that, you need to check your vitals.

WHAT ARE YOUR FIVE VITALS?

We've all been to doctor's appointments where a physician takes your vitals. Step on the scale. Let the ruler touch the top of your head. Open your mouth for the thermometer. Roll up your sleeve so the blood pressure cuff can slide over your arm. All of this information is important when a health professional is assessing your risk for obesity, heart disease, and other illnesses. It's also critical that your doctor ask you questions like "Do you smoke, drink, or do drugs?" or "Have you gotten your flu shot?" or "Are you sexually active?" But all this alone isn't enough.

When was the last time that you had your primary care provider take your vitals by asking if you have supportive friendships? Or if you're having *satisfying* sex with your partner, or whether you're treated well by your boss? I'm guessing never. Yet the data show that toxic relationships and even a lack of satisfying connections in your life can have the same negative impact as smoking cigarettes, being overweight, and drinking.[1]

I've never had a doctor ask me how many hours I spend at work or staring at a screen. But guess what? Excessive hours staring at your television, computer, phone, and watch screens can lead to poor sleep, high blood pressure, impaired vision, and even reduced bone density, according to studies.[2]

Has a doctor ever asked you about the last person you hugged? I didn't think so. You don't need me to tell you that getting hugged can make you happy (thanks to endorphins and oxytocin), decrease your stress, and wash away fears. But it does.[3] On top of that, research shows that hugs can improve your immune system, boost heart health, and reduce pain. Unfortunately, most of us aren't getting enough of them. It was no surprise to me when a tear-laden video in which a New Yorker named Mayte Lisbeth admitted that she felt like she was dying from five years of touch starvation went viral on TikTok.[4]

We all need hugs. Our skin is our largest organ, and we know from research that when people are deprived of touch, like children in orphanages and the elderly in nursing homes, it can impact their physical and mental health. Lack of touch has also been linked to asthma, diabetes, high blood pressure, depression, and anxiety.

I'm never going to tell you that your basic vitals, the ones your doctor typically takes at the start of an office visit, are useless. I will tell you that they paint an incomplete picture. I'm also certain you've never had your real vitals checked until now, because doctors aren't asking the right questions. So, allow me to introduce you to six vitals that are critical for people with High-Functioning Depression: work-life balance, sleep, relationships, nutrition, movement, and tech. These are the vitals that keep the machine of your body running. You need to honor your body if you want it to keep going. Paying attention to these vitals also challenges the negative belief that you're unworthy. Caring for your body shows you that you are. Finally, paying attention to these vitals ensures that you're in good enough physical and mental health to break the cycle of High-Functioning Depression in your life.

Unlike the traditional vitals you're used to, these vitals aren't about longevity; they're about levity. They're not about the number of years you'll have left on this planet; they're about the quality of life you'll have while you're here. Reprioritize these vitals and you'll stop High-Functioning Depression in its tracks.

VITAL CHECK: WORK-LIFE BALANCE

How many hours do you spend per week at work?

From the United Arab Emirates to the United Kingdom, countries across the globe are testing out four-day workweeks.[5] If you've got High-Functioning Depression, that idea probably sounds insane to you. Who could possibly accomplish everything they need to do in four days? Besides, what would you do with all that free time? (Probably sneak back into the office to do more work.)

Things in the United States are very different. In this post-pandemic age of technology-enabled remote working, we have access to work at all times. There's no punching a clock at 5 p.m. and leaving your job behind. Not when your boss, co-workers, clients, and teachers can reach you at any time. So many of us aren't just working from home—we're actually living at work.

Several years ago, after being in labor for thirty hours (I know!), a patient of mine who's a doctor gave birth to a beautiful baby boy. But in between contractions, she was tying up loose ends at work and taking calls from her patients from her hospital bed. Within a week of her son's birth, she was having patient charts delivered to her home so that she could review them while nursing. It was crazy! Yet such extreme stories are not uncommon—particularly for women with High-Functioning Depression. But your work habits don't have to be that extreme to take a toll on your body. Take a look at the following habits common among people with High-Functioning Depression and see how many you've adopted over the years.

- **Routinely working forty-plus hours a week.** You're staying late after everyone else has left the building and sneaking in to work on weekends; you look up from your desk or your laptop and you're all alone in the office. Or you're doing work at home late at night after your family has gone to sleep.
- **Becoming a human camel.** You don't take a bathroom break all day and end up sprinting to the toilet as soon as you get home.
- **Having a spartan office.** There's maybe one picture of your family on your desk. It's a silent sign of commitment to your job. You think your bosses won't see you as dedicated enough if there's any evidence that you have a life outside of work. Or your anhedonia is showing and you really don't take any pleasure from decorating your office.
- **Sitting. All. Day.** You're chained to your chair for Zoom meetings and phone calls—usually while answering emails or doing other work on your computer. By the time you finally get up out of your chair, you're so stiff you can barely walk normally.

- **Going it alone.** You never ask for help or admit when you're struggling with a task. You mask your true feelings at work.
- **Not socializing outside of work.** If the only parties you attend involve celebrating a birthday in the conference room, you're not living life.
- **Never taking a vacation or sick day.** You've got weeks' worth of time off accrued, with zero plans for using it.
- **Forgetting what day it is.** You occasionally wake up and start getting ready for work on a Saturday morning—only to remember after you're ready to go that it's the weekend. But it doesn't really matter because you were planning on working over the weekend anyway.

Hands down, work-life balance is going to be one of the hardest vitals for you to get control of. Work *is* life for many people with HFD. But remember: we're looking to change that. Start building firmer work-life boundaries and everything changes. Your sense of self-worth won't be tied to your performance, and you won't look up from your desk one day at age sixty wondering what you did with your life. Here are two small goals to get you started. If you're looking for more ideas, you'll find additional suggestions for each vital in Appendix B. For now, let's start here.

HFD Goal: Leave Work on Time

The most important thing for you to start doing is cutting back on your work hours. Start small. Pick just one day a week that you commit to leaving on time and then outsource some of the discipline required to make it happen by planning an event or activity (ideally one aligned with your values) right after work hours: say, volunteering at a shelter, or attending a workout class with a friend.

HFD Goal: Take Mental Health Days

Policymakers and business owners need to start giving employees ample time off from work for any kind of major surgery, family loss, mental health issue, pregnancy, childbirth, or trauma. On top of that, we all need a bare minimum number of mental health days to de-stress or simply catch up on sleep. I give my employees nine to twelve mental health days every year—no questions asked—and they're not allowed to work more than forty hours a week. That adds up to much happier employees. Until all business heads take measures to advocate for their employees, we have to advocate for ourselves. That's especially tough for people with High-Functioning Depression, who live for work. But it's not impossible, and it gets easier when we realize how much better time off makes us feel.

Some Other Questions I Ask My Patients Around Work

How physically exhausted do you feel after you finish working?
How emotionally drained do you feel after you finish working?
Do you tend to avoid social situations at the end of a workday?
Are there parts of your body that hurt (eyes, shoulders, back) at the end of the workday?[6]

VITAL CHECK: SLEEP

How many hours of sleep do you get at night?

"I had the nightmare again," my patient Sun told me with a little laugh at the beginning of her session. Then she rolled her eyes and started talking about how "illogical" it was.

She said all this with a smile on her face. But I knew that on an unconscious level the nightmare terrified her. It was part of the reason she was coming to therapy. Sun said that everything was great in her life. She just wanted help with getting more sleep. As a doctor, however, I know that sleep problems don't usually appear on their own. They are usually tied to something else, like post-traumatic stress disorder, depression, or a physical health problem like sleep apnea. So we started unpacking the nightmare to understand why it kept occurring.

Sun had the same nightmare once a week, and always at the same time: Sunday night. In the nightmare, it was the day before graduation and she was running late for a final exam she had completely forgotten about. She needed to pass to get her diploma, but as she was walking through the door to the classroom, some students had already finished the exam and were leaving. Sun would wake up in a cold sweat, and for the rest of the night she'd alternate between staring at the ceiling and staring at the second hand of her bedroom clock.

We spent several sessions looking at all of the symbolism in the nightmare: What class was the exam for? Why had she forgotten about it? What would it mean to not have a college degree? Our weeks of working together, fleshing out the details of her dream, helped her realize how stressed she was at work. She had terrible boundaries between her personal life and her professional life as a high-level editor at a publishing company. Sun couldn't wait for sex to be over with her husband so she could check her email one more time before bed. She'd take her phone with her into the bathroom in the middle of the night, scrolling through news stories for up to an hour before getting back to bed. She would skip family events to meet self-imposed deadlines.

She ignored her anxiety during the day, but it kept emerging in the form of this nightmare. She worked twice as hard because she feared being unworthy of her position and had imposter syndrome. She truly believed that her life's work could be erased by any single mistake that she might make. Sun was so ambitious, she didn't notice how much of her happiness she sacrificed to beat other publishing houses in getting prestigious authors, keep her company's revenue up, and keep everyone on staff happy.

When Sun came in seeking solutions for her lack of sleep, she didn't realize how many things she was doing to sabotage her goal of getting a good night's rest. In this, she's far from alone. Consciously or unconsciously, deprioritizing sleep is America's real national pastime. It's like we're all competing in the Exhaustion Olympics. College students brag about pulling all-nighters, new moms convince themselves that being a good parent means burning the candle at both ends, medical residents wear sleepless nights as a badge of honor, and all of us have fallen victim to a Netflix binge until 4 a.m. at some point. "I'm doing more with less sleep," we think. "That makes me amazing." In reality, we're running ourselves into the ground. Even if we don't end up with recurring nightmares, insomnia, or some other sleep problem, we still run the risk of impaired cognition because we didn't get enough rest, not to mention showing up for work with bags under our eyes looking like who shot John. The fight against High-Functioning Depression takes energy—yet we're depleting it. Take a look at the following negative sleep habits for people with High-Functioning Depression and see how many you've found yourself falling into a habit of doing.

- **Pulling all-nighters.** Then using the weekends to "catch up" on rest instead of spending quality time with friends and family.
- **Falling asleep on your lumpy couch.** You think you're just trying to decompress in front of the TV, but what you're really getting is broken, uncomfortable rest.
- **Overindulging in alcohol or unhealthy snacks before bedtime.** It could be because you haven't gotten any other dopamine hits throughout the day, but it means you'll have a bad night's sleep as a result.
- **Bringing electronics (your laptop, your phone) to bed.** Research shows that the blue light emitted from electronic devices can negatively impact your sleep quality and sleep duration.[7]
- **Doom-scrolling before bed.** You're swiping your way through social media while lying in bed looking for dopamine hits, and then an hour later you're all wound up about the latest Twitter drama when you could've been getting rest instead.

- **Staring at the ceiling, unable to fall asleep.** It's been more than twenty minutes since you went to bed, and you're still so stressed about all of the work you have to do that you're unable to drift off.
- **Working at odd hours.** Looking at your email on your phone when you wake up in the middle of the night or responding to messages as soon as you get up in the morning.
- **Destroying your own calm.** Waking yourself up with an anxiety-inducing, blaring alarm clock.
- **Sleeping your vacation away.** Working around the clock right before a vacation and then sleeping excessively or getting sick on the vacation because your body has given out.

Rather than skimping on sleep, many cultures outside the United States actually celebrate sleep. For example, people who live in warmer climates, such as in certain parts of India, take naps as a way of both conserving their energy and making sure their bodies can cope with the hottest part of the day—or perhaps because we may be hardwired to shut down when the thermometer hits a certain number.[8] In Spain and parts of Latin America, businesses close for siestas (naps) in the middle of the day. Even countries that have an intense work culture, like South Korea, prioritize naps to boost creativity and mood.[9] In Japan, people accept you taking a nap at your desk during your lunch hour or catching some Z's during your commute because *inemuri* (sleeping while present) is seen as a sign of hard work.[10]

With my patient Sun, we focused on two strategies. The first was making her aware that one mistake at work was unlikely to break her: she's allowed to make mistakes, and the chances of a massive one happening were slim to none. Then we established some new nighttime rules. We set boundaries around her sleep habits: no more bringing her phone into the bedroom, lights were out in the bedroom by 11 p.m. each night, and she changed her eating habits so that she didn't wake up to go to the bathroom in the middle of the night.

I can't tell you that her nightmares completely disappeared, but they did decrease significantly. Whenever they did pop up, she knew it was a sign that work was causing her more anxiety than usual and her High-Functioning Depression was creeping back, so she needed to double down on her mental-health-supporting habits. If you're struggling with your own sleep, consider starting with the following two sleep hygiene habits and building from there with the additional ideas in Appendix B.

HFD Goal: Take Bedtime Notes

Keep a pen and a diary or notebook by your bedside table. Before you go to sleep, write down everything that you didn't get to on your to-do list that day and anything that's causing you anxiety. For example, you might write down: "Don't forget to order groceries for the week and pick up dry cleaning" and "Don't worry about tomorrow's presentation. It'll be great." The goal is to calm your brain by getting your worries out of your head before you fall asleep so that you have peaceful dreams instead of anxiety-fueled nightmares, like Sun.

Another technique I teach my patients is worry procrastination. To do it, you designate a time and place to write down your worries every day, like 2:05 p.m. in the kitchen or 8 a.m. on the front porch. The idea is to unload your worries at a specific time—not sporadically throughout the day—so you can avoid letting anxiety take over your life. If you forget to practice your worry procrastination earlier in the day, you can do it before you go to sleep at night, too. Unloading can relieve stress—so long as you don't do it in bed and start associating being under the covers with a lack of calm.

HFD Goal: Get Up Early

One of the best things you can do to improve this vital sign is to start getting up fifteen minutes earlier. That probably comes as a surprise, since I've been talking about getting more rest, not less. But planning for tomorrow starts today. Getting up early tomorrow means going to bed a few minutes early tonight.

This small change can have a huge impact, and here's why. Rushing in the morning is extremely detrimental to people with anxiety and High-Functioning Depression. Getting up late or with barely enough time to make it to the office is like putting your body in fight-or-flight mode. It's unhealthy to dash for the door when you've had scarcely enough time to wash your face, throw on some clothes, and grab a stale bagel out of your kitchen—not to mention the unhealthy stress of spending your whole commute worrying about whether you are going to be late to work. That's the start to a day when you're destined to forget things, you're not going to think clearly, and you're so on edge that you won't appear kind to others.

Morning routines and evening routines are the most important part of the day for a person with High-Functioning Depression. Once you're out in the world at work, there's so much you don't have control over—from the rush hour traffic and the drop-off line at your kids' school to your boss's mood. How we start and end the day are the two parts of those twenty-four hours that we have the most control over. Those two times can be opportunities to find some peace, or they can be moments of chaos. Choose peace by waking up just fifteen minutes earlier. This small change in your routine is easy to stick to and enables you to start your day in a healthier way. You now have time to calmly do some stretches before getting out of bed, eat a healthy breakfast, or even walk a little slower to work. You'll have a reason to get to bed earlier, and you'll feel like you're ahead of the game when you wake up.

Some Other Questions I Ask My Patients Around Sleep

How long does it take you to fall asleep?
Do you wake up in the middle of the night?
Do you wake up earlier than you want to?
Do you feel refreshed when you wake up or are you still tired?
Do you fall asleep during the day?
Do you have bad dreams?
On a scale of 1 to 10, what is the quality of your sleep?

VITAL CHECK: RELATIONSHIPS

How healthy are the relationships in your life?

When researchers look at what makes us happy, they find that it's not how much money we have, the job we chose, the car we drive, or the house we live in. The single biggest predictor of happiness is whom we partner with in our lifetime and how happy we are in that relationship. The problem is, most of us don't get lessons on how to pick healthy partners.

If you have High-Functioning Depression, you are at an even greater disadvantage picking a partner, for three reasons. First, you're so overwhelmed by everything you have to do in a day that you may not properly vet the people you allow into your life, letting them in without considering if they're worthy of your time, attention, and love. Second, you're also struggling with anhedonia, so you're not even sure if they bring you the kind of joy you see in other couples' eyes. Finally, you're likely struggling with your self-esteem. You're so desperate to prove your love — and prove yourself worthy of love — that you end up a martyr, someone others can walk all over. Let the masochism begin.

But there's one more reason we haven't talked about yet that explains why it's so hard for people with HFD to make healthy choices in their relationships: a psychological concept called reaction formation. It's a defense mechanism whose goal is to help us avoid emotions that make us feel deeply uncomfortable. As a result, people with High-Functioning Depression will do the opposite of what they truly want to do, simply to avoid the guilt that comes with setting boundaries or saying no to someone. For example, when presented with an opportunity they will say yes even if it's the last thing in the the world they'd ever want to do — and before they realize it, they've agreed to take on a huge new project at work even though they've been putting in sixty-hour weeks already and have been imagining flipping their desk over in front of their boss every night. Or they're the maid of honor in someone's wedding, shelling out thousands on the travel, the shower, and gifts, even though they secretly hate the person. Or they find themselves in a borderline domestic violence situation with their partner, but still dream about marrying them — like one of my recent patients, Luis.

"It was so humiliating," Luis admitted to me in session. "My partner had a complete meltdown and yelled at me while we were on the train headed to a concert with friends. Everyone heard how they talked to me, and it just hit different. My friends were appalled by my partner's behavior. It's one thing when we're at home by ourselves. But even strangers sitting a few seats over turned to look."

At thirty-one years old, Luis had been dating their partner for five years. They had been looking at wedding rings, and Luis was thinking about popping the question despite the emotional abuse they suffered at home. That's reaction formation.

Things changed with the incident on the train. "They never hit me, but things have gotten really heated," Luis said, revealing threats that the partner had made to hurt themself and the two dogs they had adopted. The more Luis opened up to me, the more they realized they were in a domestic violence situation — one that I safely navigated them out of.

Take a moment to think about the relationships — romantic or not — that you're maintaining in your life. If there's any doubt in your mind about whether they are serving you or hurting you, the following list of negative relationship habits should help you figure out who's worthy of your attention and who's not.

- **Cold and closed body language.** Warm and open body language would be a partner who holds your hand, whose knees touch yours when you're seated next to each other, or who gazes into your eyes lovingly for long periods of time. On the other hand, clenched hands, folded arms, and lack of eye contact show that they're closed off from you.[11]
- **Experiencing peer pressure.** Do your friends, family members, or partner routinely pressure you into doing unhealthy things (drinking more than you want, or spending money on things you don't need and can't afford, for example)?
- **Twisting yourself into a pretzel.** Are you constantly bending over backward in a masochistic way to appease a certain friend, family member, or your partner, but they never do the same for you?
- **Being subjected to verbal abuse.** Do you have friends, family members, or a partner who emotionally abuses you by belittling how you look, downplaying your achievements, using guilt to control you, and more?[12]
- **Being subjected to physical abuse.** Do you have friends, family members, or a partner who pushes, slaps, hits, or otherwise physically assaults you, even if they pretend that it's playful?

HFD Goal: Become Less Available

Reading the preceding list, you probably thought of a few toxic people who may need to be ushered out of your life. It can be difficult to show a negative family member, friend, or lover the exit. So start slowly. Create a little distance between yourself and the toxic person—for example, by not volunteering to help them with their search for a new condo, or by not letting them emotionally dump on you for hours over the phone. Turn them down when they ask you to help them paint their apartment or plan a birthday party extravaganza. As someone who is high-functioning, you likely already have a ton of other things on your to-do list that you can use as an excuse for why you're too busy to scour Zillow or pick out paint colors or talk on the phone for several hours every night. Create more boundaries around your time with such people so that you can devote more time to your values, vision, and vitals. But note: If you are in a domestic-violence situation, creating boundaries is not easy, so please get the help of a mental health professional.

Creating some distance may take all the emotional energy you have right now, but if you have the bandwidth for more changes, you'll find additional healthy suggestions in Appendix B. There I also break down my W.A.S.H. method, which helps patients decide if it's worth trying to mend a family feud or if it's a wash.

Some Other Questions I Ask My Patients Around Relationships

How do you feel after interacting with this person?
Do you find yourself overanalyzing the interaction?
Are you giving more in the relationship than you're getting?
Do you feel heard by this person or validated by this person?
Are you afraid that this person will abandon you?

VITAL CHECK: NUTRITION

How healthy are your eating habits?

I'm raising a guilty hand here and letting you know that when my High-Functioning Depression spikes, I reach for foods that are terrible for me. I mean, really terrible — Skittles, Starbursts, and tons of other candies with a laundry list of ingredients that aren't even allowed to be used in foods in Europe: red dye no. 3, titanium dioxide, potassium bromate, brominated vegetable oil, propylparaben.[13] I know I shouldn't eat this stuff. I'm a doctor! But these foods are my weakness. Just like everyone else with High-Functioning Depression, I often opt for the fleeting enjoyment of a guilty indulgence rather than focusing on long-term satisfaction or joy. Don't worry, I'm working on it. And so can you.

The foods we put into our bodies matter. Whether we're wolfing down candy or skipping meals entirely, we're not feeding the machine. We're starving it of nutrients. When we're not regularly filling our tanks with appropriate fuel, we end up indulging at odd hours of the day and night when the hunger pains we've been ignoring become unbearable. Take a look at the following negative dietary habits for people with High-Functioning Depression and see how many you've fallen into doing.

- **Ordering out excessively.** Having a garbage can that's full of takeout containers but a sink that is empty and a stove that looks pristine is a clear sign that you need to pay more attention to your nutrition. Prepared foods generally have more preservatives and can be higher in fat than what you make at home — both of which can leave you feeling tired and sluggish.

- **Scarfing down food.** You won't be able to enjoy the simple pleasure of a meal if you're so wrapped up in work that you only step away from your computer for a second to wolf down your food before you get back to work.
- **Eating for quick energy.** Pounding high-caffeine drinks and energy bars will only work for so long. Once the high wears off, you'll have less energy than you did before your first sip.
- **Skipping bathroom breaks.** Surprise — if you're not taking bathroom breaks during the day, you may not be consuming enough water to flush out your system.
- **Bingeing at night.** You're overeating junk food and drinking alcohol late at night in front of the television for those quick hits of dopamine. In fact, people with anhedonia often consume larger serving sizes and foods like cake, cookies, and french fries in response to their higher levels of stress.[14]

There's a better way. A healthy diet can be a powerful tool for fighting depression and supercharging your brain. I hold events called Happiness Labs, in which I teach people how to implement the Five V's. We serve blueberries, because science shows they increase blood flow to the brain, which increases brain functioning.[15] When I'm working with a patient who isn't progressing or who's feeling stuck in their therapy,

I send them to a nutritionist who specializes in foods that help the brain.[16] Walnuts, berries, leafy greens (such as kale), fatty fish (such as salmon), and coffee (in moderation) and tea make the short list of foods that are good for your blood vessels and your brain and that, in the most literal sense, will leave you feeling full, fed, and content.

HFD Goal: Turn Mealtime into an Act of Kindness

If you've got High-Functioning Depression, it shouldn't be hard to convince you that everything you put in your mouth should be powering up that brain you're so eager to use. But knowing and doing are two different things.

"I ate my rabbit food today," one of my patients told me at a session. "Kale sucks."

"Let's change your attitude around good food," I suggested. "What if you said, 'I gave myself a gift today. I performed an act of love for myself'?"

Suddenly she looked intrigued. When we shift a chore into an act of kindness, it can become more appealing. Plus you don't need to eat a bowl of raw kale if you don't enjoy it. You can find foods that you enjoy that are healthy. But even if this is hard to do, reminding yourself that every bite of something is energizing you, making you stronger, and helping you be healthier might be the reframing that you need to slowly start changing your diet.

HFD Goal: Slowed-Down Sustenance

People with High-Functioning Depression tend to constantly be in a rush and eat on the go. They grab a breakfast burrito as they rush out the door to go to work, or they snack on some chips at their desk in between Zoom calls. We're conditioned to treat food in take-out containers as something you eat on the go, but food that you eat with real cutlery and glassware is considered a meal. I want you to pick one meal a week that you eat at work away from your computer and with real silverware, glassware, and a cloth napkin — not a folded-up paper towel. Make it a full-on dining experience: put on some music, then eat your food slowly and mindfully, paying attention to how it feels and tastes in your mouth before you swallow it. This thirty-minute act of self-love can help you avoid indigestion, skip the bloating, and generally add more pleasure to something we all need to do three times a day.

HFD Goal: Cook at Home

Countries or regions where people know where their food comes from (the locally grown apples, the fresh fish from the farmer's market) get the best nutrition. You don't have to make every meal a farm-to-table feast. But what if you prepped just one healthy snack each week that was unprocessed and full of nutrients? Or what if you cooked your slowed-down supper (see above) yourself instead of ordering in? Cooking with a partner or friend can also be a great way to bond. Ready for more ideas? Check out Appendix B, where you'll find additional healthy, nutritional suggestions.

Be Prepared for Some Backlash

You're making these healthy changes for yourself, but keep in mind that they may rub other people in your circle the wrong way. I had a patient who had been neglecting his health for years but decided that it was time for a change. He met with a functional medicine doctor who told him to stay away from gluten, minimize alcohol intake, and get some exercise. (More on exercise later.) He was ready to follow the plan to a T until he came up against the obstacle of his social circle. Sure, there were a few people who congratulated him for making smarter choices and even confessed that they'd never have the discipline to turn down a free round at their local bar. But with most of his friends, the realness came out. "C'mon, you can have another shot," one would tell him. "You're really bringing us down, bud," another would say. "How about you shut up with the healthy talk and grab us another order of fries so we can all have a good time?"

Once again, you've found a litmus test of who can and can't be in your life when you're recovering from High-Functioning Depression. You want to be with friends, but you can't do it when what you're eating makes you irritable, leaves you low in energy, or causes you to wake up feeling groggy the next day. Choices have to be made, and not everyone gets the pleasure of being with the healthier version of you.

Some Other Questions I Ask My Patients Around Nutrition

How does the food you eat make you feel?
How many times a day are you getting healthy foods?
What are you eating to nourish your body?
Does the food feed your soul, spirit, and brain?

VITAL CHECK: MOVEMENT

It usually starts with a health scare. Because people with High-Functioning Depression frequently work long hours and don't prioritize self-care, many don't get enough exercise.[17] As a result, here come the health issues. Our blood pressure and cholesterol spike, putting us at risk of heart disease or a heart attack. The terrible stress we're under turns into chronic migraines that knock us out of commission for a day or two at a time. Or we're trying to get pregnant and are frustrated because we can't figure out why it's taking so long to conceive.

At the same time, people with High-Functioning Depression are also a group of massive overachievers, and that can get us hurt when it comes to exercise. For example, one of my patients was starting to gain weight due to her sedentary job and lifestyle, so she decided to take up long-distance running. When she wasn't sitting at her computer, you could find her running up and down the hills of Central Park's outer loop to prepare for her next marathon. Then she got a stress fracture in her foot that led to a broken toe because she refused to stop running. She even ran her scheduled marathon with that broken toe. When she finally did make it to the doctor, he warned her that if she didn't slow down, she'd be done with marathons for good.

Whether you are overdoing it or underdoing it, here are a few negative behaviors tied to movement that people with High-Functioning Depression are prone to.

- **Getting winded shockingly fast.** When the elevator is broken at work or home and you're breathless after one flight of stairs, that's a clear sign that you're not moving enough in your daily life. It's basically the poor man's stress test.

- **Skipping the gym.** Thinking, "I have half an hour and could do a short workout," but completely lacking the motivation... then feeling guilty or stressed that you didn't do anything.

- **Getting less than ten thousand steps — all weekend.** Lying on your couch from Friday to Sunday to recover from long hours at work. You're exhausted and need rest, but you're also socially isolated and out of shape.

- **Exercising at odd hours.** Signing up for that twenty-four-hour gym so you can work out by yourself at 1 a.m. is not great for your sleep or your safety.

- **Thinking of exercise as a chore.** If you're someone who needs to get moving more often, think of exercise not as something you *have* to do but as something you *get* to do. That ups the excitement factor — you're giving yourself the chance to do something good for your body. On the other hand, if you're someone who overdoes it at the gym, this mental shift can help you listen to your body more. Instead of thinking that you *have* to go lift weights in the morning, think that you'll *get* to lift weights if your body is up for it. That way you don't push yourself to injury on days you're too tired.

I know it can be daunting to get moving, but remember that you don't have to take it to the extreme. Just seventy-five minutes of vigorous physical activity a week will improve your health.[18] Going from zero exercise to ninety minutes a week has been shown to decrease your risk of death from any cause by 14 percent and to give you a life expectancy that's three years longer.[19] Lean into doing what you love, and you won't only extend your life; you'll also improve your quality of life. Something as simple as making your bathroom Clorox clean, Marie Kondo–ing your closet, or starting a home improvement project can get you moving while also getting your house in order. Need more ideas? Check out Appendix B.

HFD Goal: The Culture Cure

A stunning 77 percent of Americans don't get as much movement as they should in a day, according to the Centers for Disease Control, and this figure is roughly reflected in other Western countries such as the United Kingdom, according to the Office for National Statistics.[20] But I've got one quick solution to solve this epidemic-level problem: tap into a cultural cure.

It doesn't have to be your culture in particular. I want you to steal movement ideas from other regions of the world with residents who are more physically active than Americans typically are. Bike culture is real in Amsterdam, for example, and it can be just as real for you wherever you are. Think about pedaling on the weekends or even back and forth to work one day a week. In some parts of Africa, people walk long distances because they lack access to cars. Even if your city has a car culture, you can still park farther away from your destination than you need to in order to walk more.

In my Trinidadian culture, dance is huge, and you have to be fit to do it—if you're going to dutty-wine all the way down to the floor and back up, you need to be able to slow-squat and gyrate at the same time (think the sexiest burpee possible). But because I grew up in a religious household, we were only allowed to do a two-step in church to praise God. It wasn't until I was in medical and business school (at the same time) that I learned how to wine. I'd turn on reggaeton dance hall music and wine in between classes to burn off steam. I still do it to this day.

Researchers are now discovering that certain types of movement help with trauma and stress, and that such movements are built into many cultural practices.[21] They're technically called bilateral stimulation. You might look at rhythmic church cries of "hallelujah," for example, as a natural form of diaphragmatic breathing. But the bottom line is that movement isn't just healthy but can also be joyful. Here are some questions to consider if you're not sure what joyful movement can look like for you.

Some Other Questions I Ask My Patients Around Exercise and Movement

What types of movement do you enjoy?
What types of movement do you dislike?
What are opportunities for movement that you haven't been utilizing?

VITAL CHECK: TECH

How many hours do you spend staring at screens in a week? This is the question that I think is most likely to end up on future health questionnaires. The average American looks at their phone 144 times a day.[22] We get so addicted to our phone that it becomes a reflex to check it. We're like little kids addicted to video games, only instead of trying to get to the next level of Candy Crush, we're endlessly checking our email inboxes for dopamine hits of excitement. We walk down the street with eyes on our phone instead of on the people around us, and we're constantly checking Instagram to see how many people liked our post.

That 144 number is just a drop in the bucket when you look at how much time the average American spends looking at *any* kind of screen in a day besides phones, including television, tablets, and computers. And if you're part of the rising number of people with online side hustles or becoming full-time influencers, that screen time skyrockets. We log nearly seven hours a day staring at those glowing bits of light. People with High-Functioning Depression probably log even more hours than that. If you feel exhausted, depleted, and anxious after being on screens all day long, there's a reason for that: humans weren't made to stare at screens all day. All of these hours add up to eyestrain and musculoskeletal problems, and ultimately take a toll on our mental health.

Stanford research shows that Zoom, which was our savior during the pandemic, was actually terrible for our health. Unlike in-person conversations, Zoom requires prolonged, close-up eye contact, and a greater level of effort to communicate, because some things (like side-eye) just don't translate across a screen. Plus staring at yourself on a screen is just…unnatural. It makes us self-conscious. Do you stare in a mirror for anywhere near the amount of time you stare at yourself on Zoom?[23]

Welcome to your toxic relationship with technology. Take a look at the list below and see if you've fallen prey to any of these other bad tech habits.

- **Following the wrong leaders.** Social media accounts that depress you, make you feel like you're not doing enough with your life, or push you toward hustle culture probably aren't helping your mood. But people with HFD gravitate toward toxic people and toxic accounts.
- **Getting addicted to email.** You don't need me to tell you why it's unhealthy to be constantly checking and responding to work emails in bed at night.
- **Falling down electronic rabbit holes.** Be honest. How many tabs do you have open in your browser right now?
- **Being overly available online.** It's tempting to want to immediately respond to people who reach out to you on your social media and email accounts, but you don't need to make yourself available to strangers at all times.

Gen Z (people born between 1996 and 2010) may be at highest risk for High-Functioning Depression purely due to being the first generation born into a world with social media.[24] It's no surprise that half of them want to be influencers.[25] The long-term data on how tech impacts our brains aren't out yet, but what we do know is that Gen Z is suffering. It's no wonder that Gen Z is said to have the least positive outlook and highest levels of mental health problems of all generations; after all, how easy is it to be happy when you're constantly comparing yourself to other people having the time of their life on TikTok, Snapchat, and Instagram?[26] Not to mention being constantly exposed to bad news such as the hazards of climate change and images of war and violence. They need a digital dopamine detox more than any other generation — but that's not to say older generations can skip that same prescription.

There's a misconception that our brains stop developing by the time we're about twenty-five years of age. Yes, it's true our brains are largely developed by then. But there's something called neuroplasticity, which allows for our brains to continue to adapt, grow, and change even when we're elderly. It's the reason that we can still improve our memory and recall ability when we are in later stages of life. We are all vulnerable when it comes to the health risks of screen time, so we all have to pay attention to protecting our mental health from digital toxins. I predict that within the next ten years, we'll see a new edition of the *DSM* that will include an emerging list of conditions related to unhealthy technology use.

In defense of technology, I will say that tech itself is not inherently harmful. It's how we use it that matters. By being mindful of our digital habits and prioritizing our mental well-being, we can achieve a healthier balance between the digital world and the real one.

Ready to shift your other detrimental behaviors when it comes to tech? Try these two small steps that can have a big impact. If you like these, I've included even more suggestions in Appendix B and guidance on my signature R.E.S.E.T. method to change your social media usage in Appendix C.

HFD Goal: Influence the Algorithm

Unfriend people and unfollow accounts that have a negative impact on your mood. Instead, follow social media accounts that encourage rest, demonstrate self-care, or even provide a more sensory experience through ASMR, for example. If you're not clicking on puppy, otter, and capybara videos, you're missing out.

HFD Goal: The One-Hour Challenge

A friend of mine was on his way to a holiday party with his wife when I issued him a challenge. "Why don't you turn your phone off for the first hour of the party?" I said.

He was stunned. "What if there's an emergency at work?" he shot back. "Or an emergency at home? Someone could die and I wouldn't know."

"Well, if you can't be reached, what would those people do?"

"I'm guessing someone would call my boss instead. Or my wife," he said. She was watching this whole conversation trying to hold back a smile. I could tell that she was excited at the prospect of getting her husband to be fully present for once. And he was. They went to the party, he actually shut his phone off for the whole thing, and the world didn't end.

I put most of my High-Functioning Depression patients on a tech diet when I start working with them. I prescribe just one hour a day during which they detach from their device and focus on something else. I encourage my patients to do something sensory during this time, whether it's having a delicious meal, practicing meditation, being present while playing on the floor with their toddler, journaling with a pen and notebook instead of a laptop, or walking through a park feeling the breeze on their skin. When you first try to cut the invisible cord to your phone, it may be too difficult to start with a full hour, so just give it ten minutes and build from there each day. You'll also want to pick an hour when it's unlikely that you'll need to be reached — maybe at night or early in the morning. Practice every day and watch tech start to loosen its grip on your life.

Some Other Questions I Ask My Patients Around Technology

Do other people in your life (partner, children, friends) complain about how much time you spend on your laptop or phone?

How do you feel after spending long periods of time on your laptop or scrolling social media?

Do you place any limits on how much time you spend on social media?

CHAPTER 9

Vision

In September 2021, I watched a heartbreaking press room inter-view with tennis phenomenon Naomi Osaka.[1] After being elimi-nated in the third round of the U.S. Open, the twenty-three-year-old was doing everything she could to avoid crying on camera while taking questions from reporters. She took long pauses to compose herself and gently slapped both sides of her face with her hands, but ultimately she had to pull her Nike visor down to hide the tears.

"When I win, I don't feel happy. I feel more like relief," said the multimillionaire athlete, who just a few years earlier had beaten her childhood idol, Serena Williams, at the 2018 U.S. Open. "When I lose, I feel very sad," she said, her voice cracking on the last word. "And I don't think that's normal. I think I'm going to take a break from playing for a while."

What would leave a world-class athlete this depressed after a loss and, worse, emotionless after a win? Osaka was the highest-paid female athlete in the world in 2020. What would cause someone at the top of their game to step away from what they'd devoted their life to?

When the interview with Osaka ended, I had the answer to those questions. Osaka wasn't experiencing anhedonia in spite of all her success; she was experiencing it *because* of all her success. To be clear, I'm not Osaka's physician, but by this point we both know that if someone is getting only relief from not losing—instead of joy from winning—that's a sign of High-Functioning Depression. In the beginning, however, it wasn't like this; competing at her chosen sport used to bring joy for Osaka (and the same was true for Tiger Woods, Simone Biles, Michael Phelps, and Tom Brady, to name just a few top athletes who have spoken publicly about their struggles with mental health). After all, we tend to love doing what we're good at, right? But as the wins keep coming and the stakes keep getting higher, a chicken-and-egg question emerges: Do you love the sport because you're good at it, or are you good at it because you love it? That reframing can happen to any of us as we progress in our chosen field. Our efforts can become less about enjoying the work that we're doing and more about winning. Less about pleasure and more about avoiding negative repercussions. Less about fun and more about avoiding disappointment. We keep striving to get to the top, but if and when we make it, that could be when everything falls apart. The more success we achieve, in other words, the harder it can be to enjoy it.

Watching Osaka, I saw not only the problem but also the solution: vision. If you want to defeat High-Functioning Depression for good, you have to master this final V. But what exactly do I mean by vision?

VISION MEANS YOU CAN TRULY "SEE" YOUR WINS

Vision is your ability to recognize wins, plan ways to celebrate them, and then take the time to actually follow through on those plans.

Read the preceding sentence twice, because if you have High-Functioning Depression, you're probably not doing even one of those three things.

When you give a stellar presentation at work that gets you a nod from your boss, having High-Functioning Depression means that you are in no danger of spraining your shoulder patting yourself on the back. More likely you don't even acknowledge how well it went. You're already on to the next task. But when you lean into vision, you actually stop and think, "Man, I nailed that!" Then you reward yourself by booking a thirty-minute massage that weekend—and you don't cancel the appointment the day before because "something came up."

When your vision is cloudy, you don't even realize that you've done something great. That major client? You landed them because you're lucky, you tell yourself. That award you won? The judges must not have looked very closely at your work, you think. When you lack vision, you certainly don't plan to celebrate these wins—you're an imposter trying not to get found out, so why draw attention to yourself? And if you do plan to reward yourself, you're probably embarrassed to follow through. After all, you don't deserve the praise; the kudos was just a big mistake. When your vision is clear, however, you can sit in the moment of achievement. Instead of assuming that there's been some mistake or that you must have fooled them again, you can stop and celebrate what you've done.

Of all the V's I've shown you for overcoming High-Functioning Depression, vision is the most essential when it comes to beating anhedonia because it forces you to focus on fostering joy in life at times when you need that extra push. Have you ever had a friend drag you to a party when you were sure you weren't up for it, but then you ended up having so much fun you closed the joint down? Well, think of this chapter as me dragging you to that party—because I know you're eventually going to kick off your pumps, let your hair down, and need to be carried off the dance floor at closing time when the bartender calls out, "You don't have to go home but you can't stay here." Vision forces you to go to the party so that you can, ultimately, have that exhilarating good time.

WHAT HAPPENS WHEN WE LACK VISION?

If you don't recognize and celebrate your wins, they become overlooked. When they're overlooked, you become numb to winning. When you become numb to winning, you don't stop focusing on winning. Wins just become joyless: something you barely notice as you refocus on the next thing to achieve. Ask yourself why Super Bowl quarterbacks have to be paid tens of thousands of dollars to go to Disney World after winning.[2] Or why Tiger Woods is famous for not knowing where his PGA trophies are.[3] Or how Naomi Osaka found herself walking away from tennis. The answer boils down to anhedonia.

Anhedonia happens to the best of us—and it also happens to the rest of us. You don't have to be a world-class athlete to feel the chill of uncelebrated wins. If you've ever considered skipping your graduation, an awards ceremony where you're being spotlighted, or a party thrown in your honor, that's classic High-Functioning Depression. I know that in those moments, your unconscious is telling you that you aren't worthy of being celebrated, so why should you attend? But when you skip those moments, you're only giving in to feelings of imposter syndrome and unworthiness.

Not attending a celebration also makes it very easy to focus on what is going wrong in our lives instead of what's going right. When we're suffering from High-Functioning Depression, we can waste so much mental energy ruminating on mistakes, we barely have the brain space to think about our successes. This is why we need reminders of the progress we're making. Instead of getting stuck in the past, we need something to pull us forward and keep us moving. Rewarding ourselves for our wins gives us something positive to look forward to, which can make us feel more optimistic, improve our mood, and reduce stress. In fact, it's such a powerful tool for improving well-being that it's even become a fundamental part of suicide prevention. Planning to celebrate wins allows us to enjoy our success in the moment while also reminding us that the best is yet to come.

WHAT COUNTS AS A WIN WORTH CELEBRATING?

I want to take a moment to point out that wins come in all shapes and sizes. Yes, a win is when you take home $3 million and a giant trophy after triumphing at the U.S. Open. But it's also a win when:

- Your boss calls you into his office to let you know you got a promotion to your dream job. Permission to head to a restaurant to party is granted!

- You get home from the most romantic date ever that ended with the two of you talking about marriage. Go ahead and celebrate with your friends!
- You call a real estate broker to put a down payment on your dream home. So why not pop the champagne?
- You finish that term paper on time for your really tough college class. Regardless of your grade, that's a major accomplishment.
- You get a standing ovation from your co-workers for planning the company's first annual conference. Definitely take a bow and treat yourself later.
- You put the finishing touches on the bathroom remodel that you've been working on for the past three months.

The first of these, winning the U.S. Open, is what I call a bucket-list win. The others are long-term wins. We're not getting a baller new job or meeting the love of our life on a daily basis. These wins are much grander and more spaced out over the course of our lives. They're few and far between.

Then there are short-term wins. Those are the everyday wins that we so easily overlook. It's a win when you:

- Get the kids to school on time in clean clothes. That's huge. It's a challenge we don't often celebrate.
- Make it to the gym for the workout you were dreading. Way

to go taking care of your body. You're a rock star! It's hard in our capitalist society to prioritize self-care.

- Set a boundary in a relationship, like asking for a dedicated date night every Thursday, and reinforcing that boundary when your partner wants to make other plans. Pat yourself on the back for not ignoring your desires.
- Delegate tasks at work and realize that you truly don't have to do it all. Letting others help you could be a win for everyone!
- Grab all the ingredients to try a new recipe for dinner. No matter how it turns out, call it a win!
- Make your bed in the morning. If you've tipped into low-functioning depression, this is a small but significant win you need to celebrate.

Celebrating all three types of wins is important for overcoming High-Functioning Depression. I practice what I preach here when it comes to celebrating wins, whether I'm headed to Washington, D.C., to be presented with a congressional award or I notice that my plants survived a season without my brown thumb killing them. By the way, my plants tend to be a reflection of what's happening in my life. If they're thriving, I'm thriving, and I buy myself another one. If they start to look like they've been left out in the Arizona desert, I talk to my local florist—and I try to cut back on work. When my daughter does well on her report card, we get dressed up and go out to her favorite restaurant for a celebratory dinner. And I put all of her graduation certificates, from pre-kindergarten on up, on the wall next to my diplomas. I want her to be proud of the hard work that she's done now so she doesn't have to relearn how to do this later in life.

It's extremely hard for people with High-Functioning Depression to acknowledge these smaller wins—that's one of the reasons I included a list of ways that you can do this at the end of the chapter (see page 242). You're welcome! The first three are my favorite ways to personally celebrate wins. You'll need to customize them to what feels good to you, but I hope you will use these ideas as inspiration to help you come up with your own list.

You need to practice celebrating short-term wins before you will be able to celebrate the long-term and bucket-list wins. On a very practical level, you have to crawl before you can walk, and walk before you can run. The small wins will help build you up so you can experience the joy of the larger ones. You are also going to encounter far more small wins in the course of a day, week, or month than you will major victories.

On a scientific level, celebrating small wins (say, having a small piece of chocolate after making a presentation at work, or listening to your favorite song after setting a boundary with a parent) can release dopamine in your brain, giving you a shot of pleasure. Research has also shown that small wins impact how people perform at work— and how they feel at work.[4] By focusing on progress (the small wins), not perfection or goals (the big wins), you can derive much more joy out of life. Research reveals that having something to look forward to (that celebration of your win) activates a section of your brain associated with a higher level of well-being.[5]

When you start honing your vision to "see" wins, it may be easier to reward yourself for them by doing something alone (leaving work fifteen minutes early, finally ordering that thing that has been on your Amazon wish list forever), rather than celebrating them publicly. You may need to build up to celebrating in ways where your community is involved and others are watching—like texting your big news on your group WhatsApp chat, posting on social media, throwing yourself a big anniversary party, or coordinating that college reunion getaway. Start with what feels most comfortable. It's more important that you focus on getting into the habit of rewarding yourself for wins as opposed to getting wrapped up in who should be there to witness it.

Two Secrets to Celebrating Wins

1. **Do it right away.** When I teach parents how to give their kids praise, I always encourage them to do it immediately. As soon as you see the good behavior, remark on it. It reinforces the good behavior in their brain, so they keep doing it. Even though adult brains don't have the same amount of neuroplasticity that a child's brain does, we are still able to learn new things as adults and strengthen the reward circuitry in our brains. Research also shows that immediately rewarding ourselves after a win reinforces positivity.[6]

2. **Make it a habit.** Anyone who has ever run a marathon or had a going-away party at a beloved job knows the sting of a low that can come after a really big high.[7] But if you're practicing celebrating small wins every single day, you can avoid this letdown — which is so important for people who are already struggling with High-Functioning Depression. Rewarding yourself on a regular basis helps moderate the fluctuations of happiness in life, as opposed to the huge ups and downs of a Six Flags roller-coaster ride.

WHY WE DON'T CELEBRATE OUR WINS

Anhedonia and imposter syndrome are just the tip of the iceberg when it comes to why people with High-Functioning Depression don't recognize and celebrate the wins in their lives. In fact, even when we recognize our victories, we still struggle to give ourselves permission to celebrate them; sometimes we even do the opposite and downplay the achievement. Read through this list of excuses people with High-Functioning Depression make to shy away from celebration and find the ones that resonate with you the most. Then follow my advice for talking yourself out of the clouds and into clearer vision.

"Win? What Win? Please, You're Making a Big Deal out of Nothing"

I'm going to start with the most basic win of all that every single one of us achieved in the past year: a birthday. It's true that you don't have to do anything to deserve a celebration other than make it to another year of life. Still, each birthday is a milestone. I'm constantly meeting with HFD patients who routinely throw huge birthday bashes for friends and family but want nothing to do with a celebration of their own. When I tried to encourage one of my clients to acknowledge her birthday last year by throwing a small party, she insisted that she couldn't. "There's not enough money," said the mom who did everything to make sure her kids didn't want for anything, were healthy, and were doing well at school. "I've had my childhood. It's got to be all about the kids now."

What changed everything for her was realizing that she was

modeling the wrong behavior for her kids. When her youngest asked my client when her birthday was, she told the child that it didn't matter. But you know how persistent kids can be. Her little one just kept asking, "But why?" and eventually she couldn't think of a good reason why it didn't matter. Not allowing herself to care about her birthday was just a rule she'd come up with in her mind that didn't make sense. She also realized that she didn't want her daughters to grow up celebrating everyone else while they ignored their own joy. That's not what she wanted to pass on to her kids.

We ended up doing a lot of work in our sessions to get her to acknowledge her birthday and pull together a small party at a local park. No expensive party hall, just free grass and benches. (Maybe for you, it's enjoying cupcakes at the office with your co-workers or sticking a candle in a cupcake at home.) When she threw that first party, her kids were thrilled because they'd never seen their mother put up a birthday banner for herself or pick the type of cake that *she* wanted at the party. She's held a park party every year since then. And just like that, her birthday parties became more than items on her to-do list. They became something to look forward to all year long. "I should be celebrating every year I'm on this earth," she eventually told me in therapy. "I do so much for my kids, so much on my own. I'm being the best mom I can be."

Celebrate yourself like you would your best friend. What makes your BFF's win a reason to pull out the streamers and yours a secret? Whether you have children or not, ask yourself if you're modeling a behavior you'd want someone you care about to watch and repeat. If it takes a little kid to drag you to that party I described earlier, then so be it!

"Celebrate Myself? That's Not How I Was Raised"

In India, it's super-taboo to have a baby shower early in the pregnancy. You have to wait at least until the seventh month before you throw any type of party around the birth; otherwise, it's believed, the family will have bad luck. Even on my social media, I see people making comments about how in their culture celebrating a win would get them the "evil eye" or people practicing voodoo against them.

I understand the cultural resistance to going on Facebook and shouting out that you got a prestigious scholarship, or even telling the waiter at Applebee's that it's your birthday so you get that free slice of cake and a few singing waiters. I understand it, and at the same time I want you to be aware that you're your own person, and it's okay to do things differently from how you were raised. What happened culturally is a part of your history. What needs to happen mentally and emotionally for you to overcome High-Functioning Depression is a part of your present and future. You need to prove to yourself that you can safely start to celebrate your wins without fear of repercussions — and with the expectation of a happier life.

Respect yourself and your culture. Would you agree that these two things can be done at the same time? Good, because if you have a cultural history that tells you not to celebrate yourself and if you are suffering from High-Functioning Depression, those two things might not be unrelated. And it probably means that celebration is an especially healthy way for you to cope.

"I Think My Masochism Is Showing Again"

Yes, it is. The sacrificial lamb in you is sticking its neck out once more. Masochism, that trait we talked about earlier in the book, is a big part of what is holding you back from allowing yourself the joy of applauding your own success. You've spent so much time giving to your work and the people around you that you're comfortable robbing yourself of any pleasure. It might feel like sacrificing your happiness for others is the ultimate good, but I'm here to tell you that's just not true.

Commit to trying something different. How has that savior complex been working out for you so far? That's what I thought. It's time to try a different path. Sometimes therapists tell people with depression to go outside for walks, especially when they don't feel like it, because it can improve their mood. I'm going to need you to celebrate yourself, especially when you don't feel like it, because it could help heal your masochism.

"I'll Celebrate When I Hit My Goal. I'm Not There Yet"

People with High-Functioning Depression are constantly thinking, "When I get X, I'll finally be happy" or "When I accomplish Y, I'll finally be successful." That's where we mess up. We can't be consumed with the idea of hitting some pie-in-the-sky goal. We need to celebrate not just the big thing at the end but also the progress along the way. It's about the milestones on our journey, not about the destination, because there's always going to be another trip and another destination.

If you tell yourself you'll finally be able to celebrate when you get a big beautiful home, then you'll find yourself moving the goalposts and aiming for a gorgeous vacation home next. And then the luxury car that gets you back and forth between them. And then wouldn't it be great to have a boat since the vacation home is near the water?

And then...There's a false narrative that all these things will make us happy when in reality they're causing stress, bitterness, depression, and lost time we will never get back.

There are also times when we arrive at that big goal we set for ourselves and it doesn't feel like enough. For example, one of my patients did a semester in Tokyo during his junior year in college. He had been obsessed with Japan since he was old enough to watch samurai movies, started learning the language in high school, and couldn't wait to immerse himself in the culture. When we would hop on Zoom for our weekly calls, though, things were not going according to plan.

"I'm having a really tough time with the transition," he said on our third call. He was beating himself up for not enjoying the city more. "I've been studying this language for years and I'm still having trouble speaking to strangers. I should be breezing through this city having the time of my life until two a.m. I used to be the party guy back home in Boston. I should be putting on Instagram the kinds of things that give people crazy FOMO."

That's when I started to help him shift his vision to smaller wins. "So, let me get this straight," I said. "You've been living as an adult on your own for the first time, and you're doing it in a foreign country that doesn't even use the same alphabet that we do?"

"Yes," he said quietly.

"What are you doing every day?"

"I go for walks and eat sushi," he replied. "Not very exciting."

"Not very exciting? You're eating sushi in Japan!" I said. "You don't need to be clubbing all night. You can go to see Kabuki or just wander around real Japanese gardens."

"But I look at everything people are posting on social media and it's not what I'm doing," he said.

"That's because they're posting things that are rewards for *them*," I replied. "You have to figure out what the rewards of being there are for *you*."

Look at the steps — not the whole staircase. Stop focusing on goals, perfection, and what other people define as success. What we see on social media is the highlight reel of someone else's life. Why should we feel less-than for not achieving a goal that wasn't even our own? It sets us up for a comparison trap that can make us feel like we're failing in life. Once you stop thinking about grand ideals and other people's progress, you'll be able to recognize realistic progress and see what wins you've accomplished. That's where the real satisfaction is.

"I Don't Want to Humble-Brag, So I Just Won't Say Anything at All"

We talked about imposter syndrome and cultural constrictions, but there's another type of barrier that people with HFD face: they don't want to seem as if they are boasting or bragging. They want to appear modest. This could've been any of my peers from medical school. They would make up all sorts of excuses (saying they "got lucky" on some exam question, or that they would've flunked the test without their study group) rather than saying they worked hard and deserved the accolades that they were receiving.

But here's the thing. Celebrating is not about bragging. It's about joy. It's about letting yourself or the world know that you set out to do something and that you made steady progress toward it or actually achieved it. Bragging is about needing adoration; it's about making other people feel bad so that you can feel better about yourself. Bragging is when you compete with others and come out ahead of them. Celebrating is what happens when you compete with yourself and win.

Get clear on your motives. When you're worried about bragging, ask yourself if your motivations for winning were intrinsic (focused on what you want for yourself) or extrinsic (focused on what you want from those around you). If the motivation came from inside you, then you can put your fears to rest.

"Celebrate? When Exactly Am I Supposed to Find Time to Say 'Yay Me!' with All That I Have to Do?"

A few years ago, I gave a talk to a group of executives at a major television network. At one point in the talk I told them to pull out their phones and take a look at their Google and Outlook calendars. Then I asked them to comb through the back-to-back meetings, "deep work" sessions, client dinners, special events, and deadline reminders and tell me about a place on their calendar where they had blocked off something that was purely for pleasure. Where had they scheduled a week in the country with friends, a family trip to a water park, a romantic getaway with their partner, or even just a work-free weekend? No one had anything remotely like that penciled in for the month.

When you put time for pleasure on your schedule, you are reminding yourself that you're worthy of that time to rest. You've earned it. And you should celebrate it.

Clear your calendar. You need to schedule time to dwell in happy moments if you want to break the cycle of anhedonia. You won't overcome your High-Functioning Depression by filling your days (and nights) with busyness. You have to schedule in satisfaction the same way that you've been scheduling in success.

"I'm Not Worthy"

Everyone with High-Functioning Depression can point to a source of trauma in their past that was the catalyst for their condition. That trauma is likely the reason you may believe that you're not deserving of a reward for any level of job well done. Surviving a trauma can make you feel defective even if you've never said those words aloud or written them down in a journal. Therapists don't completely understand why this happens. We just know there is a high correlation between the experience of trauma and the feeling of unworthiness.

Talk to a therapist. You may need some outside help with processing your trauma and reclaiming your self-worth. But know that you're not alone in your feelings and that you truly do deserve to celebrate your successes.

"If It Really Was a Big Deal, My Friends Would've Shown Up for Me"

Nope. Not true. Sometimes the problem is us; sometimes the problem is the people we surround ourselves with. Show me a person with High-Functioning Depression and I'll show you a person who has surrounded themselves with friends who do not want to celebrate their wins. You may also have been raised by narcissistic parents who pushed you to succeed because that reflected well on them, or parents who found themselves competing with you—rather than celebrating you—because of their own deep insecurity. Or you've simply spent so much time giving that you've surrounded yourself with "friends" who are constantly in receiving mode. If you're offering, they're taking—and it's never the other way around. They've grown accustomed to getting your attention and naturally have their hands out. Then when you extend yours, they don't like it.

I'm not telling you this *may* happen when you have High-Functioning Depression. I'm telling you this *will* happen. It *is* happening. You're probably creating a list of friends in your head right now who fit this description. I've seen it so many times, like with a client of mine who got a major promotion at work.

"What do most people at your company do when they move into the C-suite like you?" I asked her.

"They throw a party," she responded.

"Is that what you're planning on doing?"

She visibly cringed at the idea of holding an event in her own honor. Her reaction was a combination of so many of the barriers to rewarding yourself that I've shared with you in this chapter: confusing celebration with bragging, trauma from her childhood, having a cultural background that didn't encourage talking about her success. But the biggest barrier was the people she surrounded herself with—including her partner.

"No, my boyfriend suggested we just have a nice dinner at home," she said. And then she added, "I think he gets intimidated by my successful friends."

"But this isn't about him. And this is huge," I said, raising my voice a little. "Plus, this isn't just a celebration for you. Have you ever thought that people besides your boyfriend might want to celebrate with you?"

Suddenly she could see that she was cheating her mom, dad, siblings, and best friend from high school out of a chance to cheer her on. It took a tremendous amount of convincing, but I finally got her to throw a party for herself to celebrate the promotion.

Check your RSVPs. Once you do throw a celebration for yourself, you can learn a lot from the RSVPs. It's very revealing who shows up for you when you send out the Bat-Signal in the form of an engraved invitation. My client got an awful lot of nos from friends whose celebrations she'd not only attended but organized. Some told her they were busy on the night she'd picked, though she knew they weren't. Others showed up—because they didn't want to feel left out—but spent the whole night talking about their own promotions in the past. Or they congratulated her with backhanded compliments that downplayed her success. "Of course you were going to get the job," they said, rolling their eyes. "You keep a pillow under your desk and a change of clothes in the bottom drawer." Even her boyfriend managed to make the night about himself and an entrepreneurial pursuit he needed investors for rather than raising a glass to his girlfriend. Takers are always going to try to steal your joy.

Thankfully, she also had givers in her circle. There were plenty of people who came to the party and overwhelmed her with love. "You never celebrate yourself!" they said with genuine warmth. "I'm so glad you did this!" She had forgotten how many people did have her back—and in our subsequent sessions we worked on creating boundaries with the ones who didn't.

Whether you're throwing a party and checking RSVPs or just

HIGH FUNCTIONING

posting on LinkedIn and reading the comments, it's all important information about whom you've surrounded yourself with. If you're worried about being met with toxic reactions or rejection when you try to celebrate a win, consider that the problem isn't you, it's them. If that's the case, you may need to start investing in more positive connections.

THE ULTIMATE POWER OF CELEBRATING WINS

There's a reason vision is the last V that I've listed in this book. It's because planning for joy is a useful tool to support, enrich, and reinforce the other V's I've talked about earlier.

- Finally made some progress writing code on a project after being stuck for hours? Invite a co-worker who you know can **validate** your experience out for lunch. Did you turn your work phone off at 6 p.m. and put it out of sight until morning so you could listen to the new album by an artist you love? You're validating that you did something hard and deserve a reward—not to mention that you're introducing more fun and less work into your life.
- Made it through a manic Monday at work without flipping out on anyone? You can reward yourself with some **venting** time by journaling for fifteen minutes before bed, going to a midweek service at your church, or blocking out time on your calendar to "whine and dine" with your bestie.
- If you're walking out of your final exam feeling like you aced

236

it, don't plan a night of binge drinking or pass out in your room for the next two days. Find a way to reward yourself that upholds your **values**. If you value beauty, head to an art gallery for the rest of the afternoon. If you value humor, go to a stand-up comedy show.

- Did you avoid micromanaging your team on a project, so they actually felt some autonomy instead of the pressure of you looking over their shoulder every day? Now that you're not reviewing every move they make, you have time to focus on your **vitals**. Schedule some time to unfollow "hustle" accounts on Instagram and start following meditation ones. Block off time on your calendar for a full six to eight hours of sleep each night.

Vision is my way of making sure that I stay accountable for fighting my High-Functioning Depression—not just for today or a month from now, but forever. If we don't reward ourselves on a regular basis, we'll fall back into a cycle of anhedonia. And if we don't intentionally plan for the future, we can get stuck in a pattern of survival and sacrifice.

Just don't overwhelm yourself. From my perspective, working with patients, I know that a lot of people with High-Functioning Depression are such heavy hitters that they'll want to tackle every single V every single day. With everything that you already have on your plate, that's a one-way ticket to burnout. Instead, if you're super-motivated, try tackling just one V per month. Allow yourself time for all of the exercises, all of the experiences, and all of the self-discovery.

A NOTE ABOUT NEGATIVE VISION: PLANNING FOR YOUR WORST DAYS

It helps not only to plan to celebrate progress but also to plan to protect your mood. From the weather to your hormones, there are so many factors that impact your happiness from day to day. You can't control all of them, but you can control how aware you are of them and how you react to them. For example, I know I encouraged you to celebrate your birthdays, but for some people it's not a happy day because they fear getting one step closer to the unknown. Similarly, anniversaries can remind us of people we've lost, and holidays may have sad memories attached to them around our toxic families. You can anticipate that sadness and then put into your schedule something to distract you that leans into your values: meeting up with a rose-colored-glasses friend for connection, celebrating a holiday that's treasured in your culture, going on an adventurous trip a year to the day you and your ex broke up, or spending the day volunteering at an animal shelter on your departed pet's birthday.

Hormone fluctuations can also have a big impact on your vitals. That's why, if you don't already track your period, start using your calendar to do so, and then plan your activities around where you are in your cycle. Anxious about an upcoming meeting with your supervisor? Try to schedule it for the week you're ovulating, when you are likely to feel more confident.[8] Going through perimenopause or menopause? Understand the link between your mental health and the end of your periods. I created the acronym T.I.E.S. to help women identify their mental health concerns around menopause and to inspire them to share those concerns with their medical team.

T stands for "thinking changes," like struggling with executive functioning. You might have brain fog or problems with calculation; you might become easily distracted or suddenly have trouble with time management. *I* stands for "identity ambivalence." You might feel like you don't know who you are anymore. Body changes—in your brain, hair, skin, joints, and sexual organs—can make you question your sense of self. *E* stands for "emotions." That's the moodiness, irritability, anxiety, or apathy that can be brought on by hormonal fluctuations. *S* stands for "sleep troubles," which are common during menopause and can impact everything else I've mentioned: your thoughts, your identity perceptions, and your emotional regulation. Talk to your doctor about what you're experiencing and work with them to see if shifts in nutrition and exercise can help you to manage everything that comes with this stage of life. People going through perimenopause or menopause may have significant physical and psychological symptoms that they push through in order to stay high-functioning in their workplace or social lives. When they don't acknowledge these difficulties, they may experience internalized shame and blame. Understanding the T.I.E.S. between mental health and menopause (which I taught the first ever Master Class in) not only validates people going through menopause but also empowers them to address their symptoms and improve their quality of life.

I also encourage all my patients to forecast their mood by forecasting the weather. If you find out it's going to rain for an entire week, or if the pollen count is high and you have bad seasonal allergies, expect to be feeling down, and put some things in your schedule to lift your mood. Even sunny weather can trigger depression for some people if they're sensitive to light or heat or have body image issues. Use your vision to stay one step ahead of your mood so that you can avoid sadness and lean into more joy.

FOUR WAYS TO MAINTAIN YOUR VISION

Emotional Simmering

You're going to love this one. It's all about getting your brain primed for joy by letting the anticipation you feel simmer. It's a two-for-one, because you get to enjoy both the anticipation of the joyful experience and the experience itself. It can be romantic, like when you send a sexy text to your partner letting them know how excited you are to spend the night with them, or when you touch the small of their back on your way out the door and say "See you later" with a wink. It can also be childlike and playful, like when you're taking your kid to school and you ask them what they're most looking forward to doing over spring break or what rides they want to go on when you hit Disneyland this summer. Think about ways you can stoke anticipation throughout the day, week, or year to get your brain primed for joy that is coming.

The Calendar Review

As people with HFD, we have to force ourselves to make time for things that bring us joy. That's why I want you to do something similar to what I asked those executives to do in my presentation a few years ago. Pull out your calendar and block out time for pleasure every week. That could be anything from going to a movie to leaving work fifteen minutes early to pick up a treat before you get your child from school.

Go All In Together

For years, my office held an informal happy hour every Friday night. We'd close out our data queries and head out to a local restaurant to have a few drinks. Not only were we giving ourselves a pat on the back for the hard work we'd done, but we were also giving ourselves something to look forward to every single week. Then came Covid. Suddenly we were masked up, socially distanced, and working on a hybrid schedule that meant we didn't always see each other.

When I did see my team, however, I could sense how depleted they were. Many of them were cut off from their families, had had to cancel vacations, and had no social life whatsoever. After weeks of this, one of my team members suggested a Friday happy hour on the roof of our building. We jimmied the lock, made margaritas, and socialized safely in the fresh air. I could see that everyone was much happier and that we needed much more of this, so I planned more pandemic parties: renting an Airbnb with a rooftop garden in mid-town, taking the team to a winery upstate, and so on. I always put these events on our team calendar and brought them up in weekly meetings to prime my team for joy. Even in the face of a pandemic that could've ended our lives, I was still able to give my team (and myself) something to look forward to that kept us feeling hopeful, excited, and inspired.

You can do something similar, whether it's for your family, your college roommates, your neighbors, or your co-workers. Get some help, so it's not all on your high-functioning shoulders, and plan a retreat, vacation, reunion, or some other group gathering that everyone can look forward to as a time for letting off some steam.

Do Quarterly Vision Check-Ins

I know you've done a ton of work getting clear on your values, figuring out how to work them into your vision, and assessing what's missing from your vitals. But guess what? Everything changes. In therapy, I do quarterly check-ins with my patients to see how things are going and if what they want to focus on has shifted. You need to do the same for yourself. Through this process you may realize that you thought your values were one thing but they've actually morphed into something else. Or you thought that the vital you most needed to work on was to get more rest, but the real problem is your social media addiction. You may feel like you're doing too much work on your Five V's, or realize you're not doing enough. Regardless, put quarterly Five V's check-ins on your calendar so that you have time to review your progress and reassess your focus.

THIRTY MOSTLY FREE WAYS TO CELEBRATE SMALL WINS

Start with this list, but build out your own to make sure you never skip a rewarding chance to claim a win again.[9]

Go to bed thirty minutes early.
Buy yourself flowers.

Don't rush through (or skip) your nighttime skin care
routine.

Pick a day for restful, intentional relaxation.

Head to the movie theater (or watch a movie at home) in the
middle of the day.

Blast your favorite song.

Watch the sun rise, catch a sunset, or go stargazing in the
evening.

Play a video game.

Work on a puzzle.

Knit, crochet, embroider, or do something else creative with
your hands.

Break out the fancy cheese and crackers.

Sink into a bubble bath.

Try an expensive shower gel or lotion.

Have breakfast for dinner.

Take a nap (without feeling guilty about it).

Buy a lottery ticket or a scratch-off.

Go for a short hike or spend an hour in a park
bird-watching.

Get a gourmet cup of coffee or a nice glass of wine.

Start a book you've been meaning to read (especially if it's a
fluffy romance novel or a tell-all autobiography).

Create a playlist of songs that make you happy.

Spend quality time with a loved one.

Try a new workout class.

Spend an extra ten minutes stretching after that workout class.

Brush up on your celebrity news online.

Splurge on a new pair of shoes or a cute outfit.

Sit on a park bench or your front porch and soak in the sun.

Take a leisurely drive to nowhere.

Listen to an episode of that true-crime podcast everyone is talking about.

Make a recipe you've been meaning to try forever.

Go out for dinner and a movie with friends.

Repeat the Anhedonia Quiz

Now that you've had time to practice all Five V's, retake the anhedonia quiz on page 68 and see if your numbers have changed at all. Chances are they have. If not, I have even more tools for you in the next chapter to help.

CHAPTER 10

A Way Forward — Continuing to Heal

As a person with High-Functioning Depression, you've been pro-grammed by your trauma to focus on your flaws. But my hope is that after reading this book, you have started to break that cycle of shame and dissatisfaction. By working your way through the Five V's, you've started a shift that is allowing you to focus on your successes instead of your shame. You're no longer automatically putting others first, and you're prioritizing your own values. You've stopped sacrificing for everyone else, and you've started making time for your own health, happiness, and joy. Where your High-Functioning Depression had broken you down in the past, the Five V's have built you back stronger.

For some of you reading this, however, there still may be more work to do. Even when it looks like a row of dominos has been lined up perfectly to topple one after another, if one of them is slightly off, the chain reaction won't flow. So if you have gone through this book and still find yourself stuck, it's time to find the domino that is askew. Often that domino is validation. Can't seem to make space for your values? It's probably because you haven't acknowledged or validated the traumas that have caused you to deprioritize them. Struggling to give yourself permission to vent? Maybe you haven't fully come to terms with the fact that the feelings you need to release are valid. If your vision is clouded, maybe your masochism won't let you validate and celebrate your wins.

If that sounds like you, go back to the validation chapter, reread why people with High-Functioning Depression struggle with validation, and spend more time practicing the self-validation, verbal validation, and factual validation exercises. The last one, factual validation, might be the most impactful for you. Live in the validation for a little bit longer. Change isn't always in one direction; there can be an oscillation between progress and change, and that's okay. Even when you take one step back after two steps forward, you're still moving ahead.

The Five V's are the exact tools you need to help you pull yourself out of High-Functioning Depression—but they might not be the only tools you need. Sometimes we've done the work but something else in our life is so disruptive that we need more support to get our desired results. I need you to know that this is also okay. It doesn't mean that you've failed. It doesn't mean you're broken. It just means that you need some extra help getting some of those out-of-place dominos in line for a perfect topple. You might be working your way through the V's but find yourself in a terribly toxic relationship (say, at work or in your family) that it's impossible to get out of. Or you might find that feelings of sadness are overwhelming you—perhaps even making you question living—and making it too hard to do the Five V's work. All that means is that you need some additional support. I know, because I've been there.

Several years ago, I was going through so much emotional pain that it felt like life had pulled the rug out from under me and left me, stunned, lying flat on my back. It was the lowest point in my life. Fadi Haddad, the close friend and deeply trusted mentor I told you about earlier, had passed away unexpectedly, and I was completely shaken. When I showed up at his wake, I wept so uncontrollably and so loudly, I surprised myself. In that room, it hit me that he was gone, and I couldn't stop the tears. "Whom am I going to talk to now?" I thought. And I really needed someone to talk to. But after being assaulted by a close friend several years earlier — and never processing how that had impacted me — I became very cautious about who I let into my life.

At work, I had made a bad business decision that put my practice and my employees at risk. I felt like my career, the one Fadi had been so supportive of, the one I had worked so hard to create, was careening out of control. Things weren't much better at home. With all the distractions at work, I worried that I wasn't being a good mother to my young daughter. "She deserves better than me," I'd often tell myself. I was convinced I was failing everyone. It was a perfect storm of emotional overwhelm. Even now, writing about it, it feels surreal that all of this happened to me at once.

My therapist immediately noticed that I had careened into clinical, low-functioning depression, and escalated things from our talk sessions. "You've been through a lot of trauma," she said. "I think you should consider EMDR."

Eye movement desensitization and reprocessing (EMDR) is a therapeutic technique for helping patients heal from trauma.[1] You move your eyes in certain directions while briefly thinking about a traumatic memory in order to change your emotions and thoughts around the experience. You're going back to the time of the event and changing the narrative about yourself. Because you ultimately feel differently about it, you can also manage it better.

I had read about EMDR. I'd recommended it to patients. But now I was sitting in the patient seat and feeling vulnerable. At first I challenged my therapist.

"Aren't the data conflicting?" I asked her.

"No," she said firmly.

"How does it even work?" I asked. "There's no medicine involved."

She explained in detail, walking me through the process. "I've done it for several years," she concluded. "I've had really good success with patients."

For every question, she had an answer that chipped away at my skepticism. It wasn't just that I had to try something new. It was also that I had to let go and trust the process. I'm a control freak, so this wasn't easy. But I could see that I wasn't going to get through this depression on my own and I'd have to trust others to pull me out of it. So I gave it a shot.

My therapist asked me to imagine how I felt in moments of intense emotional pain. Then, while I was sitting in those memories, she helped me change how I felt in those moments. After three sessions of EMDR, I started to feel a difference. I was reframing the way I thought about the traumatic events I had been through. Instead of nonchalantly telling myself, "Yeah, Fadi died. Get over it," I was able to compassionately tell myself, "It sucked that this happened. It was really shitty." Instead of blaming myself for the business mistake and internalizing guilt over it, I was able to shift how I thought about it. I stopped thinking, "How could I be so stupid? Why didn't I see this coming?" and started telling myself, "Everybody makes mistakes. I know I'll get through this one." I stopped worrying about not doing enough for my daughter and reminded myself that I'm a hardworking mom trying to juggle two businesses and the caseload of my former mentor. "I shouldn't be so hard on myself," I started saying. EMDR helped me reprocess it all.

If the Five V's aren't enough for you right now — like they weren't for me then — the rest of this chapter describes additional therapies that might help you finally break through your High-Functioning Depression. Keep in mind that if you have medical issues (anything from long Covid to multiple sclerosis), you might need a holistic team approach to getting healthy, and may require a group of medical professionals to help you get back on track.

ONE-ON-ONE THERAPY

Welcome to the gold standard of care. These are online or in-person sessions with a psychiatrist (who can prescribe medicine, diagnose illnesses, and more), psychologist (providing talk therapy), or licensed or certified counselor. Consider seeking out a therapist who specializes in depression, trauma, or whatever you think may be holding you back in the healing process. As part of your treatment plan, your therapist might explore a number of different approaches, including:

- **Cognitive behavioral therapy.** CBT, a type of talk therapy typically used to challenge anxiety and depression, can be helpful for people with HFD whose anxieties make them feel like they're never enough.[2] If severe anxiety or depression is crippling you, then CBT (perhaps in conjunction with medication) may be for you.

- **Dialectical behavioral therapy.** DBT is a type of talk therapy that is helpful for people with HFD who are very reactive, have a tough time with their emotional regulation, and have lost a sense of their identity outside of work.[3] If severe hopelessness, toxic relationship dynamics, mood dysregulation, or even suicidal thoughts get in the way of validating your trauma, identifying your values, or executing your vision, DBT may be for you. (Suicide is the second-leading cause of death for people ages ten to thirty-four, which is why it's so critical to treat your depression.)[4]

- **Eye movement desensitization and reprocessing.** EMDR was originally developed to treat post-traumatic stress disorder but has been found to be helpful for anxiety disorders, panic disorders, phobias, and more. If flashbacks, nightmares, hypervigilance, or the arousal of your fight-or-flight response is overwhelming you, you may benefit from EMDR.

- **Inpatient or outpatient rehab or motivational therapy.** This might be for you if you have a substance use disorder that you're working to overcome along with your High-Functioning Depression.

- **Advanced therapy and precision medicine.** For patients who don't respond to more traditional therapies for depression, therc are more aggressive techniques, such as transmagnetic stimulation, vagus nerve stimulation, deep brain stimulation, electroconvulsive therapy, ketamine treatment, and psychedelic treatments.[5] Talk to your psychiatrist about which of these techniques might be the best next step for you.

Whom It's For

Anyone who can afford and wants the confidentiality of a one-on-one therapy experience. Even if money is tight, you might find a therapist who offers a sliding scale. Working with someone in training can also be a great way to save money on therapy while still getting quality care.

Whom It's Not For

Anyone who's been traumatized by a bad experience with a therapist in the past. Maybe one-on-one therapy became weaponized for you because your parents were going through a divorce, or you just worked with someone who was a bad therapist — we're not all saints.

How to Find It

For some reason, so many of us will Google the hell out of a restaurant or nail salon we're planning to go to, but if anyone hangs a sign on their door that says "Therapist," we're telling everyone, "I'm going! Be back in an hour!" There are so many reasons we often don't give our choice of therapist the thought it deserves. It's no surprise that with High-Functioning Depression, we might just be too busy working and caring for others around the clock that we think we don't have time to do the research. But we also might be self-sabotaging or masochistic, we might be going through the motions of improving our mental health and not really committing to it, or we might just not know how to do the work in this area. It's hard to pick the perfect stranger to whom you will be entrusting all your deepest fears, anxieties, and insecurities. But it's worth the effort to find someone whose therapeutic approach resonates with you and whom you click with.

One of the best ways to find a good therapist is word of mouth. Reach out to friends and family for recommendations. You can also consult *Psychology Today* or your insurance company's list of practitioners and then read online reviews of health professionals covered by your plan. You might also go to national organizations, like the American Psychological Association or the American Psychiatric Association, for a listing of recommended therapists in your area. Group therapists can often refer people to individual support as well. Regardless of where you get the suggestion, it's important to do a background check for accreditation, licensing, and any reports of bad practices or their license ever being revoked. You can research credentials with the Federation of State Medical Boards Physician Data Center (https://www.fsmb.org/PDC/) or the American Medical Association's Find a Doctor tool (https://find-doctor.ama-assn.org/). In the United Kingdom, websites such as those for the British Association for Counselling and Psychotherapy (https://www.bacp.co.uk/search/Therapists) and the Black, African and Asian Therapy Network (https://www.baatn.org.uk/find-a-psych-therapist) have search tools. You can also do a simple online search with the doctor's name and the word "malpractice," "lawsuit," or "complaint."[6]

Questions to Ask

There are certain questions you should ask any therapist you're considering:

- **"Can you share your level of experience with my condition?"** If they don't have many years of experience, make sure they're being supervised by someone who does.
- **"What treatment modalities do you use?"** For example, if the entire program is faith-based and only uses Bible verses, next! Even if you want faith as part of your healing, it can't be the only aspect. Look for someone who has a degree in counseling and a separate degree in religion. Whatever modalities your therapist uses, you want to make sure they are grounded in evidence-based practices.
- **"Are you trained in cultural competency?"** It may be difficult to find someone who matches your identity in every way (i.e., gender, ethnicity, sexuality, class). You can certainly try, if that's important to you. But it may be easier to find someone trained in cultural competency who is educated about your background.
- **"What is your success rate and how do you determine progress?"** You want a sense of how many cases of depression (high- or low-functioning) they've treated and what the

outcomes were. You also need to know how you'll determine if you're moving in the right direction while working with them. As a person with HFD, you will definitely want benchmarks of success.

- **"Do you have plans to move?"** It can be tough or even traumatizing to have a break in your therapy relationship if your therapist moves to a new practice or hospital and a noncompete agreement or your insurance stands in the way of you getting continuity of care. If there's a chance that the therapist will be leaving their current clinic or practice soon, you might not want to start a new relationship that could quickly end.

- **"Will I have access to support if/when you're on vacation?"** Many therapists take off the month of August for vacation, but there are plenty of other reasons your therapist might not be available when you need them. You need to know if someone else will be taking their patients in these situations. There will always be absences that no one can anticipate, but if you're serious about your treatment, you have to have a contingency plan. You want someone supporting you as diligently as you support others.

- **"Are there penalties if I miss a session?"** As you work on your HFD, it may be hard initially to prioritize your mental health over work. Being penalized for missing a session could be the incentive you need to keep coming in—or could make you resentful of the experience.

GROUP THERAPY AND SUPPORT GROUPS

Led by professionals or peers (people who have experienced the same health concern that you have), group sessions allow you to talk about your experiences and challenges with others who share your symptoms or condition.[7] They can occur in person, which aids connection but doesn't allow for anonymity, or online, which aids with anonymity but not connection. While you may not find a group focused specifically on High-Functioning Depression, you can find plenty associated with many of the behaviors associated with it: anxiety, workaholism, grief, childhood trauma, domestic violence, substance use disorders, and anger management, for example.

Your circle of peers will keep you honest, calling you out if you said last week that you were going to throw a party to celebrate your promotion but never did, or if you claimed you'd cut ties with a toxic friend but are planning a vacation with them. The circle also provides perspective. You'll see people worse off than you and think, "If I don't get control now, I'm going to end up like them." You'll see people better off than you and think, "If I keep at this like them, I'll be like them soon."

Whom It's For

Anyone who might not be able to afford one-on-one therapy, as many groups are free or low-cost. Also, as someone with High-Functioning Depression, you may be constantly thinking of others. Group therapy allows you to be verbally and emotionally supportive of the other people in your group while also receiving support from them. For some people, this can be helpful. There's a collective healing that happens. You realize you're not alone, and you get perspective on why this is happening to you and what to do about it.

Whom It's Not For

Anyone who's worried about having their business out there. While groups have privacy rules, there's no way to ensure that people keep the information you share confidential.

How to Find It

Search the websites of *Psychology Today*, NAMI, or your state or local mental health agency.

Questions to Ask

Once you find a group that you can afford and that fits into your schedule, you'll want to inquire about a few other things to make sure it's a good fit. Consider asking:

- **"Who's running the group?"** Make sure they have the necessary qualifications. Support groups tend to be led by peers, whereas group therapy tends to be led by professionals. If you need expert help, don't self-sabotage by going to a group led by a peer and risk walking away thinking, "I'm smarter than that person. They can't help me."
- **"What are the rules of the group?"** For example, is there a confidentiality clause and are there consequences for violating it? Does everyone have to participate, or are you allowed to sit

in silence? If you discover that you will have to talk, ask yourself if you're comfortable with that.

- **"What is the size of the group?"** Your experience with an intimate group of five will be a lot different from your experience with a large group of twenty-five. One may be more comfortable or beneficial for you compared to the other.

- **"Is there rolling admission?"** Do you have to wait until they're at the end of a cycle to open up the group to more people or can you jump in at any time? How long are the cycles?

FDA-APPROVED DRUG THERAPIES

Traditional drug therapies like selective serotonin reuptake inhibitors (SSRIs) and anti-anxiety meds are only approved for certain conditions in the *DSM-5*, like clinical depression, anxiety, obsessive-compulsive disorder (OCD), and PTSD. Your doctor will likely put you on one of these medications when your High-Functioning Depression crosses into low-functioning depression or when your symptoms warrant additional psychopharmacological support. Your doctor may also suggest medications if you have one of these other conditions on top of your High-Functioning Depression. Many of my patients have come to me after crossing over from HFD to low-functioning depression and are on SSRIs, but these medications don't make them feel full, fed, and content.

For patients who need a little more help, I've used ketamine (which is FDA-approved) for treatment-resistant depression.[8] Medication can mitigate symptoms of depression by helping people sleep better, by improving their concentration, or by making them feel like they have more energy. But to achieve those sensations of happiness that HFD can sap (delight, relaxation, pampering, joy, luxuriation, flow), you need to focus on the Five V's.

NON-FDA-APPROVED DRUG THERAPIES

If you've dutifully followed the Five V's and traditional standards of care (like therapy and medication) only to still find yourself going in circles or overwhelmed with treatment-resistant depression, you might consider psychedelic or hallucinogenic substances like psilocybin (also known as magic mushrooms) and ayahuasca. In general, they allow you to press a reset button on your treatment when you feel like you're hitting a wall. Using these therapies, you may be able to get your brain out of default mode so you can focus more on healing or you could gain insight into a particular problem you have. They're not a cure-all, but they can open your brain up to new possibilities and clarity. Not to mention that you can experience everything from a sense of euphoria to the feeling of seeing sounds and hearing colors while using them.[9]

I've also done research on a psilocybin-like substance for treatment of major depressive disorder (low-functioning depression) in patients. While I don't prescribe or recommend other drugs, like psilocybin (which is currently only legal in Oregon and decriminalized in a few other states) or ayahuasca (which you may need to travel outside the United States to use legally), I've seen patients benefit from the use of different types of hallucinogenic drugs.[10] These should only be used in a clinical setting or under the supervision of a clinician licensed to administer the drugs.

Whom It's For

If you're someone who has tried all of the above treatments and is still stuck, this may be your path.

Whom It's Not For

People with conditions that a psychedelic could complicate, like schizophrenia, a history of psychosis, a substance use disorder, severe brain issues (like seizures or brain injuries), or other medical conditions for which psychedelics are contraindicated. These are also not advisable for anyone who has had bad experiences with psychedelics in the past.

How to Find It

One of the safest and cheapest ways to explore psychedelic treatment is by going to ClinicalTrials.gov and searching for trials using them. You can see if you're eligible, what treatment is involved, and whether or not you would definitely have access to the medications (if it's a placebo-controlled study, you might be in the group that gets sugar pills). You can also search online for experienced facilitators and reputable organizations, like Horizons PBC (https://www.horizonspbc.com/), that can help you learn more about psychedelics.

Questions to Ask

Whether you're working with a therapist or a facilitator to help you through your experience, you should vet them as thoroughly as possible. A few questions you might want to ask:[11]

- **"What is your background and how have you successfully helped others in the past?"** Because some of these treatments are happening outside of the healthcare system, you need to have a firm understanding of the depth of knowledge of the person helping you through this experience.
- **"Is this legal?"** Because some of these treatments happen outside of the healthcare system with drugs that may or may not be approved by the FDA, you need to know what's allowed in your state.
- **"What do I need to know about how this drug could impact me?"** Your therapist or facilitator should meet with you to thoroughly explain the treatment, tell you about possible side effects, and help set expectations for the experience.
- **"What support is available to me before and after the psychedelic session?"** This could be preparation or integration work you do with the therapist days or weeks before or after the session.
- **"What happens if there is an emergency?"** If for some reason you need immediate medical care during your experience, how will that be facilitated?
- **"How much does this cost?"** Depending upon the treatment and what kind of insurance you have, you may not be covered. Make sure you can afford the likely number of treatments

you'll need so that you don't have to worry about interrupting a successful therapeutic plan.

ALTERNATIVE THERAPIES

Who am I to say that you have to go to traditional therapy? The only thing you have to do is what works for you. Some experiences may be therapeutic without exactly being therapy—and that's fine, too. I've had clients go to gurus, life coaches, and even massage therapists who have helped them work through their Five V's. You might look into art therapy, dance/movement therapy, yoga, acupuncture, reiki, massage therapy, somatic therapy, emotional freedom technique (also called tapping), and more.[12] One thing I will suggest: try to connect with a coach/instructor/facilitator/teacher who can bring you into a community of like-minded people so that you have a group that supports and encourages you to live your best life on a regular basis.

Whom It's For
Anyone who had a traumatizing experience with one-on-one therapy, group therapy, and/or drug treatments. If traditional therapy is never going to happen for you, try an alternative route.

Whom It's Not For
Anyone who needs urgent care through a medical doctor for a mental health crisis or is at risk of suicide. If that's the case for you, don't use an alternative modality as your only therapy.

How to Find It

Good old Google can serve you up lists of alternative therapies to explore, and word of mouth can help you find practitioners who come recommended or have excellent reviews. You should also ask the doctors or therapists you currently see for their recommendations. One patient I had who was seeing me due to depression over fertility problems ended up working with an acupuncturist recommended by her fertility doctor as her alternative therapy instead. She goes once a month, and it's the longest therapeutic relationship she's ever had.

Questions to Ask

No matter what alternative therapy you choose, there are certain questions you should ask any practitioner you're considering:

- **"What is your level of experience?"** You want to get a sense of how long the person has been practicing and what level of proficiency they've obtained.
- **"What is the efficacy of this as an evidence-based treatment?"** There are research studies and protocols for every treatment you can imagine. Ask about what has been proven so you can manage your expectations. You can meet with a life coach to help with life goals—but don't expect them to help you overcome depression.

No matter what path you choose for healing, know that if you stay consistent and keep moving forward, you can get to a place where you're free from your High-Functioning Depression. That's exactly what happened to me. I started this book by telling you about the Zoom presentation that opened me up to the fact that I (and millions of others) were struggling with High-Functioning Depression as Covid took over our lives. During that Zoom presentation at the beginning of the pandemic, I was a burned-out healthcare professional talking to other burned-out healthcare professionals about safeguarding their mental health. It was like the blind leading the blind. I felt like an imposter. But it led me to an epiphany about High-Functioning Depression, it inspired me to write the book you have in your hands right now—and it got me a call from the executive office of the president's staff at the White House. Four years after that epiphany, I was invited by a major social media platform to speak about Black joy for a notable mental health charity founded by Taraji P. Henson. The "Can We Talk?" 2024 mental health symposium in D.C. happened to be the exact same week that I was also asked to present to White House staff about managing stress and understanding mental health.

That pivotal Zoom meeting in 2020 that I told you about in the beginning of the book and my D.C. trip four years later couldn't have been more different. At the time of that Zoom meeting, I was teetering on the edge of my emotions and about to topple over. At the White House, I was grounded, relaxed, and focused. The Dr. Judith who showed up to give that workshop was far more aware and way more healed. While prepping for the Zoom meeting, I had to ask myself, "Am I depressed?" Prepping for the White House, I told myself: "This is special. Enjoy it!" I had fun at the presentation, and

I even cracked a few jokes! During that Zoom meeting, I felt like an imposter. At the White House, I felt like I was there with a purpose and a mission. I was excited to share what I knew about stress, anhedonia, and High-Functioning Depression after hundreds of interviews and months of research.

There had been a tremendous shift between the old Judith and the new Judith. The old Judith would've lugged two laptops (one for the lab, one for the private practice) with her on that trip to D.C. to make sure she could work on every part of her business while on the go. The new Judith brought only one. The old Judith would've left home the night before the workshop (so I could show up early and prep more) and returned home as soon as she was done presenting. The new Judith left the morning of the workshop (so I could spend more time with my daughter the night before) and then stayed the night so I could go to a themed afterparty. Yes, you read that right. Taraji's symposium had a 1980s/1990s-themed party to celebrate Black hip-hop culture. I busted out in a denim dress, matching fanny pack, and Timberland boots to dance the night away.

Are my days still incredibly full? Yes. But are they also much more balanced? Absolutely, because I've been practicing the Five V's. I spend more time prioritizing my values, like family. I lean into self-validation, like telling myself "This is a big deal!" when I get prestigious opportunities. I let myself vent to the tens of thousands of people who have downloaded my podcast, *The Vault with Dr. Judith*. I check my vitals so I know when to do deep breathing exercises to help me avoid panicking from stress. And I celebrate my wins—especially when it involves dancing to nineties R&B.

I wish I could tell you that I'm completely free from High-

Functioning Depression and that it never creeps its way back into my life. But that's not true. What I can tell you is that when I notice it edging back into my life, I have the tools to stop it in its tracks. And now you do, too. Remember, life is about progress, not one-and-done goals. You're constantly going to be experiencing good and bad days. You're going to be working on your well-being for the rest of your life. Don't think of it as being exhausting; think of it as being exciting. I asked you earlier in the book what overcoming High-Functioning Depression could make possible in your life. Hopefully by now you have the tools to understand the science of your happiness and the ability to make that dream a reality.

APPENDIX A

High-Functioning Depression Trauma Inventory
In my research on High-Functioning Depression, I use the following scale, which I designed, to determine which traumas people have been exposed to.[1] You can use this list to do the same for yourself as you build your Trauma Tree or seek to understand your HFD better.

CHILDHOOD TRAUMA
1. Childhood: Did you feel unsafe in your neighborhood growing up?
2. Childhood: Were you bullied by a peer prior to age eighteen?
3. Childhood: Have you seen anyone being beaten, stabbed, or shot in real life?
4. Childhood: Did your caretakers fail to make you feel important or special?
5. Childhood: Did your family cut the sizes of meals or skip meals because there was not enough money in the food budget for a significant period of time?
6. Childhood: Did you live with anyone who was depressed or mentally ill?
7. Childhood: Did you live with someone who was suicidal?
8. Childhood: Did you live with anyone who was a problem drinker or alcoholic?

9. Childhood: Did you live with anyone who used illegal street drugs or who abused prescription medications?
10. Childhood: Did you live with anyone who served time or was sentenced to serve time in a prison, jail, or other correctional facility?
11. Childhood: Were you ever in foster care?
12. Childhood: Did you ever see or hear a parent, a stepparent, or another adult who was helping to raise you being yelled at, screamed at, sworn at, insulted, or humiliated?
13. Childhood: Did you ever see or hear in your home a parent, a stepparent, or another adult who was helping raise you being slapped, kicked, punched, or beaten up?
14. Childhood: Did you ever see or hear a parent, a stepparent, or another adult who was helping to raise you being hit or cut with an object, such as a stick or cane, bottle, club, knife, or gun?
15. Childhood: Did you ever have a parent, a stepparent, or another adult living in the home swear at you, insult you, or put you down?
16. Childhood: Did you ever have a parent, a stepparent, or another adult living in the home push, grab, shove, or slap you?
17. Childhood: Did you ever have a parent, a stepparent, or another adult living in the home hit you so hard you had marks or were injured?
18. Childhood: Did you ever have a parent, a stepparent, or another adult living in the home act in a way that made you afraid that you would be physically hurt?
19. Childhood: Did an adult or older relative, family friend, or stranger who was at least five years older than yourself ever touch or fondle you in a sexual way or have you touch their body in a sexual way?
20. Childhood: Did an adult or older relative, family friend, or stranger who was at least five years older than your-

self ever attempt to have or have any type of sexual intercourse (oral, anal, or vaginal) with you?

21. Childhood: Were your parents ever separated or divorced?
22. Childhood: Were you diagnosed with a serious medical condition or life-threatening injury?
23. Childhood: Did you experience significant discrimination because of your sexual identity, gender identity, or gender expression?

ADULTHOOD TRAUMA

24. Adulthood: Have you ever worked in an unsupportive or toxic workplace for a significant period of time?
25. Adulthood: Were you in a relationship for a significant length of time with an intimate partner who was depressed or mentally ill?
26. Adulthood: Were you in a relationship for a significant length of time with an intimate partner who was suicidal?
27. Adulthood: Were you in a relationship for a significant length of time with an intimate partner who was a problem drinker or alcoholic?
28. Adulthood: Were you in a relationship for a significant length of time with an intimate partner who used illegal street drugs or who abused prescription medications?
29. Adulthood: Were you in a relationship for a significant length of time with an intimate partner who served time or was sentenced to serve time in a prison, jail, or other correctional facility?
30. Adulthood: Were you in a relationship for a significant length of time with an intimate partner where they swore at you, insulted you, or put you down?
31. Adulthood: Were you in a relationship for a significant length of time with an intimate partner where you were pushed, grabbed, shoved, or slapped?

32. Adulthood: Were you in a relationship for a significant length of time with an intimate partner where you were hit so hard you had marks or were injured?
33. Adulthood: Were you in a relationship for a significant length of time with an intimate partner where you were afraid that you would be physically hurt?
34. Adulthood: Were you ever sexually assaulted as an adult?
35. Adulthood: Did you ever go through a separation or divorce from your spouse?
36. Adulthood: Did you ever have a life-threatening injury?
37. Adulthood: Have you ever experienced significant debt, bankruptcy, foreclosure, or reliance on government assistance?
38. Adulthood: Have you worked in a career or job where there is exposure to violence or death?
39. Adulthood: Have you experienced significant discrimination because of your sexual identity, gender identity, or gender expression?

INTERGENERATIONAL TRAUMA

40. Intergenerational: In childhood or adulthood, did you often feel that you were treated badly or unfairly because of your race or ethnicity?
41. Intergenerational: Were you, your parents, or your grandparents survivors of genocide?
42. Intergenerational: Were you, your parents, or your grandparents refugees?

COLLECTIVE TRAUMA

43. Collective: Have you directly experienced war?
44. Collective: Have you directly survived a major potentially fatal disaster such as flood, fire, or earthquake?

45. Collective: Were you significantly impacted by a major pandemic such as Covid-19 or SARS?
46. Collective: Were you a survivor of a mass shooting?

APPENDIX B

Give Your Vitals a Boost

Ready to work on replacing more negative HFD habits in your life with positive ones? Explore this list of possibilities that will get you prioritizing your best health over busyness.

Positive Work Habits for People with HFD

- Leaving the office on time every day and treating your weekends like a mini-vacation.
- Setting an alarm to remind you to take a break—and not ignoring it when it goes off.
- Filling your work environment with plants (so that it feels more like nature), artwork, toys, and reminders that work can be fun.
- Taking the last fifteen minutes of the day to clear your desk of clutter and get better organized.
- Scheduling walking meetings so that you get more steps in every day. Ordering a standing desk so that you get exercise without even trying and break the habit of being sedentary.
- Asking for help on projects so that they're a team effort,

they're completed faster, and you avoid being overwhelmed by too much responsibility.

- Going out nights and weekends with friends you don't work with so that your entire life isn't about your job.
- Planning—and going on—vacations where you leave your laptop behind and don't bring your work phone.
- Delegating work before you go on vacation so that no last-minute surprises destroy your time off.

Positive Sleep Habits for People with HFD

- Avoiding eating food and drinking water or alcohol two to four hours before bed.[1] Cutting the caffeine eight hours before sleep.[2] These changes give your body time to digest food and prevent you from having to get up to go to the bathroom in the middle of the night. Quality of sleep is more important than quantity.[3]
- Curating your sleep experience by picking out a comfortable mattress, luxurious sheets, a good blanket (try a weighted blanket), and five-star, hotel-quality pillows.
- Designating your bedroom for only sleep and sex. Remove all electronics so you avoid blue light exposure and the temptation to do work.
- Doing a progressive relaxation exercise, some meditation, or another cognitive behavioral therapy practice to relax your body and mind.[4]
- Buying an actual alarm clock so that you can charge your phone in another room overnight.
- Tracking your menstrual cycle so that you know what phase

you are in, or what menopause symptoms you have (see page 238) so that you can manage them.

- Changing your alarm tone to your favorite song or nature sounds.
- Realizing you can't make up for lost sleep, and getting to bed at roughly the same time each night and waking at the same time each morning.

Positive Relationship Habits for People with HFD

- Choosing friends or partners who encourage you to take part in healthy behaviors (such as working out or taking vacations).
- Choosing friends who are constantly offering to help you by lending an ear, offering valuable advice, and showing up when you need them.
- Choosing friends or partners who checrlead your efforts, compliment your hard work, brag about you to others, and offer you emotional support.
- Using the W.A.S.H. method that I designed to decide whether or not to mend a family feud.
  ° *W* stands for "Why is there a conflict?" If someone did something unforgivable (like emotional, physical, or sexual abuse), the chances of that changing aren't good and you probably can't return to that situation. If they betrayed you by sleeping with a guy you'd been dating for a month, that's different.
  ° *A* stands for "agenda." What are you hoping to get out of mending fences? Maybe you're getting married and you want at least one parent there even though you feel like

your mom didn't do a great job raising you. Maybe someone died and it makes you realize you want to bury the hatchet with a sibling or cousin before it's too late.

° *S* stands for "strategy." What exactly are you going to do to repair this relationship and who can help you achieve that? Maybe you need a therapist, a lawyer, a family member who knows both of you, or a surrogate who can connect the two of you. This is important to consider if safety is a concern.

° *H* stands for "healing." We all have a fantasy that when we confront someone who has wronged us, it will bring us closure. I hate to break it to you, but 99 percent of the time that isn't the case. You may actually feel worse and it'll take you months to get over it. Be sure to book an appointment with a therapist or someone in your support system to help you heal if your attempt to mend fences leaves them still broken.

Positive Nutrition Habits for People with HFD

- Making plans to have lunch with co-workers or stepping away from weekend work to cook a dish you've been curious about.
- Eating a brain health diet or Mediterranean diet. Both have been shown to improve overall health and well-being.
- Carrying a water bottle with you so you consume the eleven to fifteen cups of water recommended each day.[5] Dehydration can impair short-term memory and attention.[6]
- Not eating within two to four hours of bedtime (which will help you avoid bingeing on unhealthy foods and, once again, get a better night's sleep).

Positive Movement Habits for People with HFD

- Opting for the stairs instead of the elevator at work (so long as it's safe) to squeeze in exercise.
- Leaving a water bottle on your desk and drinking more fluids at work, which will likely make you get up and go to the bathroom more often (for bonus movement, you could use the one at the far end of the hallway or on another floor).
- Making an inspirational playlist of your favorite songs that make you want to get up and get moving.
- Exercising with a friend. It makes working out less of a chore, can increase your motivation, and may release oxytocin, a neurotransmitter that helps you feel more connected to others.
- Figuring out how to find joy in movement.

Positive Technology Habits for People with HFD

- Using AI tools to get things done faster and organize your day so that you spend less time on screens.
- Instead of checking your work email or social media feed for the gazillionth time, send a text message or an email to check in on your friends instead.[7]
- Validating people in the comments section of social media posts when they talk about their traumas.

APPENDIX C

Time for a Tech Check

How much is too much when it comes to social media usage? It depends. There's no one-size-fits-all answer to that question because we're all different. Some of us have to use social media for work, so there's no getting around it. Some of us spend so much time doom-scrolling that our family and friends feel neglected. No matter what your situation, one thing all of us can do is develop healthy habits around social media so that we make sure it doesn't negatively impact our mental health. I created the R.E.S.E.T. method to help my adult and pediatric patients develop those habits. Here's how you can use it yourself.

- *R* **stands for "realization."** To begin, you need to think about the ways that social media is impacting you. Is it helping or hurting? Does it bring you down or make you depressed? Does it make you happy? Does it get in the way of activities you want to do? Does it give you ideas for things you can do? There are online assessment tests you can take to gauge what's happening with your social media engagement, too. They ask, for example, if you check social media as soon as you wake up in the morning, whether deleting an app would cause you anxiety, if you lose track of time on social media, and whether you rely on social media as a source of excitement.
- *E* **stands for "education."** Learn about the studies that show the direct impact social media has on your brain health.

Research shows social media use can stoke the flames of depression and anxiety. But it can also help you maintain connection with faraway friends.[1] Look at reputable sources to understand the effect that social media is having on you in particular.

- *S* stands for "strategy." How are you going to change the way that you use social media so that you have the best outcome? Do you want to cut back? Do you want to limit the number of accounts you have? What is workable for you? What is feasible? If you're in a profession like marketing or media, you can't tune it out completely. But you could decide not to use devices after 8 p.m. Or you could choose to meditate first thing in the morning instead of looking at your phone as soon as you wake up.

- *E* stands for "expectation." What are you hoping to gain by developing better social media habits? Better sleep? Less anxiety? Are you hoping to spend more time in the real world with activities with loved ones? Or do you need to be more productive? Have a very clear expectation as to what you're hoping to get from making changes to the way you use social media.

- *T* stands for "thoughtful process." After a week, see if you're making progress toward your expectations. Did it work? Did it not work? Was it too rigid or too lax? Look at the methods that you put in place to change your usage and figure out if you need to make some modifications to the plan. Also think about what you're doing with the extra time you've created for yourself. Are you spending more time with friends and family? Or have you been binge-watching Netflix more than usual? Don't replace one unhealthy habit with another.

You've probably noticed that the first and last steps of the R.E.S.E.T. method require a fair amount of reflection, but in the end it's worth it.

ACKNOWLEDGMENTS

This project came together so brilliantly thanks to the dedication of my talented book team: Heather Jackson, my agent; Talia Krohn, my editor; and Lynya Floyd, my collaborator. Deepest thanks to Heather for encouraging me to write a book about my own struggles with HFD and my research on it. I'm incredibly grateful to Talia for believing in me and sharing her own family stories about what looked like HFD in her family. And I adore Lynya for writing with me, laughing with me, and helping me put into words what so many, including myself, struggle with every day. I am also grateful to Jessica Chun and Lauren Ortiz for their hard work and creativity in marketing and publicizing the book, Julianna Lee for the beautiful cover design, Linda Kaplan for foreign and translation rights, and Betsy Uhrig for shepherding the book through all the stages of production.

This book would not have been possible without the sacrifices of my parents. I want to thank Stella and Fitzroy Joseph for leaving their warm, sunny home in Trinidad and Tobago to make a better life for myself and my siblings in New York. Trinidad and Tobago is where I was born and where I derive my inspiration.

My own journey has been made so much easier by the support of my sisters and brother: Nikeisha, Tracee, and Timothy. Thank you for letting me be the lead in our plays, for being my best friends, and for offering lifelong support. I especially want to thank my older sister, Nikeisha, for taking care of my businesses when I was traveling and working on this book. She was instrumental in working with my research team at Manhattan Behavioral Medicine to make the HFD study happen. She runs my labs and oversaw opening of our two additional research labs. Thank you to my daughter, Zara, who brings me so many moments of joy. I'm also deeply grateful to my nanny, Subarna Chhetri, who is like a second mother to my daughter and who is my family, and to Karen Lee, my best friend and godmother to my daughter.

Special thanks go out to my research team at MBM: Teresa Escobar Mendoza, my site director, who is one of the most exceptional human beings I have ever met and who inspires me to be a better person; Trisha Srigiriraju, who was with MBM from the beginning; Christine Medeiros, who helped me to start my HFD study; Dr. Deepa Voleti and Dr. Emily Shapiro, who are sub-investigators at MBM; and research coordinators Ashley Chan, Allison Degen, Margot Deregnacourt, Rachel Reiffer, and Eshna Patel, who care for patients and conduct research at MBM.

I feel so incredibly fortunate to have had the support of my Columbia University Vagelos College of Physicians and Surgeons colleagues as well as support from my colleagues at NYU Grossman School of Medicine; my social media team and podcast team (including my cousin Aquil Elijah Smith), who help me to express my creativity using various outlets; my friend circle of Black women entrepreneurs in NYC, whom I turn to when times are tough and when it is time to celebrate; and my close friends in Bermuda, who taught me to appreciate the joys in life that are free.

I'm profoundly grateful to my therapists over the years who helped me through challenges and trauma, as well as my patients over the years who taught me how to truly empathize with those who live every day with mental health conditions. You have healed me as much as I have been a part of your healing. And I can't forget to thank the Covid-19 frontline workers, including my ex-husband, for their sacrifices to the community.

Finally, I cannot express enough thanks to my mentor, Fadi Haddad, who believed in me until his last breath.

NOTES

Introduction

1. World Health Organization, *International Statistical Classification of Diseases and Related Health Problems 10th Revision (ICD-10)* (Geneva: World Health Organization, 2016), s.v. "Z73.0 Burn-out—State of vital exhaustion," https://icd.who.int/browse10/2016/en#/Z73.0.

2. Substance Abuse and Mental Health Services Administration. DSM-5 Changes: Implications for Child Serious Emotional Disturbance [Internet]. Rockville (MD): Substance Abuse and Mental Health Services Administration (US); 2016 Jun. Table 10, DSM-IV to DSM-5 Dysthymic Disorder/Persistent Depressive Disorder Comparison. Available from: https://www.ncbi.nlm.nih.gov/books/NBK519712/table/ch3.t6/.

3. Ali Watkins, "Cheslie Kryst and the Unseen Burden of Depression," *New York Times*, September 27, 2022, https://www.nytimes.com/2022/09/27/nyregion/cheslie-kryst-mental-health.html.

4. Eileen Finan, "Miss USA 2019 Cheslie Kryst's New Memoir Reveals Private Agony Before Her Suicide at Age 30 (Exclusive Excerpt)," *People*, April 22, 2024, https://people.com/cheslie-kryst-s-new-memoir-reveals-agony-before-suicide-exclusive-excerpt-8636558.

Chapter 2: Trauma

1. Douglas F. Levinson and Walter E. Nichols, "Genetics of Brain Function: Major Depression and Genetics," Stanford Medicine, Department of Psychiatry and Behavioral Sciences, accessed May 27, 2024, https://med.stanford.edu/depressiongenetics/mddandgenes.html.

2. Vincent J. Felitti, "The Relation Between Adverse Childhood Experiences and Adult Health: Turning Gold into Lead," *Permanente Journal* 6, no. 1 (2002): 44–47, https://www.ncbi.nlm.nih.gov/pmc/articles/PMC6220625/.

3. Philadelphia ACE Project, "Adverse Childhood Experiences (ACEs)," Philadelphia ACE Survey, accessed May 27, 2024, https://www.philadelphiaaces.org/philadelphia-ace-survey.

4. Hilda Bjork Daníelsdóttir, Thor Aspelund, Qing Shen, et al., "Adverse Childhood Experiences and Adult Mental Health Outcomes," *JAMA Psychiatry* 81, no. 6 (2024): 586–594, https://jamanetwork.com/journals/jamapsychiatry/fullarticle/2815834.

5. Pim Dashorst, T. M. Mooren, R. J. Kleber, P. J. de Jong, and R. J. C. Hunt-jens, "Intergenerational Consequences of the Holocaust on Offspring Mental Health: A Systematic Review of Associated Factors and Mechanisms," *European Journal of Psychotraumatology* 10, no. 1 (2019): 1654065, https://www.ncbi.nlm.nih.gov/pmc/articles/PMC6720013/; Dora L. Costa, Noelle Yetter, and Heather DeSomer, "Intergenerational Transmission of Paternal Trauma Among US Civil War Ex-POWs," *Proceedings of the National Academy of Sciences of the United States of America* 115, no. 44 (2018): 11215–11220, https://pubmed.ncbi.nlm.nih.gov/30322945/; Michael J. Halloran, "African American Health and Posttraumatic Slave Syndrome: A Terror Management Theory Account," *Journal of Black Studies* 50, no. 1 (2019): 45–65, https://doi.org/10.1177/0021934718803737; Sidney H. Hankerson, Nathalie Moise, Diane Wilson, Bernadine Y. Waller, Kimberly T. Arnold, Cristiane Duarte, Claudia Lugo-Candelas, et al., "The Intergenerational Impact of Structural Racism and Cumulative Trauma on Depression," *American Journal of Psychiatry* 179, no. 6 (2022): 434–440, https://ajp.psychiatryonline.org/doi/10.1176/appi.ajp.21101000; Teresa Evans-Campbell, "Historical Trauma in American Indian/Native Alaska Communities: A Multilevel Framework for Exploring Impacts on Individuals, Families, and Communities," *Journal of Interpersonal Violence* 23, no. 3 (2008): 316–338, https://doi.org/10.1177/0886260507312290.
6. "Hurricane Katrina," *Encyclopædia Britannica*, accessed May 27, 2024, https://www.britannica.com/event/Hurricane-Katrina.
7. Susan Kelley, "Trust in Financial Markets Was Biggest Victim of Madoff Case," *Cornell Chronicle*, July 17, 2017, https://news.cornell.edu/stories/2017/07/trust-financial-markets-was-biggest-victim-madoff-case.
8. National 9/11 Memorial and Museum, "Commemoration," accessed May 27, 2024, https://www.911memorial.org/connect/commemoration.
9. World Health Organization, "Number of COVID-19 Cases Reported to WHO," accessed May 27, 2024, https://data.who.int/dashboards/covid19/cases?n=c; World Health Organization, "Impact of COVID-19 on People's Livelihoods, Their Health and Our Food Systems," October 20, 2020, https://www.who.int/news/item/13-10-2020-impact-of-covid-19-on-people%27s-livelihoods-their-health-and-our-food-systems.
10. Haruna Kashiwase, "Female Genital Mutilation Is Still Practiced Around the World," World Bank, September 16, 2019, https://datatopics.worldbank.org/world-development-indicators/stories/fgm-still-practiced-around-the-world.html; "The Horror of Honor Killings, Even in the US," Amnesty International USA, April 10, 2012, https://www.amnestyusa.org/updates/the-horror-of-honor-killings-even-in-us/; "Honour Killings by Region," Honour Based Violence Awareness Network, accessed May 27, 2024, https://hbv-awareness.com/regions/#google_vignette; Elizabeth T. Gershoff and Sarah A. Font, "Corporal Punishment in U.S. Public Schools: Prevalence, Disparities in Use, and Status in State and Federal Policy," *Social Policy Report* 30, no. 1 (2016), https://www.ncbi.nlm.nih.gov/pmc/articles/PMC5766273; U.S. Government Accountability Office, "Military Hazing: DOD Should Address Data

Reporting Deficiencies, Training Limitations, and Personnel Shortfalls," December 15, 2021, https://www.gao.gov/products/gao-22-104066.

Chapter 3: Anhedonia

1. Jürgen De Fruyt, Bernard Sabbe, and Koen Demyttenaere, "Anhedonia in Depressive Disorder: A Narrative Review," *Psychopathology* 53, nos. 5–6 (2020): 274–281, https://doi.org/10.1159/000508773.

2. Cynthia Vinney, "Anhedonia: What to Do When You Can't Experience Pleasure," Verywell Mind, last updated May 8, 2023, https://www.verywellmind.com/what-is-anhedonia-i-dont-feel-pleasure-5680269.

3. J. Murtoff, "Anhedonia," *Encyclopædia Britannica*, February 6, 2023, https://www.britannica.com/science/anhedonia.

4. Matthew D. Lieberman, Naomi I. Eisenberger, Molly J. Crockett, Shelley M. Tom, Jennifer H. Pfeifer, and Baldwin M. Way, "Putting Feelings into Words: Affect Labeling Disrupts Amygdala Activity in Response to Affective Stimuli," *Psychological Science* 18, no. 5 (2007): 421–428, https://doi.org/10.1111/j.1467-9280.2007.01916.x.

5. Alessandro Serretti, "Anhedonia and Depressive Disorders," *Clinical Psychopharmacology and Neuroscience: The Official Scientific Journal of the Korean College of Neuropsychopharmacology* 21, no. 3 (2023): 401–409, https://doi.org/10.9758/cpn.23.1086; Siobhán R. Shaw, Hashim El-Omar, Daniel Roquet, John R. Hodges, Olivier Piguet, Rebekah M. Ahmed, Alexis E. Whitton, and Muireann Irish, "Uncovering the Prevalence and Neural Substrates of Anhedonia in Frontotemporal Dementia," *Brain* 144, no. 5 (2021): 1551–1564, https://academic.oup.com/brain/article/144/5/1551/6214168; D. Vaquero-Puyuelo, C. De-la-Cámara, B. Olaya, P. Gracia-García, A. Lobo, R. López-Antón, and J. Santabárbara, "Anhedonia as a Potential Risk Factor of Alzheimer's Disease in a Community-Dwelling Elderly Sample: Results from the ZARADEMP Project," *International Journal of Environmental Research and Public Health* 18, no. 4 (2021): 1370, https://doi.org/10.3390/ijerph18041370.

6. C. R. Damiano, J. Aloi, M. Treadway, R. Bodfish, G. Dichter, and S. B. Haas, "Adults with Autism Spectrum Disorders Exhibit Decreased Sensitivity to Reward Parameters When Making Effort-Based Decisions," *Journal of Neurodevelopmental Disorders* 4 (2012): 13, https://doi.org/10.1186/1866-1955-4-13.

7. Francesc Borrell-Carrió, Anthony L. Suchman, and Ronald M. Epstein, "The Biopsychosocial Model 25 Years Later: Principles, Practice, and Scientific Inquiry," *Annals of Family Medicine* 2, no. 6 (2004): 576–582, https://www.ncbi.nlm.nih.gov/pmc/articles/PMC1466742/.

8. John J. McGrath, Ali Al-Hamzawi, Jordi Alonso, Yasmin Altwaijri, Laura H. Andrade, Evelyn J. Bromet, et al., "Age of Onset and Cumulative Risk of Mental Disorders: A Cross-National Analysis of Population Surveys from 29 Countries," *The Lancet* 10, no. 9 (2023): 668–681, https://www.thelancet.com/journals/lanpsy/article/PIIS2215-0366(23)00193-1/abstract; World Health Organization, "COVID-19 Pandemic Triggers 25% Increase in Prevalence of Anxiety and Depression Worldwide," March 2, 2022, https://www

.who.int/news/item/02-03-2022-covid-19-pandemic-triggers-25-increase-in
-prevalence-of-anxiety-and-depression-worldwide.

9. S. B. Srivastava, "Vitamin D: Do We Need More than Sunshine?," *American Journal of Lifestyle Medicine* 15, no. 4 (2021): 397–401, https://doi
.org/10.1177/15598276211005689; Ş. Akpınar and M. G. Karadağ, "Is
Vitamin D Important in Anxiety or Depression? What Is the Truth?," *Current Nutrition Reports* 11, no. 4 (2022): 675–681, https://doi.org/10.1007
/s13668-022-00441-0.

10. "Bethnal Green WW2 Disaster—Monument," London Remembers,
accessed May 27, 2024, https://www.londonremembers.com/memorials
/bethnal-green-ww2-disaster-monument.

11. Gloria Willcox, "The Feeling Wheel: A Tool for Expanding Awareness of Emotions and Increasing Spontaneity and Intimacy," *Transactional Analysis Journal* 12, no. 4 (1982): 274–276, https://doi
.org/10.1177/036215378201200411.

12. R. P. Snaith, M. Hamilton, S. Morley, A. Humayan, D. Hargreaves, and P.
Trigwell, "A Scale for the Assessment of Hedonic Tone: The Snaith-Hamilton
Pleasure Scale," *British Journal of Psychiatry* 167, no. 1 (1995): 99–103,
doi:10.1192/bjp.167.1.99.

13. J. Breslau, E. Miller, R. Jin, N. A. Sampson, Alonso J, Andrade LH, Bromet
EJ, de Girolamo G, Demyttenaere K, Fayyad J, Fukao A, Gălăon M, Gureje O,
He Y, Hinkov HR, Hu C, Kovess-Masfety V, Matschinger H, Medina-Mora
ME, Ormel J, Posada-Villa J, Sagar R, Scott KM, Kessler RC. "A multinational study of mental disorders, marriage, and divorce." *Acta Psychiatr Scand.*
2011 Dec;124(6):474-86. doi: 10.1111/j.1600-0447.2011.01712.x. Epub 2011
Apr 30. PMID: 21534936; PMCID: PMC4011132. J. Breslau, E. Miller,
R. Jin, et al., "A Multinational Study of Mental Disorders, Marriage, and
Divorce," *Acta Psychiatrica Scandinavica* 124, no. 6 (2011): 474–486, https://doi
.org/10.1111/j.1600-0447.2011.01712.x; D. Lerner, D. A. Adler, W. H. Rogers,
et al., "Work Performance of Employees with Depression: The Impact of Work
Stressors," *American Journal of Health Promotion* 24, no. 3 (2010): 205–213,
https://doi.org/10.4278/ajhp.090313-QUAN-103.

Chapter 4: Masochism

1. Mark L. Ruffalo, "Masochistic Personality Disorder: Time to
Include in DSM?," *Psychology Today,* March 23, 2019, https://www
.psychologytoday.com/us/blog/freud-fluoxetine/201903/masochistic-
personality-disorder-time-include-in-dsm.

2. American Psychiatric Association, "Paraphilic Disorders," 2013, https://
www.psychiatry.org/File%20Library/Psychiatrists/Practice/DSM
/APA_DSM-5-Paraphilic-Disorders.pdf; "Sexual Masochism Disorder," *Psychology Today,* last updated September 15, 2021, https://www.psychologytoday
.com/us/conditions/sexual-masochism-disorder.

3. Xiaolin Xu, Gita D. Mishra, Julianne Holt-Lunstad, and Mark Jones, "Social
Relationship Satisfaction and Accumulation of Chronic Conditions and Multimorbidity: A National Cohort of Australian Women," *General Psychiatry* 36
(2023): e100925, https://doi.org/10.1136/gpsych-2022-100925.

4. Harmeet Kaur, "The Four Attachment Styles and How They Affect Your Relationships," CNN, August 29, 2023, https://www.cnn .com/health/attachment-styles-types-relationships-wellness-cec /index.html; Darlene Lancer, "How to Change Your Attachment Style and Your Relationships," *Psychology Today*, April 1, 2021, https: //www.psychologytoday.com/us/blog/toxic-relationships/202104 /how-change-your-attachment-style-and-your-relationships.
5. Mark L. Ruffalo, "Are You Masochistic? Questions," *Psychology Today*, March 23, 2019, https://www.psychologytoday.com/articles /are-you-masochistic-questions.

Chapter 5: Validation

1. F. W. Weathers, D. D. Blake, P. P. Schnurr, D. G. Kaloupek, B. P. Marx, and T. M. Keane, "Clinician-Administered PTSD Scale for *DSM-5* (CAPS-5)," 2013, https://www.ptsd.va.gov/professional/assessment/adult-int /caps.asp.
2. Rheana Murray, "Shonda Rhimes on How the Definition of Beauty Is Changing—on TV and Off," *Today*, August 1, 2017, https://www.today .com/series/love-your-body/shonda-rhimes-new-dove-project-redefining-beauty-tv-t114427.
3. Josephine Joly, Luke Hurst, David Walsh, and Giulia Carbonaro, "Four-Day Week: Which Countries Are Embracing It and How Is It Going So Far?," EuroNews, February 2, 2024, https://www.euronews.com/next/2024/02/02 /the-four-day-week-which-countries-have-embraced-it-and-how-s-it-going -so-far.

Chapter 6: Venting

1. Sophie L. Kjærvik, Brad J. Bushman, "A meta-analytic review of anger management activities that increase or decrease arousal: What fuels or douses rage?," *Clinical Psychology Review*, Volume 109, 2024, 102414, ISSN 0272-7358, https://doi.org/10.1016/j.cpr.2024.102414.
2. Monika Sohal, Pavneet Singh, Bhupinder Singh Dhillon, and Harbir Singh Gill, "Efficacy of Journaling in the Management of Mental Illness: A Systematic Review and Meta-Analysis," *Family Medicine in Community Health* 10, no. 1 (2022): e001154, https://www.ncbi.nlm.nih.gov/pmc/articles /PMC8935176/.
3. "Color Meanings in Different Cultures," Study.com, accessed May 28, 2024, https://study.com/academy/lesson/color-meanings-in-different-cultures .html.
4. Aiden Siobhan and Rachel Cash, "Are Musicals Coming Back to the Mainstream?," MovieWeb, last updated December 18, 2023, https://movieweb .com/musicals-coming-back-mainstream/.

Chapter 7: Values

1. Patricia A. Boyle, Lisa L. Barnes, Aron S. Buchman, and David A. Bennett, "Purpose in Life Is Associated with Mortality Among Community-Dwelling Older Persons," *Psychosomatic Medicine* 71, no. 5 (2009): 574–579, https://doi

.org/10.1097/PSY.0b013e3181a5a7c0; Patricia A. Boyle, Aron S. Buchman, Robert S. Wilson, Lei Yu, Julie A. Schneider, and David A. Bennett, "Effect of Purpose in Life on the Relation Between Alzheimer Disease Pathologic Changes on Cognitive Function in Advanced Age," *Archives of General Psychiatry* 69, no. 5 (2012): 499–504, https://doi.org/10.1001/archgenpsychiatry .2011.1487; Patrick L. Hill and Nicholas A. Turiano, "Purpose in Life as a Predictor of Mortality Across Adulthood," *Psychological Science* 25, no. 7 (2014): 1482–1486, https://doi.org/10.1177/0956797614531799; Patrick L. Hill, Anthony L. Burrow, and Victor J. Strecher, "Sense of Purpose in Life Predicts Greater Willingness for COVID-19 Vaccination," *Social Science and Medicine* 284 (2021): 114193, https://doi.org/10.1016/j.socscimed.2021.114193; S. M. Schaefer, J. Morozink Boylan, C. M. van Reekum, R. C. Lapate, C. J. Norris, C. D. Ryff, et al., "Purpose in Life Predicts Better Emotional Recovery from Negative Stimuli," *PLoS ONE* 8, no. 11 (2013): e80329, https://doi.org/10.1371/journal.pone.0080329; Genevieve N. Pfund, Timothy J. Bono, and Patrick L. Hill, "A Higher Goal During Higher Education: The Power of Purpose in Life During University," *Translational Issues in Psychological Science* 6, no. 2 (2020): 97–106, https://doi.org/10.1037/tps0000231.

2. Bronnie Ware, *The Top Five Regrets of the Dying* (London: Hay House, 2011), https://bronnieware.com/regrets-of-the-dying/.

3. Brené Brown, "Dare to Lead List of Values," accessed May 28, 2024, https: //brenebrown.com/resources/dare-to-lead-list-of-values/; Tchiki Davis, "List of Values: 305 Value Words, Lists, PDFs, & Excel Sheets," Berkeley Well-Being Institute, accessed May 28, 2024, https://www.berkeleywellbeing .com/list-of-values.html.

Chapter 8: Vitals

1. U.S. Department of Health and Human Services, "Our Epidemic of Loneliness and Isolation: The U.S. Surgeon General's Advisory on the Healing Effects of Social Connection and Community," 2023, https://www.hhs.gov /sites/default/files/surgeon-general-social-connection-advisory.pdf.

2. G. Lissak, "Adverse Physiological and Psychological Effects of Screen Time on Children and Adolescents: Literature Review and Case Study," *Environmental Research* 164 (2018): 149–157, https://doi.org/10.1016/j.envres.2018.01.015.

3. Erica Cirino, "What Are the Benefits of Hugging?," Healthline, last updated April 11, 2018, https://www.healthline.com/health/hugging -benefits#1.-Hugs-reduce-stress-by-showing-your-support.

4. @mayte.lisbeth, "It's been five years of touch starvation. I'll probably have some more years of it. I'm not handling this well," TikTok video, March 24, 2023, https://www.tiktok.com/@mayte.lisbeth/video/7214069179610041642.

5. Aaron Drapkin, "Countries with a 4-Day Workweek in 2024," Tech.co, January 3, 2024, https://tech.co/news/countries-with-four-day-workweeks.

6. Géraldine Fauville, Miao Luo, Ana C. M. Queiroz, Jeremy N. Bailenson, and Jeff Hancock, "Zoom Exhaustion and Fatigue Scale," *Computers in Human Behavior Reports* 4 (2021): 100119, https://doi.org/10.1016 /j.chbr.2021.100119.

7. M. I. Silvani, R. Werder, and C. Perret, "The Influence of Blue Light on Sleep, Performance and Wellbeing in Young Adults: A Systematic Review," *Frontiers in Physiology* 13 (2022): 943108, https://doi.org/10.3389/fphys.2022.943108.

8. Dillon Thompson, "Anthropologist Shares Unexpected Tip for Staying Cool During Heat Waves: 'We All Need to Study This,'" Yahoo, May 20, 2022, https://www.yahoo.com/lifestyle/anthropologist-explains-why-taking-naps-161841884.html; Win Reynolds, "Why Does Heat Make Us Sleepy?," *Northwestern Now,* August 17, 2022, https://news.northwestern.edu/stories/2022/08/why-heat-makes-us-sleepy/.

9. Katie Holliday, "In South Korea, You Snooze, You Don't Lose!," CNBC, July 22, 2014, https://www.cnbc.com/2014/07/22/in-south-korea-you-snooze-you-dont-lose.html.

10. "Sleeping on the Job: Customs from Countries Around the World," Open Access Government, February 18, 2019, https://www.openaccessgovernment.org/customs-from-countries/59117/; Bryant Rousseau, "Napping in Public? In Japan, That's a Sign of Diligence," *New York Times,* December 16, 2016, https://www.nytimes.com/2016/12/16/world/what-in-the-world/japan-inemuri-public-sleeping.html.

11. Ronald E. Riggio, "The Body Language of Couples in Love," *Psychology Today,* November 10, 2022, https://www.psychologytoday.com/us/blog/cutting-edge-leadership/202211/the-body-language-couples-in-love#.

12. Ann Pietrangelo and Crystal Raypole, "How to Recognize the Signs of Emotional Abuse," Healthline, last updated July 13, 2023, https://www.healthline.com/health/signs-of-mental-abuse#humiliation-and-criticism.

13. Jennifer Hassan, Helier Cheung, and Marlene Cimons, "Skittles and the Red Dye Debate: What You Need to Know," *Washington Post,* March 23, 2023, https://www.washingtonpost.com/wellness/2023/03/23/skittles-red-dye-titanium-dioxide/; Iris Myers, "Thousands of Children's Sweets Still Contain Additive Unsafe for Human Consumption," Environmental Working Group, October 19, 2022, https://www.ewg.org/news-insights/news/2022/10/thousands-childrens-sweets-still-contain-additive-unsafe-human.

14. Leslie Landaeta-Díaz, Samuel Durán-Agüero, and Gabriel González-Medina, "Exploring Food Intake Networks and Anhedonia Symptoms in a Chilean Adults Sample," *Appetite* 190 (2023): 107042, https://doi.org/10.1016/j.appet.2023.107042.

15. P. H. L. Tran and T. T. D. Tran, "Blueberry Supplementation in Neuronal Health and Protective Technologies for Efficient Delivery of Blueberry Anthocyanins," *Biomolecules* 11, no. 1 (2021): 102, published January 14, 2021, https://doi.org/10.3390/biom11010102.

16. "Foods Linked to Better Brainpower," Harvard Health, April 3, 2024, https://www.health.harvard.edu/healthbeat/foods-linked-to-better-brainpower.

17. Centers for Disease Control and Prevention, "Like Shift Work, Long Work Hours Are Associated with Shorter Sleep Duration," last updated March 31, 2020, https://www.cdc.gov/niosh/work-hour-training-for-nurses/longhours/mod3/23.html#.

18. "Exercise Intensity: How to Measure It," Mayo Clinic, August 25, 2023,

https://www.mayoclinic.org/healthy-lifestyle/fitness/in-depth/exercise
-intensity/art-20046887.
19. Chi Pang Wen, Jackson Pui Man Wai, Min Kuang Tsai, et al., "Minimum
Amount of Physical Activity for Reduced Mortality and Extended Life
Expectancy: A Prospective Cohort Study," *The Lancet* 378, no. 9798 (2011):
1244–1253, https://pubmed.ncbi.nlm.nih.gov/21846575/.
20. Debra L. Blackwell and Tainya C. Clarke, "State Variation in Meeting the
2008 Federal Guidelines for Both Aerobic and Muscle-Strengthening Activities Through Leisure-Time Physical Activity Among Adults Aged 18–64:
United States, 2010–2015," *National Health Statistics Reports* 112 (June 28,
2018), https://www.cdc.gov/nchs/data/nhsr/nhsr112.pdf.
21. Lucina Artigas and Ignacio Jarero, "The Butterfly Hug Method for Bilateral Stimulation," EMDR Foundation, September 2014, https://emdrfoun
dation.org/toolkit/butterfly-hug.pdf; Kellie Kirksey and Jamie Marich,
"An African-Centered Perspective on Bilateral Stimulation and Healing,"
EMDR International Association, https://www.emdria.org/learning-class
/an-african-centered-perspective-on-bilateral-stimulation-and-healing/.
22. Alex Kerai, "Cell Phone Usage Statistics: Mornings Are for Notifications," Reviews.org, July 21, 2023, https://www.reviews.org/mobile
/cell-phone-addiction/.
23. Vignesh Ramachandran, "Stanford Researchers Identify Four Causes for 'Zoom
Fatigue' and Their Simple Fixes," Stanford News, February 23, 2021, https://
news.stanford.edu/stories/2021/02/four-causes-zoom-fatigue-solutions.
24. "What Is Gen Z?," McKinsey, March 20, 2023, https://www.mckinsey.com
/featured-insights/mckinsey-explainers/what-is-gen-z.
25. G. Malinsky, "57% of Gen Zers want to be influencers—but 'it's constant,
Monday through Sunday,'" CNBC, September 14, 2024, https://www.cnbc
.com/2024/09/14/more-than-half-of-gen-z-want-to-be-influencers-but-its
-constant.html
26. Arielle Feger, "Gen Z, Millennials Grow Their Social Media Presence
Through 2027," eMarketer, August 14, 2023, https://www.emarketer.com
/content/gen-z-millennials-grow-their-social-media-presence-through-2027.

Chapter 9: Vision
1. "Naomi Osaka," Women's Tennis Association, May 28, 2024, https://
www.wtatennis.com/players/319998/naomi-osaka; Naomi Osaka, U.S.
Open interview, September 4, 2021, YouTube, https://www.youtube.com
/watch?v=YHxuYRRYVAY.
2. "Why Do Super Bowl Winners Go to Disney?," ESPN, February 12,
2024, https://www.espn.com/nfl/story/_/id/39387632/why-do-super-bowl
-winners-go-disney.
3. Adam Schupak, "Masters: Rory McIlroy Visits Tiger Woods, Who
Admits He Doesn't Know Where All His Trophies Are," *USA Today*,
April 6, 2021, https://golfweek.usatoday.com/2021/04/06/masters-rory
-mcilroy-tiger-woods-trophies/.
4. Teresa M. Amabile and Steven J. Kramer, "The Power of Small Wins,"

Harvard Business Review, May 2011, https://hbr.org/2011/05/the-power-of -small-wins.

5. Y. Luo, X. Chen, S. Qi, X. You, and X. Huang, "Well-Being and Anticipation for Future Positive Events: Evidence from an fMRI Study," *Frontiers in Psychology* 8 (2018): 2199, https://doi.org/10.3389/fpsyg.2017.02199.

6. Kaitlin Woolley and Ayelet Fishbach, "Immediate Rewards Predict Adherence to Long-Term Goals," *Personality and Social Psychology Bulletin* 43, no. 2 (2017): 151–162, https://doi.org/10.1177/0146167216676480.

7. Jeroen Nawijn, M. A. Marchand, Ruut Veenhoven, and Ad J. Vingerhoets, "Vacationers Happier, but Most Not Happier After a Holiday," *Applied Research in Quality of Life* 5, no. 1 (2010): 35–47, https://doi.org/10.1007 /s11482-009-9091-9.

8. Lara Schleifenbaum, Julie C. Driebe, Tanja M. Gerlach, Lars Penke, and Ruben C. Arslan, "Women Feel More Attractive Before Ovulation: Evidence from a Large-Scale Online Diary Study," *Evolutionary Human Sciences* 3 (2021): e47, https://www.ncbi.nlm.nih.gov/pmc/articles/PMC10427307.

9. "Self-Rewards," Bowdoin College Baldwin Center for Learning and Teaching, accessed May 28, 2024, https://www.bowdoin.edu/baldwin-center/pdf /handout-self-rewards.pdf; S. J. Scott, "205 Rewards for Yourself: Ideas and Examples for 2024," Develop Good Habits, January 1, 2024, https://www .developgoodhabits.com/reward-yourself/; Elizabeth Perry, "You've Earned It: Learn About the Benefits of Rewarding Yourself," BetterUp, February 23, 2022, https://www.betterup.com/blog/reward-yourself.

Chapter 10: A Way Forward

1. "EMDR Therapy: What It Is, Procedure and Effectiveness," Cleveland Clinic, last updated March 29, 2022, https://my.clevelandclinic.org/health /treatments/22641-emdr-therapy; "Eye Movement Desensitization and Reprocessing (EMDR) Therapy," American Psychological Association, last updated July 31, 2017, https://www.apa.org/ptsd-guideline/treatments /eye-movement-reprocessing.

2. "Cognitive Behavioral Therapy," Mayo Clinic, March 16, 2019, https: //www.mayoclinic.org/tests-procedures/cognitive-behavioral-therapy/about /pac-20384610; American Psychological Association, "What Is Cognitive Behavioral Therapy?," Clinical Practice Guideline for the Treatment of Posttraumatic Stress Disorder, 2017, https://www.apa.org/ptsd-guideline /patients-and-families/cognitive-behavioral.

3. "Dialectical Behavior Therapy (DBT)," Cleveland Clinic, last updated April 19, 2022; https://my.clevelandclinic.org/health/treatments/22838-dialectical -behavior-therapy-dbt#overview; "Dialectical Behavior Therapy," *Psychology Today,* accessed May 28, 2024, https://www.psychologytoday.com /us/therapy-types/dialectical-behavior-therapy; "Dialectical Behavioral Therapy (DBT)," Columbia University Irving Medical Center, accessed May 28, 2024, https://www.columbiadoctors.org/treatments-conditions /dialectical-behavioral-therapy-dbt.

4. "Suicide: Facts at a Glance," Centers for Disease Control and Prevention,

last updated April 2024, https://www.cdc.gov/suicide/pdf/NCIPC-Suicide-FactSheet-508_FINAL.pdf.

5. "Vagus Nerve Stimulation," Cleveland Clinic, last updated March 16, 2022, https://my.clevelandclinic.org/health/treatments/17598-vagus-nerve-stimulation; "Deep Brain Stimulation," Mayo Clinic, September 19, 2023, https://www.mayoclinic.org/tests-procedures/deep-brain-stimulation/about/pac-20384562; "What Is Electroconvulsive Therapy (ECT)?," American Psychiatric Association, January 2023, https://www.psychiatry.org/patients-families/ect; Adrian Jacques H. Ambrose, "Understanding Ketamine Treatment for Depression," Columbia University Irving Medical Center, July 14, 2023, https://www.cuimc.columbia.edu/news/ketamine-treatment-depression-what-you-need-know; Amit Anand, Sanjay J. Mathew, et al., "Ketamine Versus ECT for Nonpsychotic Treatment-Resistant Major Depression," *New England Journal of Medicine* 388 (2023): 2315–2325, https://www.nejm.org/doi/10.1056/NEJMoa2302399.

6. Trisha Torrey, "How to Check Out a Doctor for Medical Malpractice," Verywell Health, March 12, 2024, https://www.verywellhealth.com/how-to-uncover-a-doctors-medical-malpractice-history-2614988.

7. Trish Richert, "Peer Support: Helping Others, Healing Yourself," National Alliance on Mental Illness, August 6, 2018, https://www.nami.org/family-member-caregivers/peer-support-helping-others-healing-yourself/; Marla Deibler, "Understanding Group Therapy and Support Groups," Anxiety and Depression Association of America, August 31, 2022, https://adaa.org/learn-from-us/from-the-experts/blog-posts/consumer/understanding-group-therapy-and-support-groups.

8. "FDA Approves New Nasal Spray Medication for Treatment-Resistant Depression; Available Only at a Certified Doctor's Office or Clinic," U.S. Food and Drug Administration, March 5, 2019, https://www.fda.gov/news-events/press-announcements/fda-approves-new-nasal-spray-medication-treatment-resistant-depression-available-only-certified.

9. Morgan Mandriota, "What to Know Before Trying Psychedelics for the First Time," PsychCentral, February 11, 2022, https://psychcentral.com/health/what-to-know-before-trying-psilicybin-psychedelics-for-the-first-time.

10. David Culver and Jason Kravarik, "It's Legal to Use Psilocybin, or 'Magic Mushrooms,' in Oregon. But That Could Soon Change," CNN, November 4, 2022, https://www.cnn.com/2022/11/04/us/oregon-psilocybin-legalization-law/index.html.

11. Jimmy Nguyen, "How to Find Psychedelic Assisted Therapy Near Me: A Guide," Psychedelic Passage, accessed May 28, 2024, https://www.psychedelicpassage.com/how-to-find-psychedelic-assisted-therapy-near-me-a-guide/; Dana G. Smith, "What Does Good Psychedelic Therapy Look Like?," *New York Times*, last updated June 5, 2023, https://www.nytimes.com/2023/06/03/well/mind/psychedelic-therapy.html; Eric Brown, "6 Questions to Ask Before Starting Psychedelic Therapy," Mindbloom, November 20, 2020, https://www.mindbloom.com/blog/starting-psychedelic-therapy-common-questions.

12. "About Art Therapy," American Art Therapy Association, accessed May 28, 2024, https://arttherapy.org/about-art-therapy/; "What Is Dance/Movement

Therapy?," American Dance Therapy Association, accessed May 28, 2024, https://adta.memberclicks.net/what-is-dancemovement-therapy; S. Zadro and P. Stapleton, "Does Reiki Benefit Mental Health Symptoms Above Placebo?," *Frontiers in Psychology* 13 (2022): 897312, https://doi.org/10.3389/fpsyg.2022.897312; Maureen Salamon, "What Is Somatic Therapy?," *Harvard Health Blog*, July 7, 2023, https://www.health.harvard.edu/blog/what-is-somatic-therapy-202307072951; "Emotional Freedom Technique (EFT)," Kaiser Permanente, June 24, 2023, https://healthy.kaiserpermanente.org/health-wellness/health-encyclopedia/he.emotional-freedom-technique-eft.acl9225.

Appendix A
1. Manhattan Behavioral Medicine, New York City.

Appendix B
1. Danielle Pacheco, "Is Eating Before Bed Bad?," Sleep Foundation, last updated April 22, 2024, https://www.sleepfoundation.org/nutrition/is-it-bad-to-eat-before-bed#.
2. Danielle Pacheco and Dustin Cotliar, "Caffeine and Sleep," Sleep Foundation, April 17, 2024, https://www.sleepfoundation.org/nutrition/caffeine-and-sleep#.
3. M. Kudrnáčová and A. Kudrnáč, "Better Sleep, Better Life? Testing the Role of Sleep on Quality of Life," *PLoS ONE* 18, no. 3 (2023): e0282085, https://doi.org/10.1371/journal.pone.0282085.
4. Rob Newsom and Alex Dimitriu, "Cognitive Behavioral Therapy for Insomnia (CBT-I): An Overview," Sleep Foundation, last updated May 7, 2024, https://www.sleepfoundation.org/insomnia/treatment/cognitive-behavioral-therapy-insomnia.
5. "Water: How Much Should You Drink Every Day?," Mayo Clinic, October 12, 2022, https://www.mayoclinic.org/healthy-lifestyle/nutrition-and-healthy-eating/in-depth/water/art-20044256.
6. N. Zhang, S. M. Du, J. F. Zhang, and G. S. Ma, "Effects of Dehydration and Rehydration on Cognitive Performance and Mood Among Male College Students in Cangzhou, China: A Self-Controlled Trial," *International Journal of Environmental Research and Public Health* 16, no. 11 (2019): 1891, https://doi.org/10.3390/ijerph16111891.
7. Catherine Pearson, "Text Your Friends: It Matters More than You Think," *New York Times*, last updated July 25, 2022, https://www.nytimes.com/2022/07/11/well/family/check-in-text-friendship.html; Peggy J. Liu, SoYon Rim, Lauren Min, and Kate E. Min, "The Surprise of Reaching Out: Appreciated More than We Think," *Journal of Personality and Social Psychology: Interpersonal Relations and Group Processes* 124, no. 4 (2023): 754–771, https://www.apa.org/pubs/journals/releases/psp-pspi0000402.pdf.

Appendix C
1. Fazida Karim, Azeezat A. Oyewande, Lamis F. Abdalla, Reem Chaudhry Ehsanullah, and Safeera Khan, "Social Media Use and Its Connection

to Mental Health: A Systematic Review," *Cureus* 12, no. 6 (2020): e8627, https://www.ncbi.nlm.nih.gov/pmc/articles/PMC7364393/; Roy H. Perlis, Jon Green, Matthew Simonson, et al., "Association Between Social Media Use and Self-Reported Symptoms of Depression in US Adults," *JAMA Network Open* 4, no. 11 (2021): e2136113, https://jamanetwork.com/journals /jamanetworkopen/fullarticle/2786464; Mesfin A. Bekalu, Rachel F. McCloud, and K. Viswanath, "Association of Social Media Use with Social Well-Being, Positive Mental Health, and Self-Rated Health: Disentangling Routine Use from Emotional Connection to Use," *Health Education and Behavior* 46, no. 2 suppl. (2019): 69S–80S, https://journals.sagepub.com/doi /full/10.1177/1090198119863768.

INDEX

ABOUT THE AUTHOR

Judith Joseph, MD, MBA, is a board-certified psychiatrist. Dr. Judith is chair of the Women in Medicine Initiative for Columbia University Vagelos College of Physicians & Surgeons. She is a clinical assistant professor of Child and Adolescent Psychiatry at NYU Langone Medical Center. She has conducted several clinical research studies in pediatric, adult, geriatric, and women's mental health as the principal investigator of her research lab, Manhattan Behavioral Medicine. Dr. Judith developed the T.I.E.S. method to address mental health symptoms in menopause. She is on the board of Let's Talk Menopause, a national nonprofit organization that advocated in December 2023 for the Menopause Research and Equity Act in the U.S. Congress alongside Congresswoman Yvette Clarke.

Dr. Judith received a 2023 Congressional Proclamation from the U.S. House of Representatives for her social media advocacy and research in mental health. She has been a lecturer and professional speaker at prestigious institutions such as the Executive Office of the President of the United States, Ivy League universities, and Fortune 500 companies across the United States and Europe.

Dr. Judith is an expert on various media platforms and has made national television appearances on *Oprah Daily*'s "The Life You

Want" series, *Good Morning America, The Wendy Williams Show, Investigation Discovery, Today,* and CBS news. She is a medical consultant for Apple TV, where she was in the writers' room for *The Crowded Room* series. Her episode on High-Functioning Depression on *The Mel Robbins Podcast* received record ratings. She received 2020 and 2023 Share Care Awards for her MedCircle series on PTSD and a *Good Morning America* investigative special on ADHD.

Dr. Judith was named as a 2024 Black Health Hero by PopSugar. She was also named a 2024 VeryWell Mind Top 25 Mental Health Thought Leader and a 2024 NAACP Top 6 Mental Health Champion.

Dr. Judith teaches medical media courses to physicians and medical students at Columbia University and New York University. She received her bachelor's degree in biology and chemistry, cum laude, from Duke University; her medical degree from Columbia University College of Physicians and Surgeons; and her business degree from Columbia Business School. She completed her adult psychiatry residency at Columbia University, and her Child and Adolescent Psychiatry Fellowship at NYU Langone Medical Center. She lives in New York City.